Genealogy in Ontario

Searching the Records

Brenda Dougall Merriman, CG

Ontario Maps by William J. Fraser

~ FOURTH EDITION ~

Toronto 2008

Further copies of this book and information about the Society can be obtained by writing to:
The Ontario Genealogical Society
Suite 102, 40 Orchard View Boulevard
Toronto ON M4R 1B9
Canada
tel. 416-489-0734
tel. 416-489-9803
provoffice@ogs.on.ca
www.ogs.on.ca

Library and Archives Canada Cataloguing in Publication
Merriman, Brenda Dougall
    Genealogy in Ontario : searching the records / Brenda Dougall Merriman ; maps by William J. Fraser. — 4th ed.

Includes bibliographical references and index.
ISBN 978-0-7779-3414-2

    1. Ontario—Genealogy—Handbooks, manuals, etc.
I. Ontario Genealogical Society II. Title.

CS88.O6M47 2008   929'.10720713   C2008-903103-2

Cover Painting: *Opening of the First Parliament of Upper Canada (Ontario)* by Col. *John Graves Simcoe, first Lieutenant Governor, at Newark, (now Niagara- on-the-Lake) Sept. 17th 1792.* LAC copy negative C-002894. Artist unverified: "J.D. Kelly." Confederation Life Insurance Company Collection (714-32)

Also known as *Governor Simcoe Arrives in Newark* by J.D. Kelly 1931. Reproduced with the permission of Rogers Communications. Inc.

Cover Design: BG Communications.

Published with assistance from the Ontario Ministry of Culture.

Contents

Preface

This is the fourth edition in the history of *Genealogy in Ontario: Searching the Records* since 1984. Over that time, especially since the millennium, new technology and the exploding access to genealogical source material have been overwhelming. Genealogists find it an increasing challenge to monitor and review the constant flow of new information and changes. Home computer usage is at an all-time high level in North America, so it is reasonable to expect that the majority of readers are computer-literate at some level. Revisions to the content of this book had to reflect our twenty-first century world.

The Internet has become a convenient facet of preliminary planning for family history research. Its very nature is not exactly stable as we witness corporate mergers, name changes and some disappearances. Therein a conundrum: Will the websites and URLs in this edition remain "fixed" for the duration of this book? Most website addresses here are stripped to a root URL and further navigation on a site may be necessary. Frequently the reader will likely find that major websites have rapidly added databases and other finding aids that were unavailable when this book went to press.

Genealogy in Ontario now has an introductory research chapter. Although it is still not a manual for methodology, the first chapter addresses universally applicable principles which evolved to standards of excellence by the dawn of our newest century. Beginners in family history, and more experienced researchers, will find an outline in Introduction to Research. The second chapter includes background information with research and reference tips in Ontario Background.

The main object is still to introduce you to original, documentary sources in the pursuit of Ontario ancestors, along with finding aids, microfilm or digital availability, and other significant sources such as relevant reading and websites. As with former editions, the book continues to focus on the two largest resource centres in this province: Library and Archives Canada and the provincial Archives of Ontario. The most important and basic resources we use come from their holdings. This is not to dismiss other institutions—there are many facilities with a local or specialized focus. Many other institutions, organizations and agencies are fully listed in the Appendices.

The Reading and Reference Lists are now placed within each chapter. As well, the branches of the Ontario Genealogical Society have produced dozens of specialized publications relevant to their geographic areas—so many, it is not possible to mention all of them in this overview. Please visit Appendix I and explore the OGS community.

My gratitude goes to the colleagues who reviewed portions of the manuscript: Ruth Burkholder, Patricia McGregor, John D. Reid, Fawne Stratford-Devai, Glenn Wright; and Ruth Chernia, the OGS Publications Coordinator. Without the wisdom and support of Alison Hare, CG, the writing and contents would be far less comprehensible. Any errors or omissions are my sole responsibility and no reflection on their able skills.

This edition is dedicated to the memory of Ryan Taylor (1950–2006).

BDM 2008

Maps

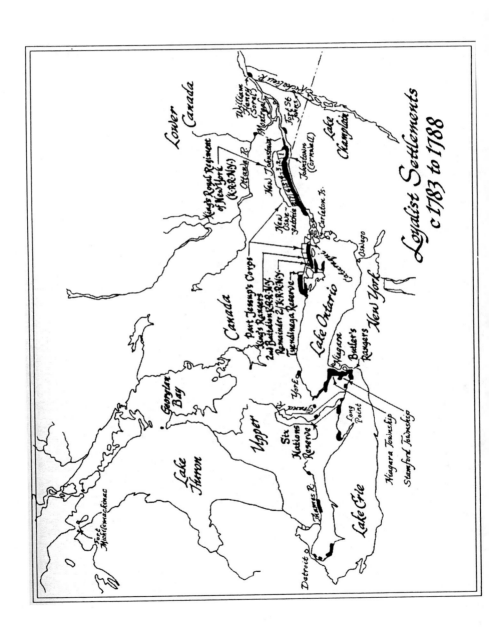

Loyalist Settlements c 1783 to 1788

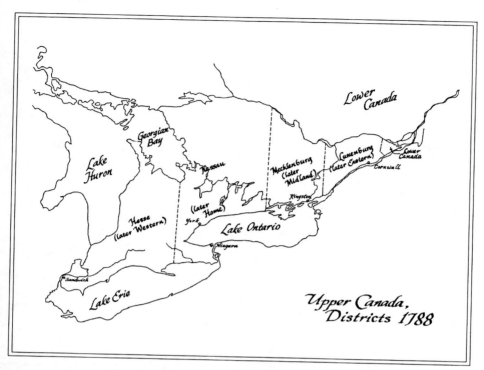

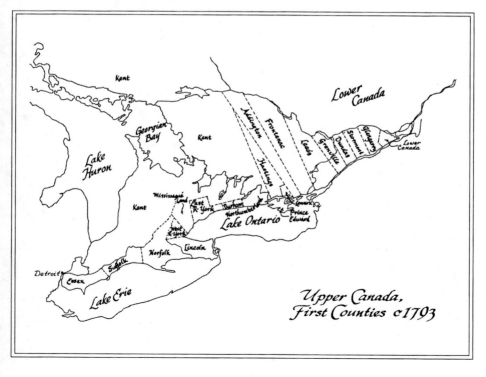

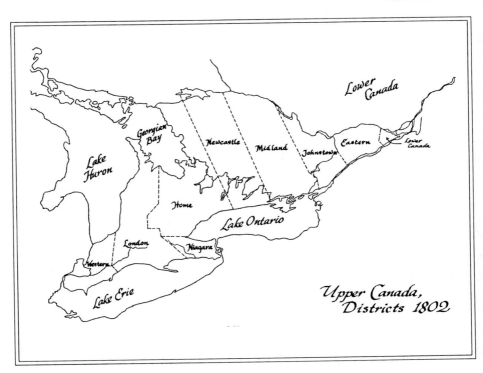

Upper Canada,
Districts 1802

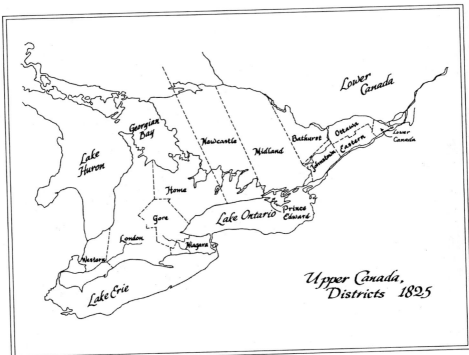

Upper Canada,
Districts 1825

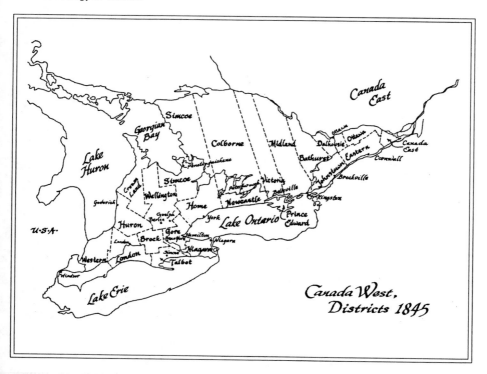

Canada West,
Districts 1845

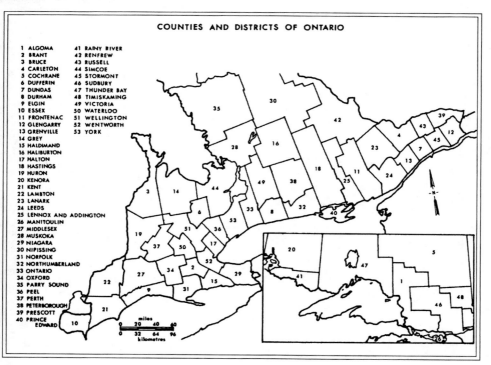

COUNTIES AND DISTRICTS OF ONTARIO

1 ALGOMA
2 BRANT
3 BRUCE
4 CARLETON
5 COCHRANE
6 DUFFERIN
7 DUNDAS
8 DURHAM
9 ELGIN
10 ESSEX
11 FRONTENAC
12 GLENGARRY
13 GRENVILLE
14 GREY
15 HALDIMAND
16 HALIBURTON
17 HALTON
18 HASTINGS
19 HURON
20 KENORA
21 KENT
22 LAMBTON
23 LANARK
24 LEEDS
25 LENNOX AND ADDINGTON
26 MANITOULIN
27 MIDDLESEX
28 MUSKOKA
29 NIAGARA
30 NIPISSING
31 NORFOLK
32 NORTHUMBERLAND
33 ONTARIO
34 OXFORD
35 PARRY SOUND
36 PEEL
37 PERTH
38 PETERBOROUGH
39 PRESCOTT
40 PRINCE EDWARD

41 RAINY RIVER
42 RENFREW
43 RUSSELL
44 SIMCOE
45 STORMONT
46 SUDBURY
47 THUNDER BAY
48 TIMISKAMING
49 VICTORIA
50 WATERLOO
51 WELLINGTON
52 WENTWORTH
53 YORK

1

Introduction to Research

Genealogy *is* family history. And vice versa. For the most part, I use these two terms interchangeably. The beginning genealogist who is eager to explore ancestral connections with Ontario, and who picked up this book, may not have read any "how to do it" books about genealogy or family history. Such instruction books are available at or through a nearby library, wherever you live. A few introductory recommendations or warnings are not amiss here.

Novice genealogists are advised to collect family information from living relatives and other "at home" sources. We all must begin with who we are and what we know from readily available family sources. Ask, and look, for family memories, papers and artifacts. Learn how to interview elderly relatives, asking open-ended questions that encourage them to reminisce. Seek documentary verification of oral information whenever possible. Start filing the collected information into surnames and family groups. Your quest has begun—to proceed step by step from one generation to another in the past, documenting your progress.

New family historians frequently look first to tracing the ancestors of their birth surname. This is called direct-line ancestry, or building a pedigree, discovering the one immediate ancestor in each generation. Good advice tells you not to ignore the siblings in each generation. A stumbling block in your direct line can often be overcome by looking at brothers and sisters. Records for them might provide the wanted information about parents or a birthplace. Beyond such collateral considerations, the families of spouses can also reveal unexpected and welcome clues.

Networking

Working at family history in isolation is extra time-consuming and unnecessary. Kindred spirits abound and you don't have to re-invent the wheel! This is why you should explore attending an instructional course or lectures; they might be conducted as evening classes, or weekend seminars, one-day workshops or major conferences. Online courses are also available. Sponsors could be groups like genealogical societies, public libraries, archives, museums, school boards or post-secondary educational institutions.

Joining at least one genealogical society cannot be overrated for making personal contacts and receiving the benefits of collective experience. Your choices are usually the group nearest to where you live, or a distant group where one of your ancestors lived. Some people do both. The former can give you immediate networking support and assistance while you are learning. The latter will give you insights into the places where your ancestors originated. Both choices will keep you current on changes in the availability of records, new books and special published material, their own library collections, and many more benefits. Personal research experiences and case studies in society journals and newsletters can be very illuminating with regard to sources and research techniques.

Spelling

Searching for names as you know them today is not always successful because of spelling and phonetic variations. Our ancestors were not necessarily literate, although some learned to make a signature. The people who created written records for them—the clergymen, government clerks, schoolmasters, solicitors, census enumerators—by and large wrote names down as they heard them unless they were acquainted with the individuals. Even if our ancestors were in the literate minority 150 years ago or more, they lacked the same concern about spelling that we have. You could find one man's signature with different spellings throughout his lifetime.

This is a fundamental issue to be kept in mind at all times, whatever type of source you are searching. You can miss a vital reference or breakthrough if you are narrowly focused on one spelling only.

Making Each Step Count

Identification

For each ancestor the ideal minimum is the three basic events of birth, marriage and death. Each of those events needs his or her name together with a date and a place. Each is a genealogical statement or assertion that satisfies us as to its factualness. Frequently that assertion can only be made after examining information pulled from a number of sources. We seek relationships of child to parent and parent to child. Thus identities are built. Eventually, more sources will add the biographical, social and historical text to make our people come alive.

"Name collectors" are those who latch onto any and every reference to their family names, claiming "ancestors" indiscriminately. The pause to evaluate new information and establish identification is lost in the excitement of finding names in an index or database. Family history normally works one step at a time, and each step back in time involves clearly framing a specific quest or goal. Ancestors need dates and places, events and relationships, to place them in their rightful family positions. Pausing, evaluating and analyzing as you move along is absolutely central to genealogical procedure.

Sources provide us with *information* that can become *evidence* in answering a genealogical question about an event, identity or relationship.

Sources

Sources are the material or form *in which* we find information. Think of a source as a container of information. For example, a death certificate is a source. Genealogists can now categorize sources more clearly as either original or derivative. Original sources are the first recording of an identity, relationship or event; they are still in the form in which they were created. In genealogical research, these are usually paper documents, but they can also be oral material or physical artifacts.

On the other hand, all else is a derivative source—material that is based on a previously existing source. This includes books and compilations such as family histories, family "trees" on websites and other publications. Transcriptions, abstracts, indexes and databases are also derivative.

Photocopies, microfilm and scanned or digital images are *image copies*, generally considered faithful reproductions of original sources and usually treated as such. The researcher must consider the condition of an image and evaluate whether it indeed has quality equivalent to an original. Microfilm can demonstrate flaws such as inexpert focus, under-exposure, over-exposure and/ or wording lost in tight register bindings. An electronic or digital image should give assurance that it is a matching copy of an original and has not been altered at some point. The legibility of the item and the credibility of the image's provider are key points. See Mills's *Evidence Explained* for more discussion on treating these sources, and for expert details regarding *duplicate originals*.

Information

One source, such as a death certificate, can contain multiple pieces of information. Each piece needs to be examined and analyzed with regard to the source it came from and its relevance to the particular goal, whether it's establishing a parent-child relationship, identifying an ancestor among several individuals of the same name or other genealogical questions. Therefore, information is judged on its quality within the context of its source and in relation to a particular family issue we want to solve.

Primary information comes from someone involved in or witnessing an event. A doctor's report of the date and cause of death is primary (and official) on a death certificate. He was either there when death occurred or shortly after. Secondary information comes from secondhand knowledge. The same death certificate might have information given by the doctor about the decedent's age, parents, place of birth and so on, which the doctor probably did not have firsthand knowledge about (unless he was a close family friend or witnessed the birth of the decedent). Repeated family traditions and hearsay are secondary information.

We also have to be aware that primary information, no matter how welcome, is not above suspicion. Our ancestors were human too, and they made unintentional mistakes or deliberately misleading statements in official records. Government requirements, social acceptability or personal sensitivities could lead a person to alter, for example, age, place of birth or date of marriage. All information needs to be carefully evaluated: who created it, in what context, for what purpose, how soon it was recorded after the event and so on.

Evidence

The more or less exhaustive collection of information we have gathered provides the basis for evidence that we hope answers our immediate goal. We evaluate the sources, and analyze and compare the information. In a few cases we will have stand-alone, direct evidence to give us what we seek—for example, a birth record that establishes parentage without a doubt, or a marriage record that clearly identifies the bride and groom.

Very often, though, we find information that only *implies* the details that would answer our question or goal. This is indirect evidence. For example, a woman's age on her death certificate is indirect evidence of her year of birth. We need much more than this to draw a realistic conclusion about her date of birth. If a record of birth or baptism seems impossible to locate, many additional bits of indirect evidence about age or birth are needed for reinforcement—such as from census returns, her marriage record, newspaper notices and so on.

Other times (more often than you expect, if you are inexperienced), we will find discrepancies among our pieces of information, about names or ages or parents or dates. We have to try to resolve those discrepancies by examining all the available evidence. These are steps 4 and 5 in the Genealogical Proof Standard below. Writing out your thoughts about the evidence is beneficial to help you clarify your reasoning.

Genealogical Proof Standard

The Genealogical Proof Standard (GPS) has replaced Preponderance of Evidence (POE) as a more rigorous measurement of proof argument. POE is a legal principle that was widely applied in the study of genealogy in the last half of the twentieth century. It was used to weigh evidence of a conflicting nature, or indirect evidence, as above, when the researcher drew genealogical conclusions from a variety of hints, inferences or indirect references to the subject at hand. A genealogical decision was based on which pieces of evidence outweighed the others (the preponderance "wins"). Preponderance means that *only a balance of probability* was the criterion.

Now, serious genealogists subscribe to the Genealogical Proof Standard (GPS), which sets a higher bar and greater confidence in the credibility of our work. There is nothing mysterious about the GPS. It outlines a series of five logical steps that apply to most of our genealogical conclusions:

1. making a reasonably exhaustive search of sources for information;

2. citing each of the sources accurately for future reference or retrieval;
3. evaluating the information and correlating the evidence;
4. resolving any contradictions in the evidence;
5. describing your conclusion convincingly and clearly, in writing.

"In writing" can mean anywhere your concluding statement is made—in your notes, in your family history, in your software report, to a client and so on. When contradictions *are* present, it's a very helpful exercise to work it out in writing.

The BCG Genealogical Standards Manual describes standards for data-collection, evidence-analysis and compilation, among others.

The Internet

This section follows closely behind methodology principles simply because even the mildly curious about family roots have likely already sampled the tempting smorgasbord of cyberspace. Our computers have led us to a revolution in communications and information, whether we are beginners or more experienced researchers. The Internet has definitely changed the way both hobby and professional genealogists go about their work, especially in the early stages of a family project. Name indexes and searchable databases have proliferated and are almost impossible to ignore. More and more digital images of original sources are being uploaded. "Family trees" are everywhere. The vast offerings of the Internet can be overwhelming or even hypnotizing. How much do we think about where such information is really coming from?

We now have online memberships, newsletters, subscriptions, finding aids, forums, podcasts, vidcasts, blogs, email lists (listserves) and bulletin boards, not to mention a variety of software programs for managing our ancestral projects. Name collectors can download everything of surname interest without any system or methodology in mind. The result is often not knowing where these names might fit, or not, into their own ancestry, besides not knowing where the names came from in the first place. Researchers need to pick their way carefully through a great deal of chaff before finding fertile grain.

To be able to find your ancestors in databases may also require imagination and patience. It was mentioned earlier that names—both forenames and surnames—are not always spelled the same way in original documents. Databases that index or transcribe original records are all derivative sources, no matter who created them. Indexing and compiling is done by employees or volunteers who are susceptible, like all of us, to mistakes and misinterpretations. Difficult old handwriting, stained or poorly filmed documents or unfamiliarity with some ethnic-language names all contribute to potential errors. Some imagination can be useful in spelling names for a search engine or refining your searches.

To provoke us into thinking about where Internet information comes from, it may be helpful to consider the Internet as composed of three kinds of providers: *institutional*, *commercial* and *personal*.

Institutional providers are the websites of libraries, archives, government and other credible organizations that hold materials of interest to family historians. The Archives of Ontario, the Government of Ontario, the Ontario Genealogical Society and the Family History Library are examples. Using their online tools and finding aids prepares you for onsite research, microfilm borrowing or photocopy requests. Links to digital images are an even greater benefit. Sometimes knowledgeable staff members have created online educational research guides. Some institutions and some non-profit concerns offer digitized books online; some are free and some are pay-per-view. Certain organizations, such as the National Genealogical Society and the Board for Certification of Genealogists, provide instructive information about standards and education.

Commercial providers, such as *Ancestry.com* (*Ancestry.ca* is its Canadian component), are an example of a subscription-based service. New providers continue to appear in this growing but still slightly unstable industry. Mergers, corporate name changes and disappearances are not unusual. Besides offering online databases, some produce newsletters and other related sidelines. However, databases are their big selling points. Searchable databases as a product are as reliable as the competency of the people hired to decipher original records. Many commercial concerns are partnering with institutions and important genealogical societies to create new databases, some of which are linked to digitized images.

Personal providers are those websites and electronic communications created by fellow family historians and related interests. The material may range from extensive genealogies, charts and family stories to items such as newsletter articles, mailing list messages, blogs and GenWeb information. The educational value and integrity of such sites can vary widely. Some genealogies, family histories or charts may be well-documented but many are not. One way to judge credibility is by learning the reputation and credentials of the author/creator. Use your best judgment on this score. Even though the information might look promising, a serious genealogist will follow up with confirmation from original sources, whenever possible. No matter who created them, they are considered published, *derivative* sources that beg verification from original sources.

"Lookups" are popular electronic requests in the genealogy world. They serve us best when we are unable to access a rare or distant source, a source that may be available to a relative, colleague or stranger in the requisite location. Requests are often made via mailing lists, or perhaps directly to one person. Your acquaintance (or not) with a correspondent, and especially his or her ability in transcribing or citing the source, will have an impact on what you receive. Treat the results with caution as not entirely satisfactory research. Your citation for this circumstance should clearly note that you did not view the item firsthand.

Online course offerings from colleges, genealogical societies and commercial companies are becoming more common. Again, look for credentials of the sponsors and instructors. Word of mouth and peer recommendations can help with choices. It is important that any educational courses incorporate evaluation of sources and analysis of evidence.

The Internet has given exciting new possibilities to genealogists. Now we can do more from our home computers. We can access material we might never have been able to reach before. We can pick up a family's trail with only meagre clues. We can save much time and aggravation by consulting online information sites. However, not everything you want to inspect is online yet and may not even be microfilmed. Nothing replaces the family historian's own evaluation of sources and analysis of evidence to make conclusive genealogical statements.

Once you understand the basic steps of genealogy, working back through each generation with satisfactory identifications, you will be better off in the long run if you lay your own groundwork by traditional methods. If you use Internet resources in the best possible way—a thoughtful, objective way—they can often give you a jump-start into good research. Using the Internet carefully requires conscious evaluation of what you are looking at. Keeping track of where you found information, *and* the source it cites, is absolutely essential.

Citing Documents and Research Sources

How do you cite a source? How do you create a citation? Why bother? This topic can barely be touched on here, but is fundamental to any work you do, right from the beginning. In any given research period—at a resource centre or on the Internet—it's essential to keep track of what you were looking at and where you found it! Citations are also called source notes.

Citations are not only to be used in footnotes or endnotes in a lengthy genealogy or published article. Whether you only keep notes for yourself or whether you plan to compile a family history, or something in between, it is not good enough to cite merely "Archives of Ontario" for your ancestor's property deed, or "Scarlet O'Hara's blog" for a piece of vital information. You want to record details of exactly what you saw if you need to return to it later (this happens!). Citations reveal the quality of the material on which our genealogical statements and conclusions are based. They help our descendants, readers, or peers understand the value of our evidence.

Citations are needed for every genealogical statement that is not "common knowledge." For example, *John Smith was born at Kingston on 29 January 1839* needs a source citation. *Kingston is upriver from Montreal* does not. Citations are needed on photocopies, printouts and scans of documents, preferably not on the reverse side where they can be lost in additional copying.

A citation has elements that say where the source is located and in what medium it was viewed, that is, the actual form of the record you used. Some citations need a date, such as for personal correspondence or website usage. Titles or names are needed for the original document, the record series, the book or the online site and digital image. Document or entry numbers, page numbers, microfilm numbers—all these things are also important.

A citation follows some logical order in description. There are no rules set in concrete, but it's important that you cite a set of records the same way each time you use them—be consistent in one piece of work. The semi-colon often serves to separate two major components.

- Example citing a birth registration:

Kate Mabel Dougall, Ontario birth registration 029867 (1880); microfilm MS 929 reel 45, Archives of Ontario, Toronto.

- Example citing a census return:

William Dougall household, 1851 census Canada West, Prince Edward County, Hallowell Township, page 3, line 30; microfilm C-11750, Library and Archives Canada, Ottawa.

- Example citing a database:

Ron Demaray, *Ontario Cemetery Finding Aid*, database (www.island. net.com/~ocfa: accessed 8 August 2007); entry for John Porter, Trinity Anglican Cemetery, Elma Township, Perth County.

- Example citing a digital image:

John Porter, Ontario death registration 035429 (1910), digital image, *Ancestry.ca* (www.ancestry.ca: accessed 20 June 2007); citing Archives of Ontario microfilm MS 935 reel 160.

Earnest researchers will look for Elizabeth Shown Mills's guides from Genealogical Publishing Company. Her *Evidence Explained* does exactly that: giving the reasoning behind the usage and construction of citations and how they make our work credible. See also Alison Hare's article "Citations for Canadians" in *Families* Vol. 42, No. 3 (2003). Many examples are specific to this province and include a variety of common sources.

Ethics

Sharing family research has always been a hallmark of the genealogical community. Nevertheless, forethought must prevail with regard to over-eager dispersal of information, correspondence and files, whether they are your own work or came from someone else. The nature of electronic media, especially, lends itself to rapid circulation and duplication of information (too often without the knowledge of the first researcher). Besides the copyright questions, errors and omissions are repeated along with anything accurate. It is not ethical to "adopt" and circulate or post someone else's family research without permission. It's also unethical to post vital information about living people. The National Genealogical Society (U.S.) has the excellent "Genealogical Standards and Guidelines" on its website under Learning Center. Every responsible family historian should be aware of these.

- Standards for Good Genealogical Research
- Guidelines for Using Records, Repositories, and Libraries
- Standards for Use of Technology in Genealogical Research
- Standards for Sharing Information with Others
- Guidelines for Publishing Web Pages on the Internet

Genealogical Standards & Guidelines

Standards For Sound Genealogical Research

Recommended by the National Genealogical Society

Remembering always that they are engaged in a quest for truth, family history researchers consistently—

- record the source for each item of information they collect.

- test every hypothesis or theory against credible evidence, and reject those that are not supported by the evidence.

- seek original records, or reproduced images of them when there is reasonable assurance they have not been altered, as the basis for their research conclusions.

- use compilations, communications and published works, whether paper or electronic, primarily for their value as guides to locating the original records, or as contributions to the critical analysis of the evidence discussed in them.

- state something as a fact only when it is supported by convincing evidence, and identify the evidence when communicating the fact to others.

- limit with words like "probable" or "possible" any statement that is based on less than convincing evidence, and state the reasons for concluding that it is probable or possible.

- avoid misleading other researchers by either intentionally or carelessly distributing or publishing inaccurate information.

- state carefully and honestly the results of their own research, and acknowledge all use of other researchers' work.

- recognize the collegial nature of genealogical research by making their work available to others through publication, or by placing copies in appropriate libraries or repositories, and by welcoming critical comment.

- consider with open minds new evidence or the comments of others on their work and the conclusions they have reached.

- Guidelines for Genealogical Self-Improvement and Growth

Major Resource Centres

Most of the fundamental genealogical sources discussed in this book are in the custody of national or provincial repositories. This does not necessarily mean a personal visit to these centres is the only option for accessing their records. Many important sources have been microfilmed and can be borrowed through interlibrary loan. Some of this material has been distributed to, or bought by, other institutions. Last but not least, researchers increasingly have the convenience of consulting digital images, transcriptions and indexes to their key resources online. Be sure to bookmark these major sites, which keep expanding. You can lay a good foundation for your family research by using the comprehensive resources of these institutions.

Interlibrary loan is a service that benefits family historians at a distance. Participating repositories make available certain popular resources from their books and microfilm. A participating public library in your area can borrow those resources for you directly from the institution, if you provide the details from their catalogues and inventories. For viewing microfilm, the local library must necessarily have a microfilm reader.

Library and Archives Canada

Library and Archives Canada (LAC) combines the resources of what used to be the National Library of Canada and the National Archives of Canada. Despite the amalgamation of the two institutions in 2004, the physical location remains at 395 Wellington Street in Ottawa. The former national archives began collecting documents about Canada's history in 1872. Until 1987 the institution was known as the Public Archives of Canada. References to PAC and NA or NAC will still be found in older publications and on microfilm footers. It was only 1953 that the federal government decided to create a national library. Until the recent merger, the archives' mandate was to collect unpublished material while the library's focus was on publications. Now all documentary material is collected and preserved by one bureaucratic structure.

With its extensive collection of unpublished and published material under one roof, LAC is a researcher's paradise. Census returns, passenger lists, Loyalist material, military records and documents about early land grants in Upper Canada and Canada West are among the archival sources heavily used by family historians. Newspapers, city directories, local histories and cemetery transcriptions are highlights of the published collection. The LAC website should be an often-consulted bookmark on your computer. Searching the site for all online descriptions is easily done from the home page, or you can choose separate search engines for the library or archives only. The "Ancestors" search relates to material that has been nominally indexed on the Canadian Genealogy Centre site (see below).

First-time visitors to LAC will need to come by during weekday hours to obtain a no-cost research pass. After that, you can take advantage of the evening and weekend hours. Not all services are open during the extended hours but most genealogical resources are available then.

Canadian Genealogy Centre

The Canadian Genealogy Centre (CGC) is the special unit through which LAC delivers many of its genealogical services. The centre first came into being as a website but now has a physical home as well. The website features numerous databases and information on topics relevant to Ontario and Canada. The physical centre is located in the LAC building and should be the first stop for new visitors. Here you will find the genealogy reference desk, manned

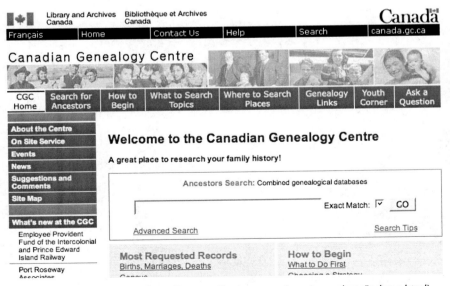

Canadian Genealogy Centre (http://www.collectionscanada.ca/genealogy/index-e.html)

by weekday staff who will answer your genealogy questions and help you get oriented.

Archives of Ontario

The Archives of Ontario (AO) is moving its public services in 2009 from the familiar site at 77 Grenville Street in Toronto to a new location at York University. The campus is located in the northwest corner of the City of Toronto. For more information and updates about the new facility, check the AO website.

The premier repository for Ontario sources, AO has records documenting many facets of our collective and individual pasts. A large part of the institution's mandate is to preserve select records of every provincial ministry. Since provincial governments are responsible for vital statistics (births, marriages, deaths), wills and probate matters, land registration, education and many other areas of residents' lives, you can imagine how large the holdings are. The extensive collection of Crown land records has special interest for researchers with early Ontario ancestors. AO accepts donations of personal papers from Ontario citizens representing many walks of life, and company business records. Written documents are not the only source you can consult. Art works, photographs, films, architectural plans, maps, a library and more are all there for you to discover. Not the least of its treasures are the online exhibits that serve as excellent consulting tools for various subjects and collections within its holdings.

Although AO did not have a genealogy reference desk at the time of this writing, it does have excellent on-site genealogy guides and pathfinders. These are available on the AO website along with a growing number of databases, finding aids, record

A drawing of the new Archives of Ontario building to be constructed in Toronto on the campus of York University at 4700 Keele Street. The Archives will be housed in a purpose-built facility that will both meet international archival standards and make it easier to showcase some of the Archives' most valuable collections. Rendering by Bregman + Hamann Architects.

descriptions, special exhibits and news about current events. Moving from the home page to "Genealogical Research" opens a selection of research guides, No. 299 "Sources of Family History," being the basic introduction. There are several search engines to use online: Archives Descriptive Database for archival materials, BIBLiON for library holdings, the Visual Database for scanned images and others for specialized collections.

The archives is open during the day and evening Monday to Saturday but some services are only available during regular hours. A research pass is required but can be obtained at the security desk any time the archives is open. As is the case with LAC, the staff cannot do research for you but will answer telephone or e-mail questions about their collections. There is also an online query form.

Family History Library

The Family History Library (FHL) in Salt Lake City, Utah, is the largest genealogical library in the world. It is the depository for the microfilming program of the Genealogical Society of Utah (GSU), the educational arm of the Church of Jesus Christ of Latter-day Saints (widely known as Mormons or LDS). As part of its program to preserve historical records worldwide, the GSU has crews microfilming material in more than 40 countries. They have partnered with LAC to index Canadian records such as the 1881 census and passenger lists, while a partnership with AO led to the filming of civil registrations, land records and probate files. AO patrons will recognize their work by the GS and GSU cataloguing designations. Microfilmed Catholic parish records are another great asset for researchers. These and other Canadian and Ontario resources can be found by exploring the online FHL catalogue.

The Family History Library has more than 4,000 branches around the globe. These local Family History Centers sometimes have small collections onsite, but more importantly, you can use them to order material from Salt Lake City. Any of the main library's vast microfilm holdings can be borrowed through a local centre. The only cost is a small fee to cover shipping. A Family History Center near your home would be the most geographically convenient place for you to work.

The FHL's popular website, *FamilySearch,* offers many useful resources including databases, research guides and the just-mentioned catalogue. Among the databases on the main page in the Search for Ancestors are the International Genealogical

Index, Ancestral File and the Pedigree Resource file. Those databases contain material submitted by individuals, therefore are of unproven reliability. While the IGI contains information extracted from original records, it too has individual submissions. Thus caution is required because all these resources are not a substitute for the real thing. Ontario researchers appreciate the 1881 Canadian census database, keeping in mind that it is not an error-free transcription. Above all, remember that one of the most important tools at *FamilySearch* is the library catalogue. With this you will be able to identify the original sources essential for quality research. As an added bonus, some of the Family History Centers have a subscription to *Ancestry.com*.

Ontario Genealogical Society

The Ontario Genealogical Society (OGS) is a province-wide organization with 30 branches under its umbrella. It also boasts a fine library and publishing program. The society's headquarter office is in Toronto. More information about OGS appears in Appendix I.

Other Research Centres

In addition to LAC and AO, there are many other centres in Ontario with genealogical or historical collections. Some counties or districts have archives with records specific to their regions. Their holdings frequently include microfilm copies of basic LAC and AO material, such as census returns and civil registrations. A few examples of such archives are Grey Roots near Owen Sound, Simcoe County Archives near Minesing, Norfolk Heritage Centre in the town of Simcoe and The Lambton Room Archives in Wyoming.

Certain universities libraries have material intended for their own history and social science programs that are of interest to family historians. The D.B. Weldon Library at the University of Western Ontario in London and Queen's University Archives in Kingston both have a wide variety of genealogical material. The James A. Gibson Library at Brock University in St. Catharines features a Loyalist Collection and the Thomas J. Bata Library at Peterborough's Trent University holds material related to aboriginal studies.

Smaller facilities may also have valuable resources. Some public libraries build special collections celebrating the histories of local families, communities, churches, schools, businesses, industries and so on. Then there are the museums. While we might think of these as a place for artifacts, most of them offer more than changing visual displays. Municipalities or counties may have successfully combined museums, archives and libraries. The Markham Museum, the Brockville Museum, the Penetanguishene Centennial Museum and Archives and the Wellington County Museum and Archives in Fergus are but a few. No slight is intended by not listing every one! A real blessing is that all of these more localized or special resource centres may have one-of-a-kind material.

Often these facilities have been organized and operated by volunteers from the area's historical society or a branch of the OGS. In fact, many OGS branch libraries are partnered with a public library or other willing repository.

A comprehensive listing of resource centres can be found in *Ontario Heritage Directory*, published and updated regularly by the Ontario Historical Society. Centres are also listed county by county at the Ontario GenWeb or at various OGS branch websites where you can choose a county of interest to find out where their resources are. Finally, university and public libraries can be found through the Canadian Library Gateway. A link is given at LAC's website under "What We Do For—Libraries, Archives and Publishers."

Reading and Reference

The BCG Genealogical Standards Manual. Orem, UT: Ancestry, Inc., 2000.

Canada, Department of the Secretary of State. *The Canadian Style: A Guide to Writing and Editing.* revised edition. Toronto, ON: Dundurn Press, 1997.

Colket, Meredith B. *Creating a Worthwhile Family Genealogy.* Arlington, VA: National Genealogical Society, 1985

Curran, Joan Ferris, Madilyn Coen Crane and John H. Wray. *Numbering Your Genealogy: Basic Systems, Complex Families and International Kin.* Arlington, VA: National Genealogical Society, 2000

Dollarhide, William. *Managing a Genealogical Project.* 3rd edition. Baltimore, MD: Genealogical Publishing Company, 2001.

Fitzpatrick, Colleen. *Forensic Genealogy.* Fountain Valley, CA: Rice Book Press, 2005.

Hatcher, Patricia Law. *Producing a Quality Family History.* Salt Lake City, UT: Ancestry, Inc., 1996.

Merriman, Brenda Dougall. *About Genealogical Standards of Evidence: A Guide For Genealogists.* Toronto, ON: Ontario Genealogical Society, 2nd edition, 2004.

Mills, Elizabeth Shown. *Evidence Analysis: A Genealogical Process Map.* Baltimore, MD: Genealogical Publishing Company, 2006.

_____. *Evidence! Citation and Analysis for the Family Historian.* 1996. Reprint, Baltimore, MD: Genealogical Publishing Company, 2006.

_____. *Evidence Explained! Citing History Sources from Artifacts to Cyberspace.* Baltimore, MD: Genealogical Publishing Company, 2007.

_____. *QuickSheet: Citing Online Historical Resources, Evidence! Style.* Baltimore, MD: Genealogical Publishing Company, 2007.

_____, editor. *Professional Genealogy: A Manual for Researchers, Writers, Editors, Lecturers and Librarians.* Baltimore, MD: Genealogical Publishing Company, 2001.

Rising, Marsha Hoffman. *The Family Tree Problem Solver: Proven Methods for Scaling the Inevitable Brick Wall.* Cincinnati, OH: Family Tree Books (F+W Publications), 2005.

Smart, Susan and Clifford Duxbury Collier, compilers. *Using Forms for Canadian Genealogical Research.* Toronto, ON: Ontario Genealogical Society, 2006.

Ancestry.ca. www.ancestry.ca

Archives of Ontario. www.archives.gov.on.ca

Canadian Genealogy Centre. www.collectionscanada.ca/genealogy/index-e.html

Canadian Library Gateway. www.collectionscanada.gc.ca (see "Archives, Libraries and Publishers")

Family History Library. www.familysearch.org

Genealogical Publishing Company. www.genealogical.com

Library and Archives Canada. www.collectionscanada.ca

National Genealogical Society. www.ngsgenealogy.org

Ontario Chapter, Association of Professional Genealogists. www.rootsweb.com/~onapg

Ontario GenWeb. www.geneofun.on.ca/ongenweb

Ontario Historical Society. www.ontariohistoricalsociety.ca

2

Ontario Background

Reference Dates

1763	Treaty of Paris; New France (including present day Ontario) became a colony of Britain
1775–83	American Revolutionary War
1783	Treaty of Separation; influx of Loyalist refugees and British soldiers into Nova Scotia and Quebec
1783–84	Spreading of Loyalists and soldiers into western Quebec (now Ontario) under supervision of Governor Frederick Haldimand
1786	Guy Carleton (later to become Lord Dorchester) became the new Governor of British North America, for the next ten years
1788	Western Quebec divided into four administrative districts (see maps), each with an appointed judge and sheriff
1789	The Governor in Council created UE (Unity of Empire) designation and privileges for Loyalist settlers
1791	Canada (Constitutional) Act; Quebec divided into Upper and Lower Canada
1792	John Graves Simcoe became the first Lieutenant Governor of Upper Canada; the first meetings of the Executive Council and Legislative Assembly, at the capital, Newark (now Niagara-on-the-Lake)
1793	York (now Toronto) was named the capital of Upper Canada

1794	Jay's Treaty: one condition was the ceding of British Forts Detroit, Michilimackinac and Niagara to the United States
1812–14	War between Britain and the United States
1829	Welland Canal opened, Port Dalhousie to Port Robinson
1832	Rideau Canal opened, Bytown to Kingston; Burlington Bay canal finished
1837–38	Rebellion in Upper and Lower Canada; American invasions
1841	Act of Union: Upper and Lower Canada became Canada West and East, with an elected assembly
1849	The district system was abolished in favour of county administration
1850	The Municipal Act came into effect: municipalities (towns and townships) became officially responsible for local administration
1851	Great Western Railway construction began, Toronto to Buffalo
1866	Fenian raids into Canada from the United States
1867	British North America Act: Canadian confederation of four provinces; Canada West became Ontario
1885	Canadian Pacific Railway was completed across Canada

An excellent and more detailed historical outline can be found at the Global Genealogy website. Click on columnist Rick Roberts and scroll down to "A Chronology of Ontario History for Family Historians."

Geography

Knowing the lay of the land is essential, whether you know where your ancestor lived within the province or not. The 1783–1784 arrival of Loyalists across the Detroit and Niagara Rivers, and especially the majority who came up the St. Lawrence River to its juncture with Lake Ontario, initiated permanent European settlement in the region to be named Upper Canada in 1791. "Upper" Canada refers to its relative position along the St. Lawrence, above the already-populated downriver areas.

The eighteenth and early nineteenth century pioneers travelled by water routes, so the first communities clustered along the Great Lakes and the rivers that feed them. Later, roads and eventually railways would enable colonization to reach further inland to expand farming, mining and timber operations.

Topographical features account for diversions and quirks in land surveys and influenced travel between two points. For instance, without some geographic knowledge of the Niagara Peninsula, you would not understand the customary routes westward across the Niagara Escarpment. Poor soil, rough land and swamps affected the viability of certain areas for farming. Sites for the first mills and market centres were affected by terrain and location. Human changes to the environment, such as canal construction, manufacturing, town planning and so on, further affected an individual's choice of settlement or employment.

Planning a visit to the ancestral location is a natural outcome of your research, as you discover where the family lived. And there's no question that soaking up the local environs and viewing the historical buildings, farms, places of worship, schools and cemeteries can be a unique experience. However, do not expect to find original birth, marriage, death, census, wills, land or military records in a nearby village or a town, even if it is a county seat. Village or town administrators rarely have records of a genealogical nature. While many records were created at such a grassroots level, they were mandated by a higher level of government that collected and preserved them. This system is contrary to the expectations of American researchers, who generally rely on county level courthouses and offices for obtaining many different kinds of rewarding sources.

Agricultural ancestors might have remembered a nearby village or town as their place of residence due to their social and economic ties with it. However, sometimes that village may not even be in the same township or county as the family farm. You will hear repeatedly that the township and county locations are the keys to finding and using most basic genealogical sources.

Location

Some searchers may be approaching their family research with no idea *where* the ancestor lived in this large province. This happens when descendants have moved away from Ontario. You may only have a vague reference like "born in Canada" or "Upper Canada" or "British Canada" or "English Canada" or "Canada West." You may not be able to access any meaningful sources until you can determine the name of a county, but preferably a township or town. The standard advice is to go back to your relatives and home sources for more possible clues. The next advice is to exhaust sources for the ancestor who left the province, and all his or her siblings or children. To trace anyone in the family who was born in Ontario and died elsewhere, you need to search out records at the next place of residence or eventual place of death. Although your direct ancestor may not have inspired a newspaper obituary, or had an exact birthplace mentioned in a death record, one of his twelve brothers and sisters may have.

Name indexes to original or published sources can be helpful, the more wide-ranging the better. At the very most they might locate your ancestor or, at the least, show you where your surname was clustered if it is not too common. Consult library collections of Ontario genealogical and historical material, which are discussed further in the Publications section of this chapter. Here are a few useful suggestions for original sources, discussed later in the appropriate chapters. The range of time for each source differs.

- Registrar General's Indexes to Births, Marriages and Deaths
- Census indexes for 1851, 1871, 1881, 1901, 1906 [Western Canada only but might hold clues], 1911
- Ontario Land Records Index created by the Archives of Ontario
- Index to Upper Canada Land Petitions
- Indexes to Probate and Surrogate Courts

When you do know where your ancestor lived, but have no idea where that place is within the province, there are some online resources for help.

- *Ontario GenWeb's* "Ontario Locator"

This part of the Ontario GenWeb allows you to search for a place name alphabetically, or by typing a name into the search engine. It takes names literally (exact searches), so you may have to try more than once with spelling variations.

- *ePodunk The Power of Place*

Be sure to check the "include former names" box. This site often includes historical postcard views.

- *Geographical Names of Canada*

This official federal government site does not necessarily include obsolete historical names.

Historical Plaques

Plaques commemorating a geographic or historical site could be an unexpected source of information for family historians. The Provincial Plaque Program began over 50 years ago as a project by the Ontario Heritage Foundation, now the Ontario Heritage

Trust. Their blue and gold signs have been erected throughout the province in appropriate locations to increase public appreciation for the natural environment and notable historical events. The text of the plaques can be viewed online on the Heritage Trust website by searching a location name or choosing from the site's theme menu. While the Trust's website has some photographs, another website called *Ontario's Historical Plaques* has perhaps a larger collection of well over 1,200 plaque photos, also searchable by subject or location.

The Trust publishes the updated *A Guide to Historical Plaques in Ontario*. You can request background research papers about the subjects of the plaques. Exercise caution about relying on the facts reported on some of the older memorials. The Trust has the similar Local Marker Program to honour particular communities, their founding families or significant buildings.

Maps, Atlases, Plans

A family historian cannot work without maps. A good map will help you visualize the province and the township (or town) and surroundings where your ancestor lived. A pre-1968 map of

Wellington County Court House

Photo by Alan L Brown - June 1, 2005

Photo used with permission from the website www.ontarioplaques.com.

Ontario is recommended. Maps after this date show the trend to amalgamation and larger regional governments that changed some names and boundaries. Gartner and Prong's *Townships of the Province of Ontario, Canada* is a useful reference list with maps.

Historical map suggestions:

- Joan Winearls' *Mapping Upper Canada, 1780-1867*

This book is the ultimate map reference work for the province, covering all known pre-Confederation maps of Ontario, including those held in Special Collections at the Archives of Ontario. It will be found at all major libraries.

- "Online Learning Project" at *Historical Atlas of Canada*

The publishers of the original 3-volume set have designed a website, still under development in late 2007. The site specializes in numerous themes such as exploration, boundary changes, military and regional patterns. The interactive maps and other features are supplemented by text from the print volumes.

- *Perly's Detailed Atlas, Provincial Atlas of Ontario*

This excellent atlas is out of print but can be found in libraries or second hand. It shows late twentieth century place names, roads and other features, but also pre-1968 county maps with township, town, village and railway station details. All place names are alphabetically indexed, along with lakes, rivers and other natural geographic features.

- Eric Jonasson's "The Districts and Counties of Ontario, 1777–1979, Two Centuries of Evolution," in *Families* Vol. 20, No. 2 (1977) was also reprinted in *Families* Vol. 45, No. 4 (2006). The article is a more complete reference than the maps in the front of this book, and focuses on the county level.

- *Canadian Heritage Gallery.* Several maps are of 1788 and 1798 vintage.

- County maps with township details were created in the 1860s by cartographer George Tremaine. Some OGS Branches sell reproductions.

- See also "Cartographic Records" on the Archives of Ontario website for a list of township, town and city plans in their holdings. They are non-circulating, to be viewed in the Special Collections Reading Room.

On the national level, the federal government has numerous map publications to choose from, including topographic maps.

You can explore many offerings at *The Atlas of Canada* website. The map collection at Library and Archives Canada website is huge, with thousands listed on the LAC website. A growing number of digital images are linked to the maps. The more specific you are in your keyword search, the fewer hits you will have to work through. "Canada at Scale" is an online LAC exhibit featuring a selection from their collection.

A current road map used in conjunction with an older version will help you correlate locations you may want to visit. Try the online sites of the Ontario Ministry of Transportation (road maps) and the Ontario Ministry of Natural Resources (specialized maps and aerial photographs). If you want to home in on specific coordinates from modern satellite images, you can download the popular Google Earth program.

Genealogy, Geography and Maps by Althea Douglas is especially valuable for both beginners and seasoned family historians, and beautifully illustrated. See also Stratford-Devai's *Using Maps in Family History Research.*

Historical Atlases

The historical atlases of Ontario counties are a treasured resource for genealogy and history in the nineteenth century. Thirty-two atlases cover forty counties. Published in oversize format in the 1870s and 1880s, they bring you right down to a township level. They usually show each township map on one or two pages, with plans of towns and villages. Individual properties are well marked in the expected concession and lot patterns; concessions are in roman numerals and lots are in arabic numbers. Often schools and churches are shown, although not named. Railway lines, rivers and roads add to the sense of surroundings. Ask yourself where the rural ancestors would go for shopping, banking, post office and religious services. As a bonus, many of the atlases begin with a map showing the whole province as it existed then.

Perhaps of most interest to family historians are the names of the occupants on each farm lot. In general, we assume that these are the property owners of the time—but that assumption should be verified from other land records. You will also see who the neighbours are, an added interest if their surnames appear in family marriages. Condensed historical accounts of the overall area mention pioneer milestones, and each township and major town has a more detailed settlement description. Portraits of prominent residents or officials, and sketches of model county

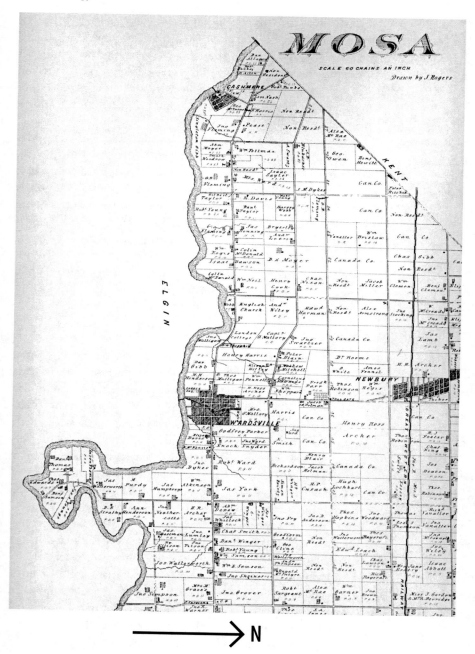

Detail of Mosa Township, Middlesex County, from the Historical Atlas of Middlesex County, Ontario. *Originally published by H. R. Page & Co., 1878; reprinted by Mika Silk Screening Ltd, Belleville, Ontario, 1972. Note that north is not always at the top of old maps.*

farms and businesses are sprinkled throughout, the owners having paid a premium for the privilege. Many atlases include a list of patrons in each town or township at the end. Just be aware these are names of people who subscribed to the publication and are not all the residents. A few of the books lack some of these elements and sometimes two or more counties are combined in one publication.

The atlases can be consulted in Canadian libraries that have Ontario genealogy collections, and at LAC and AO. Global Genealogy publishes and sells reprints for some counties. Most convenient of all, McGill University has scanned the atlases and the digital images can be searched by an individual's name or by place name. The township maps can be magnified for easy reading. A different atlas, the *Electoral Atlas of the Dominion of Canada* (1895), is online at the Canadian Genealogy Centre to show county and township boundaries for electoral districts. The districts correspond to census returns on both sides of the turn of the twentieth century.

Fire Insurance Plans

These maps, plans, and records were created by insurance companies to assess underwriting values in cities, towns and villages. They are a special resource that genealogists consult infrequently. The earliest surviving Ontario fire insurance map is for Guelph in 1875, housed at McLaughlin Library, University of Guelph. The plans were usually copyrighted and published or registered by the creators or companies that produced them. Charles Goad was an eminent cartographer of the time, well-known for his work across Canada. Most of his fire insurance plans created between 1895 and 1917 were fortunately preserved in the British Library, London, England.

The Canadian plans of the Charles E. Goad Company, including 319 locations in Ontario, can be viewed on microform at Library and Archives Canada. They are in the form of atlases, arranged by province and then by town and village. Larger cities have street indexes. What do the plans show, exactly? The detail of "the built environment" can be astounding—construction materials, architectural features and neighbourhood items regarding fire risk management, such as street and water access to buildings. If you have a street address in the right time period, you can learn a great deal about your ancestor's home and surroundings. See the list of available plans and locations by searching the name Charles Goad at the LAC website or consult *Catalogue of Canadian Fire Insurance Plans* by Dubreuil and Woods.

Place Names

Numerous place names occur more than once in Ontario. Unless you are aware of this, you could start your investigations off on the wrong track. One example is the Grand River that runs for 290 kilometres from near Georgian Bay on Lake Huron into Lake Erie. In very early times both the St. Lawrence River and the Ottawa River were called Grand River. Other well-known names that cause confusion are:

York	a county now absorbed by the City of Toronto
	a township formerly in the County of York
	the name until 1834 for the City of Toronto
	at one time, a village on the Grand River in Haldimand County
Toronto	capital (and largest city) of Ontario
	townships called Toronto and Toronto Gore, formerly in Peel County, now absorbed by the City of Mississauga
Oxford	a county in southwestern Ontario
	townships Oxford East, Oxford North and Oxford West in Oxford County
	Oxford Township, aka Oxford-on-the-Rideau, is in Grenville County
Hamilton	the city in Wentworth County
	a township in Northumberland County
Perth	a county in central western Ontario
	a town, county seat of Lanark County
Prescott	a county along the Ottawa River
	a town, county seat of Grenville County
Simcoe	a county on the west of Lake Simcoe
	a town, county seat of Norfolk County
Clinton	a township in the former Lincoln County
	a town in Goderich Township, Huron County
Bothwell	an artificial county created for 1871 census purposes
	a town in Zone Township, Kent County

In addition to confusing place names, some of the old names for places have disappeared. Most often this was due to a name change or annexation into an expanding urban area. Now that we are in the twenty-first century, even some of the townships are being renamed as administrative needs are consolidated. Gazetteers and books, as well as the online sites for maps mentioned above, exist to help you. Here are a few of the large or important historical centres that changed names:

Present Name	Former Name
Burlington	Wellington Square
Cambridge	Galt, Hespeler (aka New Hope), Preston
Cornwall	New Johnstown
Grimsby	Forty Mile Creek (The Forty)
Halton Hills	Acton, Georgetown
Hamilton	Cootes Paradise
Jordan	Twenty Mile Creek (The Twenty)
Kingston	Cataraqui, Waterloo
Kitchener	Berlin
Mississauga	Toronto Township, including the villages and towns of Lorne Park, Port Credit, Cooksville, Malton, Streetsville, among others
Nanticoke	Waterford, Port Dover, Jarvis, with all or parts of surrounding townships
Niagara Falls	Chippawa, Clifton, Drummondville
Niagara-on-the-Lake	Newark
Orillia	The Narrows
Oshawa	Kerr's Creek
Ottawa	Bytown
Port Hope	Amherst, Smith's Creek
Paris	Forks of the Grand
St. Catharines	Twelve Mile Creek (The Twelve)
St. Thomas	Stirling
Thunder Bay	Fort William and Port Arthur
Toronto	York
Wallaceburg	Baldoon
Whitby	Perry's Corners, Windsor
Windsor	Sandwich

Numbered Townships

When the province was first being surveyed, original townships were hastily numbered to accommodate the overwhelming numbers of Loyalists and discharged soldiers who needed land. Indeed, some settlers had moved onto lands before survey work was completed, or in some cases, before it began. Researchers using eighteenth century material will see these numbered references on documents or maps. By the 1790s most townships had been named.

Referring to the first map of the series in this book, numbered townships along the north shore of the St. Lawrence River were (known as the "royal townships," named after King George III's children or their titles):

1 — Charlottenburgh	5 — Matilda
2 — Cornwall	6 — Edwardsburgh
3 — Osnabruck	7 — Augusta
4 — Williamsburgh	8 — Elizabethtown

The "Cataraqui townships" in the Bay of Quinte area were originally measured as being above or below Cataraqui, the first name for the town of Kingston:

1 — Kingston	7 — Ameliasburgh
2 — Ernestown	8 — Sidney
3 — Fredericksburgh	9 — Thurlow
4 — Adolphustown	10 — Richmond
5 — Marysburgh	11 — Camden
6 — Sophiasburgh	

Some early townships in the old Nassau District (Niagara Peninsula area):

1 — Niagara	5 — Clinton
2 — Stamford (earlier, Mount Dorchester)	6 — Grimsby
3 — Grantham	7 — Saltfleet
4 — Louth	8 — Barton

Along both banks of the Thames River (previously called Rivière la Tranche) in western Ontario, now in Kent County:

South side:	North side:
1 — Raleigh	1 — Dover
2 — Harwich	2 — Chatham
3 — Howard	3 — Camden

Publications

When approaching any new geographic region for family history, the researcher familiarizes herself with the diversity

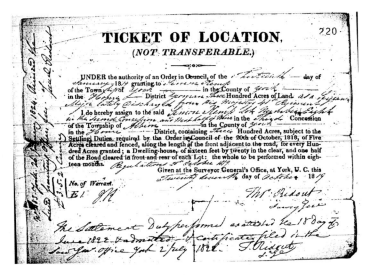

Simon Kemp
Location Ticket for
land. AO, RG-1-58,
Township Papers,
Albion, p. 220;
MS 658, reel 5

of publications. Books are a major category of interest to the genealogist. Newspapers give fascinating insights into daily life of the past and sometimes mention family members. Directories zero in on specific locations for an ancestor. Biographies are of special interest for an ancestor who was prominent in provincial or national life.

Books

"How to" books are essential for a personal reference library. They include basic texts about research methodology and creating acceptable source notes. Anyone compiling a family history should not overlook a style manual. Also, genealogists have taken the time to write guides to the records and resources of a region or country. The best ones help you plan your research steps and keep you on track as you go along. Many society journals feature book reviews that assess the instructional value of such guides. And the term "reviews" refers to thoughtful critique, not the ubiquitous book notices that merely summarize a book's content.

Local histories of counties, townships, towns, churches, schools, organizations and more are another category of useful books. Every genealogy and family history benefits from background detail about an ancestor's life and times. Local happenings, and often events of a broader nature, could have influenced decisions about moving from one place to another, or opportunities for employment, for the environment in which he raised his family, where he conducted his business, where he worshipped and so on. Flipping to an index at the back of a book to find a name is tempting, but not true research. How much can be missed without reading about the author's or compiler's scope, and understanding the context where a name is found! The compilers of many local histories relied on family memory and word of mouth, or previous publications. As derivative material, it can provide important clues to a family's whereabouts or activities, but demand further investigation on your part.

The digitization of historical books is increasing rapidly to produce some interesting sites. Only a few are mentioned here.

- *Early Canadiana Online* is a digital library for making scarce publications more widely accessible. The Canadian Institute for Historical Microreproductions, which morphed into *Canadiana.org*, created the bibliography microfiche set called *Genealogy and Local History to 1900*. The set can be found at many Ontario libraries or purchased from the ECO website. It became the basis for selective digitization on the ECO website. Digitized images include government reports, acts, sessional papers and other documents about people in the past. A search engine gives limited free access to digitized pages. A subscription, which supports the ongoing work, is necessary for full use of the site.

- The Champlain Society has a digital collection of its own published volumes that include some early books about Upper Canada. Its pages are freely accessible.

- *OurRoots/Nos Racines* is dedicated to local histories. The content can be freely searched by title, author or subject. Ontario is represented with some lesser-known books of community or family history.

- *Google Book Search* has been rapidly scanning books for on-screen reading. Full viewing is available for books in the public domain. Partial viewing of such things as title page, table of contents and perhaps an opening page of a book are allowed dependent on copyright and publisher restrictions. The selection is huge, and most useful for obtaining information about obscure books.

Possibly an ancestor's family history already exists, compiled by someone you never met. These can be found in genealogical libraries and on personal websites. Keep up with new additions to the *Family History Archive,* a joint digitization project by Brigham Young University, the Family History Library and Allen County Public Library. Sometimes such finds open a door to new family connections and the potential for sharing and combining research efforts. Nevertheless, the same catch-22 applies here as with local histories—the information was often gathered from derivative sources or sources were not cited, but the information may hold morsels worth investigating. The ever-present caution about apparent credibility emphasizes your own need for research that supports or rejects such information. Countless genealogies were published in the past without today's more exacting standards. They might have captured wonderful clues for your own research, but the provenance of each genealogical statement may not be clear. Even when sources are cited, you will want to examine those sources yourself.

Another type of publication is name indexes for commonly consulted regional histories that originally had no indexing. Also, some individuals or groups have compiled abstracts or extracts from historical manuscript material or serial publications. Genealogical publishers' catalogues and OGS branches are places to look for them. Publishers of genealogical material are listed in Appendix V. Most have websites you can browse.

One method to find out-of-print or limited-edition books and manuscripts is through *Information Network For Ontario*, an interlibrary loan service on the Internet among collaborating public libraries. Although not each and every library is represented, this is a way to find family histories that may not be on legal deposit with Library and Archives Canada. Searching for a book's existence or location can be done from your home computer by author, title or subject using the "INFO" log-in screen. The search results give complete bibliographic information and circulation status. If the material is available for loan, take the search results to a participating local library to make the request for you.

LAC's online library search engine leads you to a comprehensive catalogue of Canadian publications including both the LAC and library collections across the country. Via interlibrary loan your local public library can borrow books, with certain exceptions, from LAC. The library of the Archives of Ontario, the Family History Library and the OGS Library do not lend print publications on interlibrary loan. These places have specific family histories, some of them published in very limited editions or even manually produced. At the very least, all have catalogues to make you aware of what is available and where to find it. Some researchers prefer to search for books using *WorldCat*, the expanding network of world-wide libraries.

Periodicals

The journals and newsletters of genealogical societies contain countless references to surnames and families. The content and quality of articles depend on the contributing authors. Here again, someone else may have written an article about one of your families. The OGS quarterly *Families* has been indexed for names and subjects from its inception in 1962 up to 2007.

An article about a family with Ontario connections could also have appeared in distant publications where descendants settled. Then the great tool called PERSI (PERiodical Source Index) comes to the fore. Created at the Allen County Public Library, Fort Wayne, Indiana, it is an index to thousands of English-language genealogy-related serial publications. PERSI is searchable through a subscription to *Ancestry.com* or through *HeritageQuestOnline*, the latter accessible only at subscribing libraries and institutions. Some libraries have institutional subscriptions to both sites. When articles of interest are located this way, photocopies can be obtained from the Allen County Library.

The publishing of commercial magazines aimed at genealogists has increased. *Family Chronicle* is one that often includes Canadian or Ontario content. Web newsletters, or e-zines, have also become popular. While they seem to rarely feature a family history as such, they do have stories about ancestors. Rootsweb and Ancestry produce two of the better-known online magazines.

Newspapers

Most small-town newspapers in the nineteenth century were weekly publications. The relatively brief birth-marriage-death notices are of chief family interest, although not every newspaper had a regular BMD column in earlier times. A newspaper notice can be a complement, or sometimes an alternative, to a BMD record.

Do not limit yourself to scanning BMD columns alone. Many notices were reported elsewhere in the newspaper, within the local town items and small columns from outlying areas. Sometimes the reporter for a village or rural township did not get his copy published until a week or two after an event.

Death notices, especially obituaries, are usually the most rewarding finds. Even people who were not prominent might have deserved a local tribute by virtue of old age, long residence, a pioneering history, exemplary conduct or community service. The best obituaries mention a person's place of origin, age or date of birth, date of settlement, occupation, marriage information, possibly a local claim to fame and surviving kin and their locations. When obituary searches are unsuccessful in newspapers published near the ancestor's residence, you may have some luck in newspapers where some of the children lived.

After death notices, marriage notices are probably the most prevalent. They too are worth looking for outside the BMD columns. In the twentieth century, weddings might be described in grand detail. It's not unusual to see the wedding gowns, guests and gifts described. Notices of births are fewer, especially if they took place outside the immediate town of publication. Often they only tell us that Mrs. John Smith delivered a baby boy last Tuesday.

Certain newspapers appealed to immigrant sensibilities, such as an Irish Catholic or Protestant readership. Canada's cultural mosaic policy encouraged ethnic newspaper publishing among other activities. Some of those papers may be in English, but many are in the language of the readers' country of origin.

The Archives of Ontario holds the wide-ranging collection of the Multicultural Historical Society of Ontario, including numerous microfilmed newspapers. The great majority are from the twentieth century and titles can be explored through AO on-site or online reference aids.

The *Upper Canada Gazette* began publishing in 1793 as a quasi-government organ. It became *Canada Gazette* in 1841 with official status for the legislative assemblies of Canada West and Canada East. After 1867 it became the voice of the federal government. The *Gazette* published all government

MARRIAGES.

STEPHENS-STEPHENS.--At Christ's Church, on Wednesday, May 10th, by the Rev. Canon Pentreath, Francis, son of the late Thomas Correy Stephens, of Owen Sound, to Maria Kathleen, eldest daughter of T. W. Stephens, of Winnipeg.

DEATHS.

WAGG.—At Collingwood, on Monday, May 22, 1893, Bertha, eldest daughter of Charles and Susan Wagg, aged 20 years, and 4 months.

BATTEN.—On the 21st inst., at Kirkville, Walter Ross, youngest son of Mr. Chas. Batten, aged 14 years, 7 months and 24 days. Died of pleurisy and inflammation of lungs.

Detail from The Enterprise *(Collingwood, Ontario) 25 May 1893, p. 8, col. 3.*

proclamations and appointments, new statutes and regulations, proposed legislation, committee decisions, names of people who became naturalized citizens and other announcements of public interest. Notices of bankruptcies, real estate and sheriffs' sales, divorces, chartered banks and corporate information also appeared. A complete series of *Upper Canada Gazette* no longer exists, but LAC and AO and several other libraries have a microfilmed series, as per Gilchrist's *Inventory of Ontario Newspapers 1793-1986*. The *Canada Gazette* is more complete in its run. Library and Archives Canada is already making available a searchable index of the *Gazette* 1841–1997 with links to digital files.

Both Library and Archives Canada and the Archives of Ontario have fine collections of nineteenth and twentieth century weekly and daily Ontario town newspapers. Gilchrist's Inventory is the guide to consult. In an alphabetical arrangement by place name, the book shows all newspapers that existed, and the repositories that have extant copies. LAC published *Checklist of Indexes to Canadian Newspapers (1987)* from a survey of archives, historical societies, libraries and newspaper offices. The Checklist provides detailed information about which newspapers were indexed, which material within a newspaper was indexed and how researchers can access it. Updates can be seen on the LAC website. Bur-Mor Publications, available through Global Genealogy, has extracted BMDs from dozens of Ontario's first newspapers.

The *Paper of Record* website bills itself as "the world's largest searchable archive of historical newspapers." The website requires registration, but you can freely search digitized images of newspaper pages. The key word(s) you enter is highlighted on the page results. The collection for Ontario is good and growing. You can explore the possibilities of other companies or the newspapers themselves that are digitizing historical issues. Some sites are accessible only by paid subscriptions. Some are available at libraries requiring a membership card for access.

Denominational newspapers for the major religions commenced publishing in the nineteenth century. They too featured BMD items with particular regard paid to obituaries for their own members. *The Church* (Anglican), the *Christian Guardian* (Methodist), the *Presbyterian Record*, the *Catholic Record* and the *Catholic Register*, and the *Christian Messenger/ Canadian Baptist* are to name a few. They are available at the appropriate church archives, which may have some nominal indexes; for example, the *Christian Guardian* starting in 1829 at the United Church of Canada Archives. Hamilton Branch OGS has indexed Baptist newspapers beginning in 1854. Many of the microfilmed religious newspapers are also available at AO and LAC. The Ontario Jewish Archives has copies of Jewish newspapers in Yiddish, Hebrew and English dating from the early twentieth century until the present.

Hunterdon House of Lambertville, New Jersey, published several volumes of newspaper extracts by compilers Thomas B. Wilson and William D. Reid. The extracts come from a mixture of religious and secular newspapers and are name indexed. See Chapter 4 for specific titles. Donald A. McKenzie's remarkable work includes ten volumes of extracts from a variety of Methodist newspapers, from earliest days to 1890. These publications are available at libraries and through Global Genealogy.

Directories

The value of city, town or county directories is self-evident in placing an ancestor in a specific location and year. Few were published in Ontario before the middle of the nineteenth century, with the notable exceptions of Toronto in 1834 (the year it was incorporated and its name changed from York) and the 1837 *City of Toronto and the Home District Commercial Directory and Register.* The latter included all the developed townships then within the old Home District, with residents' names, street addresses and lot and concession descriptions if they were farmers. More directories for Toronto and other cities began to appear in the 1850s. Later, directories for large counties, or groups of counties, followed the same pattern.

City directories often have an alphabetical street listing, so you can see if other individuals or families occupied the same house as your ancestors, or who their neighbours were. If a resident is listed as an employee of a certain company you can then look up the company listing to find its location. There are alphabetical listings of businesses, both large commercial concerns and smaller shops. Maybe you will find a paid advertisement for a business or factory where the ancestor worked. If the directory includes ward boundaries, your city census searching is facilitated.

Directories can also be a source for much additional material about the areas they represent. Government agencies and offices, banks, schools, churches, hospitals, post offices and community organizations are usually listed with addresses and principal officials.

Publishers occasionally produced province-wide compilations like *Directory of the Province of Ontario* (1857), *Province of Ontario Gazetteer and Directory* (1869) and *Lovell's Province of Ontario Directory* (1871) but they do not list every resident. They tended to concentrate on business, professional and trades people. Reading the detailed sub-titles or the explanatory introductions that appear in some reprint editions will alert you to the directory's limitations.

Both LAC and AO have good collections of historic directories for this province. The ready reference shelves at LAC extend the city collections through the twentieth century. A selection of older directories is searchable at the CGC website. Public and genealogical libraries also have directories for general interest and for their immediate areas.

Telephone Books

In more modern times, name searching can be effective with telephone books. Phone service began before the turn of the twentieth century, with urban service first and rural service following. Using phone directories obviously requires knowing which city or area telephone book to consult. Sometimes the telephone area coverage was or is geographically wider than you might expect from the title on the cover of the book. Both LAC and AO have the microfilmed Bell Canada Telephone Historical Collection. The phone books for Ontario span approximately 1878–1980. The microfilms are non-circulating, and can be consulted with in-house guides.

Biographies

Searching for published references to people should include the massive and scholarly *Dictionary of Canadian Biography*. Each of the 14 volumes in print up to 1920 spans a chronological time period, with entries made according to the year a person died. The arrangement in each volume is alphabetical by surname. From 1851 each volume covers a decade. Noted historians are participating in this ongoing project. While the thousands of people with individual entries were contributors in some degree to Canadian history, the indexes include all names, even those mentioned peripherally in each biography. The DCB website is searchable for every name and keyword. The home website at the

University of Toronto has detailed information about the scope of the project. Print volumes can be consulted in many libraries, and can also be purchased as a CD-ROM created in 2000.

A relatively modern type of biographical and serial directory is the *Who's Who* format, which has been imitated in dozens of variations. Originally intended as "social registers" of the prominent, powerful, and wealthy, they were issued by publishing companies for a country, region or city, usually in a chronological series. Prepaid subscriptions ensured the subscriber's inclusion. Now it is common to see them for professional occupations, businesses, government bureaucracies, religious institutions, membership organizations and many, many other categories. Browsing the library sections of the LAC and AO websites gives a large selection from *Canadian Who's Who* (from 1910) to *Who's Who in Ontario* (1996).

The nineteenth century historical atlases have been described on page 35. Some interesting commemorative biographical works were published near the turn of the twentieth century for a few counties in the province (Essex, Kent, Lambton, York). The publications were intended to feature prominent local families whose descendants were still in the area. A typical family biography will include several generations descending from the pioneer ancestor. The genealogical information was generally provided by family members living at the time the commemorative biographies were published. Later research has uncovered a number of factual errors in them. These books will also be found in genealogy collections of many libraries.

Reading and Reference

Aitken, Barbara B. *Local Histories of Ontario Municipalities, 1951-1977: A Bibliography*. Toronto, ON: Ontario Library Association, 1978.

_____. *Local Histories of Ontario Municipalities, 1977-1987: A Bibliography*. Toronto, ON: Ontario Library Association, 1978.

_____. *Local Histories of Ontario Municipalities 1987-1997, A Bibliography*. Toronto, ON: Ontario Genealogical Society, 1999.

_____. *Local Histories of Ontario Municipalities 1997-2008, A Bibliography*. Toronto, ON: Ontario Genealogical Society, 2009.

Armstrong, Frederick H. *Handbook of Upper Canadian Chronology*. Revised edition. Toronto, ON: Dundurn Press, 1996.

Bond, Mary E. *Canadian Directories: A Bibliography and Place-name Index.* 3 volumes. Revised third edition. Ottawa, ON: National Library of Canada, 1989.

Burkholder, Ruth. *Starting Out in Genealogy.* Campbellville, ON: Global Heritage Press, 2007.

Burrows, Sandra and Francine Gaudet, compilers. *Checklist of Indexes to Canadian Newspapers.* Ottawa, ON: National Library of Canada, 1987. See also www.collectionscanada/8/12/index-e.html.

The Canadian Style: A Guide to Writing and Editing. Revised edition. Toronto, ON: Dundurn Press, 1997.

Carter, Floreen Ellen. *Place Names of Ontario.* 2 volumes. London, ON: Phelps Publishing, 1984.

Cook, Ramsay and Réal Bélanger, editors. *Dictionary of Canadian Biography.* 14 volumes, 1000-1920. Toronto, ON: University of Toronto Press, 1966-1998. Also www.biographi.ca

Craig, Gerald M. *Upper Canada: The Formative Years.* Toronto, ON: McClelland & Stewart, 1968.

Douglas, Althea. *Here Be Dragons! Navigating the Hazards Found in Canadian Family Research.* Toronto, ON: Ontario Genealogical Society, 1996.

_____. *Here be Dragons, Too! More Navigational Hazards for the Canadian Family Researcher.* Toronto, ON: Ontario Genealogical Society, 2000.

_____. *Tools of the Trade for Canadian Genealogy.* Second edition. Toronto, ON: Ontario Genealogical Society, 2003.

_____. *Genealogy, Geography and Maps: Using Atlases and Gazetteers to Find Your Family.* Toronto, ON: Ontario Genealogical Society, 2006.

Dubreuil, Lorraine and Cheryl A. Woods. *Catalogue of Canadian Fire Insurance Plans 1875-1975.* Occasional Papers of the Canadian Map Libraries and Archives, No. 6. Ottawa, ON: ACMLA, 2002.

Gartner, Muriel and Frederick Prong, compilers. *Townships of the Province of Ontario, Canada: A Complete Index of the Townships in All the Counties & Districts of Ontario.* Revised edition. Toronto: OGS, 2007.

Gilchrist, J. Brian and Clifford Duxbury Collier, compilers. *Genealogy and Local History to 1900: A Bibliography Selected from the Catalogue of the Canadian Institute for Historical Microreproductions.* Ottawa, ON: Canadian Institute for Historical Reproductions, 1996.

A Guide to Provincial Plaques in Ontario. Toronto, ON: Ontario Heritage Trust, 2006.

Hayward, Robert J. *Fire Insurance Plans in the National Map Collection.* Ottawa, ON: Public Archives of Canada, 1977.

Morley, William F.E. *Ontario and the Canadian North.* Volume 3: *Canadian Local Histories to 1950: A Bibliography.* Toronto, ON: University of Toronto Press, 1978.

Perly's Detailed Atlas, Provincial Atlas of Ontario. Toronto, ON: Perly's Valprint, 1978.

Rayburn, Alan. *Place Names of Ontario.* Toronto, ON: University of Toronto Press, 1997.

Stratford-Devai, Fawne. *Using Maps in Family History Research: Lessons and Links.* Campbellville, ON: Global Heritage Press, 2005.

Taylor, Ryan. *Important Genealogical Collections in Ontario Libraries and Archives: A Directory.* Toronto, ON: Ontario Genealogical Society, 1994.

_____. *Books You Need to Do Genealogy in Ontario: An Annotated Bibliography.* Fort Wayne, IN: Round Tower Books, 2000.

_____. *Researching Canadian Newspaper Records.* Toronto, ON: Heritage Productions, 2002.

_____. *The Canadian Genealogical Sourcebook.* Ottawa, ON: Canadian Library Association, 2004.

Whyte, Donald. *Dictionary of Scottish Emigrants to Canada Before Confederation.* 4 volumes. Toronto, ON: Ontario Genealogical Society, 1986-2005.

Wilson, Thomas B., editor. *The Ontario Register.* 8 volumes. Lambertville, NJ: Hunterdon House, 1968-1990.

Winearls, Joan. *Mapping Upper Canada, 1780-1867: An Annotated Bibliography of Manuscript and Printed Maps.* Toronto, ON: University of Toronto Press, 1991.

Allen County Public Library. www.acpl.lib.in.us

Ancestry.ca. www.ancestry.ca

The Atlas of Canada. atlas.nrcan.gc.ca/site/index.html

Canada at Scale online exhibit. www.collectionscanada.ca/maps/index-e.html

Canada Gazette. canadagazette.gc.ca/index-e.html

Canadian Heritage Gallery. www.canadianheritage.org/galleries/mapsplans0300.htm

Canadian Library Gateway. www.collectionscanada.ca/genealogy

Champlain Society. www.champlainsociety.ca

Early Canadiana Online. www.canadiana.org/cihm

Family Chronicle. www.familychronicle.com

Family History Archive. www.lib.byu.edu/fhc

Federal government map publications. www.fedpubs.com/maps/ontario_maps.htm

Geographical Names of Canada. geonames.nrcan.gc.ca

Global Genealogy. www.globalgenealogy.com

Google Books. books.google.com

Google Earth. earth.google.com

Information Network For Ontario. info.hostedbyfdi.net:80/en/vdx/index.html

In Search of Your Canadian Past: The Canadian County Atlas Digital Project. digital.library.mcgill.ca/CountyAtlas

Ontario GenWeb. www.geneofun.on.ca/ontariolocator

Ontario Heritage Trust. www.heritagefdn.on.ca

Ontario's Historical Plaques. www.ontarioplaques.com

Ontario Historical Society. www.ontariohistoricalsociety.ca

Ontario Ministry of Natural Resources. www.themnrstore.mnr.gov.on.ca/english.asp

Ontario Ministry of Transportation. www.mto.gov.on.ca/english/traveller/map

Our Roots / Nos Racines. www.ourroots.ca

Paper of Record. www.paperofrecord.com

The Power of Place. ca.epodunk.com

Rootsweb. www.rootsweb.com

WorldCat. worldcat.org

3

Post-1869 Vital Records

Reference Dates

1869	Vital Statistics Act introduced civil registration of births-marriages-deaths to Ontario
1892	Children's Aid Society opened its first shelter, in Toronto
1896	Marriage Act amended; municipal clerks required to provide clergy with official books for marriage registrations and to keep copies in their local offices
1921	Adoption Act; Children of Unmarried Parents Act; Children's Aid Society assumed authority for adoptions
1930	Divorce Act; divorce became available in provincial Supreme Court as well as through the federal parliament

Beginning 1 July 1869, the province of Ontario required that births, marriages and deaths (BMD) be registered with the government. We call these civil registrations. Earlier attempts to collect such data had been generally ineffective, apart from limited success with marriage returns. Mid-1869 marked a real genealogical watershed, even though family historians may experience missing entries after this date. Initial compliance with the new edict was erratic. The population had more or less become accustomed to the registration of marriages, but collection of birth and death information was a newer phenomenon.

Basically the system involved the municipal clerk who

acted as the local registrar under the supervision of what became the Office of the Registrar General of Ontario (RGO). The town or township clerks recorded details of each vital event on an eventually standardized form. The completed forms were returned to the RGO where the information was copied into large books, with separate volumes for births and marriages and deaths. Each registration book contains several counties, divided into town and township pages. The format of the registrations changed slightly over time. Local clerks were authorized in 1896 to keep a duplicate set of records in their offices. However, municipal legislation for the protection of privacy bars researchers from consulting them.

By 1897 every clergyman and congregation was issued a standard register for marriages, with the onus on them to submit half-yearly returns to the local clerk. As well, anyone who solemnized a marriage was required to register it with the clerk within thirty days. Later on, it appears that the original forms for marriages, with signatures of bride and groom, were sent to the RGO and bound into books along with the marriage license.

The above is a simplified overview. The relevant legislation and the Registrar General's annual reports contain much more detail about the policy and practice of the system. The classic reading on this subject is George Emery's "Ontario's Civil Registration of Vital Statistics, 1869–1926: The Evolution of an Administrative System" in the *Canadian Historical Review* Vol. 44, No. 4 (1983) and his more recent book, *The Facts of Life: Social Construction of Vital Statistics, Ontario, 1869–1952.*

You will not find a record if your ancestors failed to register an event. There are any number of reasons for failure, including ignorance of the law, indifference or difficulty travelling to the town or township office. Overworked municipal clerks generally expressed little interest in enforcing compliance. Only by the turn of the twentieth century were government officials satisfied that most events were being registered.

Privacy legislation limits public access to post-1869 vital records documents to specified date ranges. It is necessary to understand the difference between the holdings of the Archives of Ontario (AO) in Toronto and the Office of the Registrar General (RGO) in Thunder Bay. AO holds the historical records and they are accessible. The RGO retains the more recent, tightly controlled records.

Historical Records at Archives of Ontario

For many years family historians could not view civil registration records firsthand. All these records were in RGO custody and only by submitting an application and paying a fee could members of the public obtain information from them. Even then, the transcription typed by an RGO staffer while viewing the actual record was not always accurate or complete. Then in 1991, the RGO released the earliest civil registration records into the custody of the Archives of Ontario for conservation purposes and public access. For genealogists, the new arrangement was a milestone second only to the introduction of the system in 1869.

Before beginning research, you need to know which records are where. The custodial split allows AO to offer researchers access to registrations for births up to 96 years after the event, marriages up to 81 years after the event, and deaths up to 71 years after the event. As of the end of 2007, AO had the following:

Births	1869–1910
Marriages	1869–1925
Deaths	1869-1935

Another year's worth of registrations are transferred to AO annually. After microfilming, the records are then opened to researchers. The records are catalogued in AO's RG 80, Records of the Office of the Registrar General, with births in MS 929, marriages in MS 932 and deaths in MS 937.

Registrations

Vital records are rich in genealogical detail. They are the building blocks of ancestral identification, for names, dates, places and relationships. Although the details they reveal are sometimes vague, they can also lead to major research breakthroughs. The information that was collected varied by type of event. Each record also gives the date and place of registration and the name of the local registrar.

Births: These give the name of the child, sex, date and place of birth, names of parents, the father's rank or occupation and sometimes his address, name and address of the informant, and the name of the *accoucheur* (physician, midwife or other birth assistant). In 1908 new questions were asked for date and place of the parents' marriage and whether the mother had been married more than once.

Sarah Eliza Cooper, Ontario birth registration 013310 (1881); AO microfilm MS 929 reel 49

Marriages: These records name both the bride and the groom and give each one's age, marital status, place of residence, place of birth, religion and names of parents. Also recorded are the date and place of the marriage, who performed the ceremony, whether it was by banns or license and who stood as witnesses.

Deaths: These are the forms that have changed the most over time. For about the first 40 years of registration, the information was a dry recital of name, age, rank or occupation, religion, place of birth, name and description of informant and cause of death. After 1907, however, the form began to add more requirements: the birth date of the deceased, place of death and burial information, the names and birthplaces of the deceased's parents. Even later death registrations ask other useful questions such as how long the deceased had lived at the place of death, and how long the person had lived in Ontario.

Genealogists especially value new clues that can appear in vital records. A birth record might provide the birth surname of the mother. Witnesses or informants can be previously unknown relatives. Sometimes the record will show not just the country of birth but a village, town or county—a real bonus when the ancestor originated outside Ontario or Canada. But not even the smallest details should be overlooked. The date of the

Mary Law, Ontario death registration 021870 (1888); AO microfilm MS 935 reel 53

registration can provide insight into timeliness of the record. For example, if a father registered a child's birth six months late, he might have slipped a bit on the exact date of birth.

Cause of death (and contributing illnesses, if available in death records) for ancestors is important in tracing a family health history. Elizabeth and Colin Briggs' *Before Modern Medicine, Diseases and Yesterday's Remedies* helps interpret former names for diseases and conditions we are familiar with. A little more on this subject is in Chapter 9 under Health and Welfare.

Don't assume that all of the information on vital registrations is accurate. Much depends on whether the informant—the person who provided the information—was knowledgeable and truthful. Also, not every event in which you are interested will have been registered. At the other extreme, we find that some events have been registered more than once. In one case, the death of a man was registered three times. It was registered a week later by his son from out of town, two weeks later by the brother he lived with and six weeks later by the parish priest. Each informant gave a different day of death and a different cause of death!

Indexes

Researchers can choose between two indexes, the handwritten originals or a computerized version created in the late 1950s. The latter is the most heavily used, being easier to browse, but can have omissions. Births, marriages and deaths are each indexed separately. Entries are arranged on microfilm alphabetically by year, with "A" surnames for 1869 followed by "A" surnames for 1870, and so on. More than one microfilm will be necessary to follow all the "A" entries until more recent microfilming placed each year's indexes all on one film. The AO finding aid "Vital Statistics: Birth, Marriage and Death Records" is essential for finding a microfilm number (for on-site usage and AO or FHL interlibrary loan) and is a Reading Room handout as well as on their website.

Also given in the index are the date and place of the event, the year of registration and a six-digit number, usually beginning with a zero. The registration number and the year of registration are the keys that will lead you to the full registration on microfilm. Other columns provide for the number of the registration district and internal coding systems. The occasional asterisk (*) denotes a registration that has been altered, such as a corrected spelling or date.

The original handwritten indexes are useful as backup for questionable or missing entries on the computerized version. Their organization differs slightly. They are sorted first by year, then surname (not necessarily in alphabetical order under each initial letter), then county. Rather than a registration number, they provide a *liber* (volume) and *folio* (page) reference to the registration books.

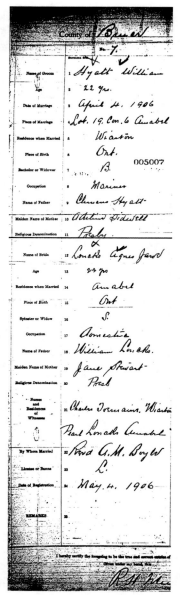

Hyatt-Sidwell, Ontario marriage registration 005007 (1906); AO microfilm MS 932 reel 121

Births indexes do not show the name of the parents; marriage indexes do not show the name of the spouse; death indexes do not show the age of the deceased. Women who were marrying for a second time or more were normally indexed under their previous married surname.

Marriages from 1869 to 1872 are not covered in the computerized index. For these you will need to use the original indexes. Another option is to consult the six-volume *Index to Marriage Registrations of Ontario, Canada, 1869-1873* published by Ontario Indexing Services. This series is the most complete index to marriages for this period. It even includes some 1869 marriages missing from *both* the original and computerized indexes. The addition of the spouse's name in five of the six volumes is a special bonus, making it easier to identify the entry you want.

Delayed Registrations

Delayed registrations are births, marriages, or deaths that were registered *after* the year in which they happened. For example, a December event might not be registered until early in the new year. Longer delays took place for a variety of reasons. Delayed registrations are listed in the indexes in the same way as regular events, except for two things. First, the registration number will begin with the digit 2, 3, 5 or 9. Secondly—using as an example an 1896 birth registered in 1897—the birth will be grouped with other 1896 index entries but will show a registration year of 1897. And the microfilm you want for actual birth registrations is the one for 1897, not 1896.

Once you have located a delayed registration in an index, your next step will depend on how long the registration was delayed. The digits 2 or 3 were used to flag events the year after they happened. To find the full registration for one of these, drop the initial 2 or 3 from the registration number then search for the number on the microfilm that covers the year of registration (not the year of the event). The digits 5 or 9 denote registrations delayed for several decades. The records corresponding with these index entries will be found in separate volumes of delayed registrations. Very late registrations may still be held by RGO.

Tips

If you cannot find a registration for which you are searching:
- Remember, the registration number must be sought in the

year of registration in order to locate the correct microfilm with the entry you want.

- Check all possible spelling variations of the surname.
- Look for possible entries under "U" for "unknown," where illegible surnames were indexed.
- Don't ignore entries with unexpected first names. A child registered as Henrietta Mary may have been known as Nettie all her life. A male known as William Edward may have been registered as Edward William. It sometimes happens that an individual was registered with forenames he or she never used.
- A woman who is marrying for a second time or more should be listed under her previous married name. If not, try her maiden name or other married surnames she may have had.
- Consult the original handwritten indexes as well as the computerized version.
- Try making a page-by-page search of the registration books. This requires knowing approximately when and where the event occurred.
- Keep in mind that the event may never have been registered.

Miscellaneous

AO has miscellaneous clergy returns of interest in the RG 80 collection:

- Registers of various clergymen dating from 1896, seven of them Methodist, five Presbyterian, four Baptist, one Anglican and one from a justice of the peace. The majority relate to Toronto and its environs.
- Roman Catholic marriage registers for thirteen parishes or missions, mainly in the Toronto and Home District area from 1833 to 1870, but also some for the Niagara Peninsula and Simcoe and Dufferin counties.
- Some miscellaneous death registers for Toronto 1911-1913.
- Wesleyan mission records for the New Credit Native Reserve in Brant County 1859-1931.

Access

The options for researching civil registrations are numerous. The indexes and registrations are available on microfilm in the AO Reading Room, in the OGS Library and at many libraries with Ontario genealogy collections. Some may have the indexes only. AO has very complete pathfinders on its website and as print handouts in its Reading Room. If your public library has a microfilm reader, you can also borrow the films from AO using interlibrary loan. There is a limit of three reels per request. The borrowing procedure and film numbers are on the AO website. Note that AO staff cannot research these records for you.

The films are also available at the Family History Library in Salt Lake City and can be borrowed for you through one of the FHL's Family History Centers. Due to popular demand, some centres in Ontario have obtained the series on permanent loan. If you only have access to the indexes, copies of the registrations can be obtained using the FHL's copy service. Requests must be submitted using their online form or a form from one of the centres. Failing all else, both AO and FHL can send you lists of independent professional researchers in Toronto and Salt Lake City who can conduct searches and make printouts.

Be aware that the FHL and AO number these microfilms differently. The FHL numbers can be found in the library's online catalogue. A conversion list is available in the AO pathfinders. For individuals or institutions wishing to purchase vital statistics microfilm, OGS sells both the indexes and the registrations.

Ancestry.com

Vital statistics research changed considerably when the commercial giant *Ancestry.com* entered the Canadian genealogy picture in 2006. Ancestry's Canadian website *Ancestry.ca* offers not only a powerful search engine for Ontario civil registrations but also digital images of them. Access is by subscription only. Births are available to 1909, marriages to 1924 and deaths to 1934. The site periodically keeps up to date with new AO releases. Advanced search options allow for searches that were previously impossible. For example, the birth database can be searched by specifying one or both of the parents' names but not the child's. It is also easier to search for events of unknown date or place.

However, the enterprise is not without its drawbacks. Chief among these is the quality of the indexing. Some names are so garbled they are unrecognizable. Even seemingly straightforward names can be masked by strange spellings. The problem can sometimes be overcome by creative use of the search options. If you have the exact date of an event, do a search using only the date, or try dropping either the first or last name. If you aren't satisfied, revert to using the AO indexes.

⟨🖋 **ancestry**.ca

| Home | My Ancestry | Search | Publish NEW | Community | Learning Centre | Store |

You are here: Search > **Ontario, Canada Births, 1869-1909**

Ontario, Canada Births, 1869-1909

☐ Exact matches only   Search tips

First Name   Last Name

Birth

Day   Month   Year
All ▼   All   ▼   +/- 0 ▼

Gender   Birth County
Any ▼   All   ▼

Father

First Name   Last Name

Mother

First Name   Last Name

Other

Keyword(s)

▲ **Hide Advanced Search Options**   **Search**

Source Information:

Ancestry.com. *Ontario, Canada Births, 1869-1909* [database on-line]. Provo, UT, USA: The Generations Network, Inc., 2007. Original data:

- Archives of Ontario. *Registrations of Births and Stillbirths – 1869-1909.* MS 929, 206 reels. Toronto, Ontario, Canada: Archives of Ontario.

- Archives of Ontario. *Delayed Registrations and Stillbirths, "50" Series, 1869-1907.* MS 930, 51 reels. Toronto, Ontario, Canada: Archives of Ontario.

- Archives of Ontario. *Delayed Registrations of Births and Stillbirths, "90" Series, 1869-1907.* MS 933, 50 reels. Toronto, Ontario, Canada: Archives of Ontario.

- Archives of Ontario. *Direct Clergy Returns for Simcoe County Births, Marriages, and Deaths, 1892-1896.* MS 936, 1 reel. Toronto, Ontario, Canada: Archives of Ontario.

- Archives of Ontario. *Evidence for Delayed Registrations of Births, 1861-1897.* MS 946, 2 reels. Toronto, Ontario, Canada: Archives of Ontario.

- Archives of Ontario. *Division Registrar Vital Statistics Records, 1858-1930.* MS 940, reels 1-4, 10-15, 17-20, 22-25, 27-28. Toronto, Ontario, Canada: Archives of Ontario.

Ancestry.ca search screen for Ontario births. Used with permission.

Some marriages are listed twice, once with an image, once without. Occasionally a marriage listed twice, with images, indicates the addition of an image where one side of a double folio had previously been missed. The marriage database also covers some in the pre-1869 period, without images.

Ontario Vital Statistics Project

The OVSP was established in 2000 with the goal of providing free Internet access to information from the AO civil registrations. Hundreds of volunteers have contributed to the site, which has separate categories or pages for births, marriages and deaths. Births can be searched by first letter of the surname. Search engines are available for marriages and deaths. The marriages section consists of two parts, post-1869 registrations and marriages 1800-1924 from sources *other* than civil registrations. The majority of the latter are generally transcriptions of marriages from an earlier period. Post-1869 entries for each type of event are abstracted from the registration books, providing most of the pertinent detail. The registration number is given so you can verify your find with the original record.

Certificates

Many of us are in the habit of calling a provincially registered birth, marriage or death entry a "certificate," but most of the digitized or microfilmed records we use are more accurately called "registrations." Of the two types of records, a certificate is often assumed to be the most desirable. But for genealogical purposes, the reverse is often more true. Although certificates are legally acceptable, they are prepared by a government clerk whose work may contain transcribing errors. Now we have a welcome number of digitized or microfilmed images that are free of this intermediate processing.

In the genealogical world, emphasis is placed on the earliest available source, and higher value is thus placed on the registrations. The distinction is pointed out even though the word "certificate" is likely to continue in common usage. The registration books themselves may be second-generation copies, but they are official government documentation.

AO does not issue certificates for the civil registration records in its custody. However, if you need documentation of an event for some *legal* purpose, you can obtain a certified copy of the registration. This involves you (or your agent) making a printout from the microfilm under the supervision of an AO archivist. The printout will be officially stamped and then requires the signature of the Archivist of Ontario, which can take up to two days and entails a fee.

Registrar General of Ontario

As of late 2007, births registrations dated after 1910, marriages after 1925 and deaths after 1935 continued to be held by the Registrar General's Office. The RGO comes under the provincial Ministry of Government Services and is located in Thunder Bay (see Appendix II). All the forms, precise details, up-to-date fees and a variety of services can be reached through the Government of Ontario website in a search for Registrar General. Online application forms can be submitted for quick service. Application forms for vital events can also be obtained at Service Ontario centres at 60 locations throughout the province.

Access

However, family historians should recognize the limitations for genealogical purposes. Indexes to these RGO records are not open for public viewing. The records themselves are subject to "entitlement/authorization" restrictions, listed below under births, marriages and deaths. A request for a confirmation letter is often the only viable choice.

The types of documents currently available are

- a *certificate* (short form) is a wallet-size extract from the record, containing only basic information for name(s), date, place.

- a *certified copy* (long form) is a photocopy of the full original record. This is the form of most interest to genealogists.

- a *confirmation letter* stating that a certain record exists. This is what you will receive if you request a search for an event of unknown date. Such searches cover a five-year period and can be requested by anyone. A successful search depends on a) how much information you can provide and b) whether office staff are able to identify a particular entry. If a search is successful, you may proceed to apply for one of the other forms—if you are entitled to one. If a search is not successful, you will receive a negative Search Notice. It implies either the event was never registered or the details you supplied may not have matched with any registration.

Births: A birth certificate for a living individual will only be issued to the person named on the record or the parents. Family historians more often want a birth certificate for someone who is deceased. In that case, you must be the next of kin or the executor or administrator of the deceased's estate. You must provide proof of death, preferably a death certificate or funeral director's statement. The policy of restricted access to short and long forms reflects North American concerns about terrorist activities, because a birth certificate is such a fundamental piece of identification.

Marriages: Applications for a marriage certificate are restricted to the bride and groom, their children, their parents or a legally authorized representative acting on their behalf. Proof of such authorization must be presented. If either the bride or groom is deceased, or both, then the surviving next of kin can apply for a certified copy of the registration. Next of kin may include surviving descendants or extended family members.

Deaths: There are no restrictions on who can apply for a certificate. The more desirable certified copy is, again, only available to next of kin or an authorized representative as with marriages.

On an application, you are expected to provide a date and a location along with the name for each event you are seeking. When you do not know the exact date, you can request a five year search. Providing a location is important for the RGO to distinguish among several entries of the same name. Most events were recorded, and identified on the index, by town or township and date. Experienced researchers advise that you not leave blank spaces on an application form. If you don't know the location of the event, it's better to say "unknown."

In the "old" days prior to about 1993, the RGO issued *genealogical extracts* from a BMD registration. If you have such documents for events that now fall within the AO range, you are urged to obtain your own printouts from the microfilm or digital images for comparison. Genealogists have discovered discrepancies between the now-available registration books and the information earlier abstracted by RGO staff.

Other Post-1869 Sources

Divorce

This chapter concentrates on post-1869 vital records, and divorce is more common in this period. But a process for divorce existed earlier and begs some historical explanation. A person wanting divorce had to petition for the passage of a government act to obtain it, incurring some expense, perhaps considerable waiting time and public attention. For many of our early ancestors, it was simpler merely to abandon the matrimonial home—frequently explaining the disappearance of the head of a family. In the case of an unexplained disappearance, researchers could try looking in local newspapers for potential information. Notices appeared from time to time announcing no further responsibility for debts incurred by a spouse who "has left my bed and board." More often it seems the notices were inserted by disavowing husbands. "Pioneer Divorce" by Helen Weaver in *Families* Vol. 25, No. 2 (1986), discusses some situations like this. Only five divorces were recorded between 1841 and 1867, as acts of the legislative assembly. The text of the acts was published in *Journals of the Proceedings of the Legislative Assembly of the Province of Canada* in the year the act was passed. The *Journals* are found in the AO library and other reference libraries.

After Confederation (1867), a private act of the Canadian parliament was necessary to obtain a divorce. Because of the expense and delay in this system, and the rigidity of the required grounds, normally it was only couples with strong financial or child custodial motivation who undertook divorce proceedings. The original proceedings for this period up to about 1930 were destroyed but the parliamentary acts that summarize them remain available. Depending on the year, the least you should be able to learn is the names of the parties, their residence, marriage date and place and date of the judgment absolute or decree. The birth surname of the wife is available if it was mentioned in the original proceeding.

From 1931 until 1968, divorces could have been granted federally or provincially. For the family researcher, this could mean seeking divorce information in two different ways. Firstly, the Canadian Genealogy Centre has a database that streamlines the search for divorces granted by parliament from 1841 to 1968. The database covers actions in all Canadian areas. The sources for the database are transcripts of parliamentary acts in federal government publications. The citation in the database gives a reference number to the act published in that year, enabling you to consult the publication or order a copy from LAC. Copies of an act can also be obtained from the Law Clerk at the Senate of Canada (Appendix II).

Secondly, the Supreme Court of Ontario has also granted divorces since 1931 and took sole jurisdiction from 1968 onward. These actions are *not* in the CGC database. Ontario divorces are registered with the RGO, which does not issue copies of documents. The Archives of Ontario has custody of divorce files created provincially from 1931 to 1978. Filing for divorce in Ontario was usually begun by a party in his or her county of residence. A petition initiated the divorce action and a judgment or decree absolute completed it. Only the information from these two sources is public. The necessary keys to obtaining divorce information are the file number with the year and county or district of the action. Indexes are available to provide this necessary information but they are not necessarily province-wide or all arranged the same way. The online and paper handout AO "Research Guide 210" gives step-by-step procedures for navigating the indexes. Files at AO may be stored off-site, so you must allow several days' retrieval time for these documents.

From 1979 onwards, divorce files are held at county courthouses in the Superior Court of Justice, as the Supreme Court of Ontario is now called. Courthouse addresses and telephone numbers are listed in AO "Research Guide No. 210." Before being able to enquire locally for a file, you must learn the place a divorce was granted, with the key information of year and file number. Again, consult AO "Research Guide No. 210."

Funeral Homes

The funeral industry grew along with increasing regulations concerning burial and cemetery standards. Genealogical societies now work in cooperation with funeral homes to transcribe information from their documentation. Fortunately for us, numerous funeral establishments—especially those, it seems, which were family businesses for more than one generation— have saved their older records. Many of the OGS Branches are good resource points for such compilations. Names and dates from existing index cards are the least they reproduce, or perhaps more complete information relating to funeral payment, burial location, cemetery plot ownership, next of kin and so on. The Ontario Association of Cemetery and Funeral Professionals (Appendix III) represents a membership of many cemetery operators, large and small, and related death-care industries in the province. Their website has a search engine based on business name or location keys. A good article called "Funeral Records" is posted on the *Ontario GenWeb*.

Adoption

In Ontario, in the nineteenth and early twentieth century, most adoptions were unofficial and unrecorded. In many cases, orphaned children were taken in by someone in their extended family or kind neighbours. Such fostering of children was quite informal. An illegitimate birth frequently took place away from "home" and the child was then passed off as the child of the mother's mother or a married sister. Later, shelters for single mothers and births may have arranged a baby's placement. Such placements were called indentures and the child automatically assumed the surname of the adoptive parents. However, the baby's birth may have been registered by the surname of the mother. After 1920, birth records were amended or registered in the surname of the adoptive parents.

In 1921 an adoption law was passed to ease the plight of overburdened orphanages and deserted or destitute mothers with large families. From the point of adoption, the birth parents lost all rights and obligations for that child and the court orders for adoption became sealed documents. The Children's Aid Society became involved in pairing qualified parents with a child. Hearings have been held since the 1920s on disputes about children of unmarried parents, but few case files date back to that time. Some existing custody case files are at AO but are subject to written requests to the AO Information and Privacy Unit.

The provincial government later acknowledged the desires of adoptees to seek their birth information and the potential to reunite with biological parents. The Adoption Disclosure Register was set up, operated by the Adoption Unit of the Ministry of Community and Social Services. An adoptee is allowed to acquire non-identifying information on his or her birth parent(s), such as age, marital status, education and religious or ethnic heritage. Identifying information is available only if the adult adoptee and a birth parent had both registered. If a natural parent is not registered, the Register staff can perform searches to try to find parents or other biological relatives. Consent by adoptive parents is not required for this process. The Unit provides mandatory counselling for emotional impact before any information is disclosed.

In 2005 the Ontario government passed further legislation to recognize the importance of biological identity. This necessarily involved working with the Registrar General's Office and the Vital Statistics Act. Full implementation of the changes was not complete until the fall of 2007. Adult adoptees were to have access to their original birth registrations. Birth parents would have access to the same, as well as the adoptive order, which could identify the child's adoptive name (without the names of the adoptive parents). For family historians, the law would have applied retroactively to any adoption order in Ontario since the first one was registered in 1921.

However, this new law was struck down by the provincial Supreme Court within days of its implementation. The court declared the legislation was in violation of the Canadian Charter of Rights and Freedoms. It is possible the Ontario government will re-examine the matter. Balancing an individual's right to information with another's right to privacy is a complex manoeuvre.

Since the first adoption law was enacted in 1921, some Ontario baby or orphan adoptions were and are arranged by individuals such as doctors or lawyers. They are responsible for submitting the appropriate vital information for official registration, and would have been known to a local Children's Aid Society, which monitored the child's placement at least once. If one of your ancestors was adopted after say 1890, it's barely possible a local CAS will now have records of their involvement. Since inception, the primary concern of the CAS has always been the welfare of neglected, abused or abandoned children. The present Ontario Association of Children's Aid Societies (Appendix III) is a non-profit advocacy group representing over 50 local societies.

An option could be researching the AO Archives Descriptive Database for "children's aid." Among the variety of results are the Children's Aid Society of Brockville fonds 1894-1944 and the Ontario Association of Children's Aid Societies fonds 1912-1975. Search results will also present numerous references to county court cases under the 1921 Children of Unmarried Parents Act. Currently all files before 1954 are open to public access.

The article "Canadian Adoptions and Discharges in Erie County, New York, Records, 1876-99" by Joyce S. Jewitt in *Canadian Genealogist*, Vol. 7, No. 2 (1985) gives a rare glimpse into a historical part of this subject.

BMD Alternatives

Alternate sources might be available as unofficial substitutes for government vital records. Even if you do have a copy of a registration, thorough research entails seeking additional sources to support your evidence. Many of the sources discussed in Chapter 4 could also apply to the post-1869 period. Any source that required the ancestor to supply his or her vital information is a potential option to be examined.

- Church registers are an obvious option, especially for baptismal and marriage recording.

- Cemetery stones or transcripts provide a year or date of death, and sometimes clues to date and place of birth.

- Funeral home or morticians' records will have date and place of death and, usually, the age of the deceased.

- Estate files give place and date of death in the petition for probate.

- Newspaper notices and obituaries; birth, marriage and death announcements.

- 1901 and 1911 census returns have a date of birth column, although the information may prove to be inaccurate.

- The National Registration Act of 1940 required personal vital details (more in Chapter 5).

- Professional and school yearbooks, social registers, biographical dictionaries and so on, have explicit or implicit information about vital dates or ages.

DNA

DNA testing does not fit easily into any category of research sources or strategies but, increasingly, its results are being utilized by family historians. Sometimes it is called genetic genealogy, molecular genealogy or even "genetealogy." DNA is nature's genealogical record, an ancestral heirloom found in every cell of the body. Testing can provide another source of information for evaluation, along with traditional research methodology, in constructing a family genealogy. DNA testing does not *replace* traditional genealogical research, nor can it tell you exactly *who* your direct ancestors are.

Children inherit a mixture of genetic material from their parents. The Y chromosome appears only in males, passed intact from father to son. Mitochondrial DNA (MtDNA) is passed from a mother to all her children, but only her daughters continually pass it on in turn, unchanged by or mixed with each father's Y-DNA. That means it can resolve questions of maternity, which are rarely a genealogical issue. Both Y-DNA (male) and MtDNA (female) testing are available. For family historians, Y-DNA testing is presently of most interest because it relates well to the customary genealogical tracing of one direct-line surname at a time.

By sharing the testing among a pool of potentially related individuals and comparing the results, science can determine if or which of those individuals share a common ancestor. Results are measured by genetic markers and, within the same testing pool, the markers can show anything from a match with another person to more distant probabilities. Thus, testing contains the possibility of discovering new cousins to some degree or it can eliminate having a common ancestor. Analysis of haplotype results for an individual are a way of identifying inherited strains from ancient origins. See *Kerchner's Genetic Genealogy Glossary* website for introductory terms of reference.

This is a rather simplistic description but there are some good sites to learn additional information on this subject. Megan Smolenyak's website *Genetealogy* and the Sorenson Molecular Foundation are but two of many resources. A number of commercial companies, such as *FamilyTreeDNA*, have been formed to provide testing services. The ability to analyze and understand DNA is constantly improving and expanding. As it does, we may expect other components of our DNA to become useful for family history. Genealogists intensely interested in the subject may like to keep up with the free online *Journal of Genetic Genealogy*. The Geneographic project of the National Geographic Society may also be of interest to some readers.

Reading And Reference

Briggs, Elizabeth and Colin J. Briggs. *Before Modern Medicine: Diseases and Yesterday's Remedies*. Winnipeg, MB: Westgarth Publishing, 1998.

Emery, George. *Facts of Life: Social Construction of Vital Statistics, Ontario, 1869-1952*. Montreal, QC/Kingston, ON: McGill-Queen's University Press, 1993.

Fitzpatrick, Colleen and Andrew Yeiser. *DNA and Genealogy*. Fountain Valley, CA: Rice Book Press, 2005.

Gilchrist, J. Brian and Nancy J. Duffy, compilers. *Index to Canadian Parliamentary Divorces, 1867-1930*. Etobicoke, ON: A. Gilchrist, 2001.

Hinckley, Kathleen. *Locating Lost Family Members and Friends: Modern Genealogical Research Techniques for Locating the People of Your Past*. Cincinnati, OH: Betterway Books, 1999.

Kerchner, Charles F. Jr. *Genetic Genealogy DNA Testing Dictionary*. Emmaus, PA: Charles Kerchner and Associates, Inc., 2004.

McNab, Luanne, Elizabeth Curtis and Kathleen Barclay Bowley. *Family Health Trees:Genetics and Genealogy*. Second edition. Toronto, ON: Ontario Genealogical Society, 2005.

Rumpel, Renie A., compiler and editor. *Index to Marriage Registrations of Ontario, Canada, 1869-1873*. 6 volumes. Waterloo, ON: Ontario Indexing Services, 1995-1996.

Smolenyak, Megan S. and Ann Turner. *Trace Your Roots With DNA: Using Genetic Tests to Explore Your Family Tree*. Portland, OR: Rodale Press, 2004.

Stratford-Devai, Fawne. *Canadian Family History in the 21st Century: Lessons, Links and Resources*. Campbellville, ON: Global Heritage Press, 2005.

Archives of Ontario. www.archives.gov.on.ca

Ancestry.ca. www.ancestry.ca

Canadian Genealogy Centre. www.collectionscanada.ca

Family History Library. www.familysearch.org

Family Tree DNA. www.familytreedna.com

Genetealogy.com. www.genetealogy.com

Journal of Genetic Genealogy. www.jogg.info

Kerchner's Genetic Genealogy Glossary. www.kerchner.com/anonftp/pub/glossary.pdf

Ministry of Community and Social Services, Adoption Disclosure. www.mcss.gov.on.ca/mcss/english

National Geographic Society Genographic Project. www3.nationalgeographic.com/genographic

Ontario Association of Children's Aid Societies. www.ocas.org

Ontario Association of Cemetery and Funeral Professionals. www.oacfp.com

Ontario GenWeb. www.geneofun.on.ca/ongenweb

Ontario Vital Statistics Project. www.rootsweb.com/~onvsr

Registrar General of Ontario. www.cbs.gov.on.ca/mcbs/english/forms.htm

Sorenson Molecular Genealogy Foundation. www.smgf.org

4

Pre-1869 Vital Records

Reference Dates

1790	By this date, active congregations were established in the original Loyalist settlement areas—Anglican, Catholic, Presbyterian, Lutheran—or being served by travelling preachers or missionaries
1793	Marriage Act; the right to perform marriage extended to justices of the peace in addition to the authorized Catholic and Anglican clergy
1831	Recognition of marriage sacraments performed by "non-conformist" clergy; district marriage registers began
1854	The first Cemeteries Act made provision and regulation for non-religious burying grounds
1858	All legitimate clergy in Canada West allowed to perform marriages; county marriage registers began
1861	Union of United Presbyterians and Free Church (Kirk) became the Canada Presbyterian Church
1875	Union of Canada Presbyterians and Church of Scotland
1882	The first Salvation Army meeting was held in London
1884	Methodist Church union of Wesleyan (British and Canadian), Episcopal, New Connexion, Primitive, Bible Christian groups

| 1925 | United Church of Canada formed from the Methodist union, Congregationalists, the majority of Presbyterians and the Council of Local Union Churches |
| 1968 | Evangelical United Brethren joined the United Church of Canada |

Religious Records

If you are looking for evidence of vital events in an ancestor's life before the significant date of 1869 when civil registration began, the main source is religious registers in the form of baptism, marriage and burial records. These records are generally regarded as direct evidence of a specific event—when the church register entry or document was presumably created. However, sometimes events were entered in a church register after some delay, for various reasons. You can often deduce from the source itself whether entries were made on a regular chronological basis, or if some were inserted post facto.

Canadian population census returns, unlike many countries, usually recorded the religious denomination of each member of the household. This requirement gives family historians a felicitous head start on pre-1869 sources.

Although the three rites of baptism, marriage and burial are sacramental in nature, the British tradition of imposing some political control over the institution of marriage was continued in Canada. Bruce S. Elliott's "Utility and Variety of Early Church Records" in *Families* Vol. 16, No. 4 (1977) is recommended reading for more historical detail. Originally, the Church of England made some effort to be seen as the state or established church of Upper Canada. Adherents are known as Anglicans. However, Roman Catholic rights and privileges from the French Regime had been confirmed by the Quebec Act in 1774, leaving the door open for equal demands by dozens of other denominations.

Mobile missionaries and circuit riders travelled considerable distances in early days. Baptisms, marriages and burials are frequently mixed together in one notebook or register. A clergyman may have entered the events on the spot on the day he performed them, but obvious chronological disorder in old registers can indicate that some entries were added after the fact and not perfectly remembered. The careful researcher will differentiate between a birth and a baptism, between a death and a burial or funeral record in his or her notes and charts.

Aside from the government collection of marriage records, religious records were and are created for ecclesiastical purposes. They are private, as opposed to public, sources. Therefore, access to them is a privilege, not a right. The records and their keepers must be treated with due respect.

Baptisms

Each denomination or religious congregation followed their own customs in the recording of events. A baptismal or christening entry might range from simply naming the child and the father and the date of baptism to a more encompassing record with the names of both parents, date of *birth* for the child (as well as baptismal date), names of the sponsors or godparents and additional remarks about the father's occupation or where the parents resided. Some denominations such as Baptists do not practise infant baptism. Other denominations, like the Society of Friends (Quakers) had a somewhat different approach by compiling "family records."

In searching for where these religious events occurred, it is a rewarding exercise to imagine your ancestor's precise lifestyle and times. If the desired baptismal record is not found in the logical place, use your imagination in conjunction with other evidence you have collected. Did the father and mother of the child have different religious affiliations in census returns? Did the mother's parents live in another parish or distant place? Could she have gone to stay with her parents for the birth or baptism? Did the family change their religious affiliation between census returns? Should you be looking for more than one set of church records?

Another consideration with the family you are seeking is whether their location was contiguous with another colony, province or country. There are numerous instances where family members from one generation to another regularly crossed borders between Ontario and Quebec, or between Ontario and neighbouring American states. "Missing" baptisms and marriages may have occurred outside this province.

Marriages

While the Church of England and the Roman Catholic Church were the original ecclesiastical authorities in Upper Canada for the legalization of marriage, people often still sought a clergyman of their chosen faith whenever possible. Early marriages did take place among Methodists or Baptists or Mennonites and so on,

Baptisms in Niagara 1793

April

27 Catherine Alms of Christian & Magdalane
   Christina Smith of Henry & Mary
28 John Rice of John & Esther
   Mary Davis of Thomas & Deborah

May

2 Martha Parslow of William & Catherine
5 Catherine Barrow of William & Mary
   Mary Molyna of William & Ann
12 Priscilla Bassey of Robert & Mary
   John Read of William & Catherine
19 Jane Crooks of Francis & Elizabeth
26 Elizabeth Bassey of Jacob & Elizabeth
27 Francis Fryder of Francis & Margaret

June

5 Mary Smith of David William & Ann
   David Smith of David William & Ann
12 Mary Camden of William & Elizabeth
16 John Jones of John & Jane

St. Mark's Anglican Church (Niagara-on-the-Lake, Ontario), Baptism, Marriages and Burials Register 1, 1792–1850, unpaginated (1793); AO microfilm MS 545 reel 1

but surviving registers are rare. When seeking the marriage for a nonconformist couple in the eighteenth or early nineteenth century without success, it is always wise to check nearby Anglican or even Catholic registers.

Local justices of the peace (also known as magistrates) were licensed early on to perform marriages when there were fewer than five Anglican clergymen in a particular district, and if none were available within eighteen miles of the couple. Such records survive only sporadically, and surface occasionally. Most of those found have been published as transcripts or extracts in *Ontario Historical Society* journals, *The Ontario Register* or the district marriages and vital records series.

In the usual course of events, a marriage took place in the bride's home territory, but there may be almost as many exceptions. The problem of not finding a marriage record can sometimes be solved by studying where the bride and groom each resided in relation to the nearest towns, and the churches or clergy of their choice(s). It was not uncommon for a couple to travel by train for half a day or so, to exchange their vows and have a head start on a wedding trip. Many couples crossed Lake Ontario or the St. Lawrence and Detroit Rivers to marry in a U.S. state, and eastern residents sometimes had marriages performed across Ottawa River in Quebec. Elopements can also be taken into account when at least a day's distance from disapproving parents would have been advisable.

Banns, Licenses, Bonds

Several denominations practised the calling of banns in church to announce a couple's intention to marry. Banns, as written records, may perhaps exist only if an individual church or minister preserved them. The alternative to banns was the procurement of a license to marry, from a magistrate or justice of the peace, after the signing of a bond. Early marriage licenses have seldom survived before before 1867.

A bond was not issued to the couple in question, but rather it was executed between the groom and two friends or relatives (the sureties), whose signed consent assumed liability if any impediment to the proposed marriage was uncovered. Parental consent is included if an under-age daughter is involved. It cannot be assumed that a marriage always followed from this proceeding; nor can it be assumed that the marriage took place that day. There are instances when the prospective bride or groom married a different person after a bond or license was recorded.

You may ask what happened if a bond was forfeited? Is there a source that recorded the circumstances if the bondsmen did become liable? The discovery of an "impediment" such as one party already being clandestinely married, or having made a similar promise to another person, was likely a rare occurrence. The bond is addressed to the Crown, and would have been held by a provincial representative of the Crown as a financial asset. The provincial attorney general would have been ultimately responsible for ensuring due process. Also, as a related issue, civil actions have occasionally been brought to court to sue for breach of promise. The Archives of Ontario holds material for both the attorney general and court records, the latter needing in-depth searches under district or county headings.

A collection of Protestant marriage bonds has been preserved at Library and Archives Canada. The Canadian Genealogy Centre has a searchable online database, combining the surviving marriage bonds for Upper Canada 1803-1865 and Lower Canada 1779-1858. The search results show the names and residence of the intending parties, the date and place of the bond, the names of the bondsmen, and the archival reference number for the microfilm. The bond itself may also have a witness to the proceedings. Part of the Upper Canada collection has been extracted in Wilson's *Marriage Bonds of Ontario 1803-1834*. Microfilm copies of the LAC bonds collection are also at AO where a few small collections of marriage licenses issues from 1853 to 1911 can be found.

Burials

For obvious reasons, burials in pioneer societies were effected as quickly as possible. Members of a faith or congregation who died some distance away from church and clergy were usually interred on the family farm by relatives and neighbours. Burial services or sacraments were performed only when the local minister or priest was near enough. Hence, we do not find many burial entries in an early church register unless the incumbent had conducted a service, and little information can be expected from them.

Cemeteries

Cemeteries, like church records, are not solely relegated to the pre-1869 era. After a period of burials on farms or in relatively small churchyards, church congregations gradually acquired land for longer-term burial needs. Often the property was donated, or transferred for a token sum, by a member of the church or a prominent local resident. At this stage, an appointed trustee or sexton may have started a cemetery log or plot location map or plot owners' list. By the second half of the nineteenth century we find an increase in "union" cemeteries or non-denominational municipal cemeteries. Cities, towns and townships began to own and operate cemeteries and, quite often, a register of interments exists only from the date of their management. This topic overlaps with the previous chapter's post-1869 material as sources for death information began to expand to include registers of plot owners and interments, administered by public or private companies, and the increasingly detailed documentation of funeral establishments.

Gravestones can provide evidence that may not be found elsewhere—date of death, age at death and sometimes, fortuitously, place or date of birth. The latter should be treated as a clue only. Birth information from this source is definitely secondary and needs additional evidence. It is possible to access cemetery information without physically visiting the cemetery. Transcriptions of individual cemeteries and occasionally photographs of headstones are now appearing on some GenWeb pages or personal websites, but here are the main research aids.

Hannah Hutchins, 21 May 1841(?) Kent county. Photo by Tom Malott.

All branches of the Ontario Genealogical Society have worked for years on transcribing the more than 6,000 cemeteries identified in the province. The *Ontario Cemetery Finding Aid* (OCFA) is a popular site, initiated as a private venture, with more than two million names entered from OGS transcriptions and other sources. It is an index of names, a guide to locating a necessary transcription. *Not all OGS Branches have participated in this project.* For example, Toronto Branch developed its own database for cemeteries transcribed within the boundaries of old York County, and they are not part of the OCFA input.

OGS has created two finding aids for burial information. See "Resources" on its website. Ontario Cemetery Locator is a directory to all known cemetery locations in the province. There are several ways to search, browse and query with this tool. The results will also tell you if that cemetery has been transcribed and where the transcription is. The OGS Ontario Cemetery Ancestor Search is similar to the OCFA but with wider branch participation. Also, information is added about plot location within the cemetery, when available, and a link to the branch that produced a transcription. It will take time to complete the database entries for names from so many branch publications. The most up-to-date OGS transcriptions can be purchased from the branches or viewed in branch libraries or in the main OGS library. Another option is viewing the transcriptions that AO makes available on 147 reels of microfilm.

Unhappily, we all know that cemetery stones can succumb to years of weathering, neglect or vandalism. Making a personal search in a cemetery might not yield what you are looking for. Several generations ago, W.G. Reive recorded many cemeteries, mainly in the Niagara Peninsula. The collection is available at AO. It is very noticeable how many stones have disappeared since the more recent OGS recordings were made. The Perkins Bull Collection at the Peel Region Archives contains similar material for Peel County with some now-vanished information.

The Ontario Association of Cemetery and Funeral Professionals (Appendix III) has a website with a page "Contact a Member/Directory" to assist in finding local funeral homes. The Mount Pleasant Group of Cemeteries, which superseded the former Commemorative Services of Ontario, cares for ten major cemeteries within the greater Toronto area, including Toronto Necropolis and Mount Pleasant. We are now told that genealogical information from any of their cemeteries is available by phoning their office. The website includes stories by historian Mike Filey about some of the interesting people interred in the area. Toronto Branch OGS has transcribed and published the entire Toronto Necropolis Cemetery.

Some websites that concentrate on cemetery transcribing or photography are *Interment.net* and *Saving Graves*. Both have an Ontario section at different stages of development. The popular *Find A Grave* website has a limited selection of Ontario burials. *Northern Ontario Gravemarker Gallery* is working on the province's northern districts. Another online site of interest to readers may be *Ontario Cemeteries Resources*, which is also building an obituary collection.

Other than date and place of death, the genealogical details about a deceased person on a cemetery stone are considered secondary information. Who provided additional information for the burial register, the cemetery stone, the death certificate, the newspaper obituary and so on? You must ask yourself whether that person could have been personally involved or present at the birth of the deceased. Thus, data like the age of the deceased, date and place of birth, names of parents, previous residence(s), date of emigration to this country, while providing important and useful clues, are open to question.

Remember that religious institutions created more records than just registers of baptisms, marriages and burials. Lists of members or communicants, professions of faith, certificates of removal from another congregation, minutes of meetings of church or congregational officials (for some denominations this includes reprimands for moral transgressions, assistance for poverty, and so on), cemetery trustees, building fund information and pew allocation are some of the extra material you might find.

Family Bibles

Family Bibles are somewhat relevant to church records and were perhaps more common in family homes of the past. A family member would make entries of vital events in the special insert provided for this purpose. The family historian who finds one will treasure it for an ancestor's penmanship as well as for the entries. The information that was recorded needs evaluation and, of course, some support from other sources.

- Check the date of the Bible's publication. Do some or all of the entries precede the publication date? Logically this implies the recording came some time after the events, from memory, however accurate that may be.

- Note the legibility and variety—or lack of variety—in the handwriting. Entries entirely in one hand can indicate that all the information was written by one person and perhaps at one sitting. Older events would therefore again be from memory. Depending on the age of the Bible and/or the writer, the writing may be difficult to decipher according to the person's literacy level or how handwriting was taught. Unfamiliar forms of written letters can be misconstrued by the undiscerning eye. Numbers, also, may have different loops and whorls than we are accustomed to.

- The usage of ambiguous abbreviations can mislead us. Short forms for the names of months can sometimes be inadvertently confusing. All these considerations affect a reliable interpretation of the entries.

Newspapers

Religious newspapers were mentioned in Chapter 2. The major denominations were publishing them by the second half of the nineteenth century. Announcements of births, marriages and deaths among the members appeared fairly regularly and encompassed most areas of the province or beyond. Obituaries were often featured, for more prominent or notably pious adherents. It is not unusual to see details about places of birth and marriage. If applicable, the date of settling in Ontario and the year of conversion to that faith may be included.

Knowing a date or even the year of death is most helpful for searches because few of these newspapers have extensive nominal indexes. The great exception is the work of Donald A. McKenzie with Ontario's variety of nineteenth century Methodist newspapers. Hamilton Branch OGS has extracted BMDs from the Baptist newspaper *The Christian Observer*, re-named *Christian Messenger*, from 1851 to 1885 in 21 volumes. Consult LAC's *Checklist of Indexes to Canadian Newspapers* or OGS branches for more newspaper indexing projects.

Finding Religious Records

Locating the appropriate religious register for your ancestor or your family may be easier said than done. The procedure from scratch may be described as

- determining the family's location at a given time;
- knowing their religious affiliation (census is a good source);
- discovering the location and name of the appropriate congregation, minister, circuit or mission through historical reference material;
- Learning whether the relevant registers still exist and where they are currently housed.

Some church records remain with the original building while it is still in use. Some records have been lost, damaged or destroyed through calamities of nature. Some have disappeared through the generations, particularly in cases where they were regarded as the property of the clergyman or, as the responsibility of a church appointee, rather than the congregation at large. Sometimes records were returned to superiors at a clergyman's base of operations, for example, a headquarters based in the United States. When a church building was closed or congregations were amalgamated, earlier records may be found at the new congregation's building. Otherwise, they may have been sent to a neighbouring place of worship where a majority of the former congregation had transferred, or they may have been sent to a central archives.

Once again, a contemporary map is an essential working tool when you have located the ancestors in a census return with their religious affiliation. Studying a definitive religious history book can give you valuable insight, and perhaps even grass-roots details. City and county directories of the period may list the local churches by name. Histories of the county, town, township or community will frequently have a section on the development of local religious life. To bring it down to the most particular level, the very congregation you are interested in may have published its own history to commemorate a special anniversary.

Perhaps your research will reveal only one obvious local site that claimed your ancestor's devotion. On the other hand, the larger the surrounding population, the more possibilities you may find within the area.

To generalize, there is more chance of finding records of the large religious denominations that have a hierarchical structure. They tend to form policies that centralize, at least on a regional basis, the preservation and conservation of their historical records. Denominations that hold meetings of autonomous congregations may encourage safekeeping efforts without actively soliciting the central deposit of records. Family historians should remember that religions have their own reasons for creating records, which may not coincide with genealogical expectations.

Finding Aids

One source of addresses for current organized religions is the *Yearbook of American and Canadian Churches*, published each year by the National Council of Churches in the U.S.A. Most large denominations publish an annual report, directory or yearbook with names and addresses of churches. The Yellow Pages of telephone companies usually list existing religious institutions with addresses. Beginning on page 86 you will find guidance to some of the larger religions and their archives.

On a more local level, a number of OGS branches have published or are preparing genealogical finding aids to historic churches in their areas, as per the OGS Places of Worship Records Inventory. Rosemary Ambrose's *Waterloo County Churches* is an admirable example. If you become a member of the branch catering to your interest you will receive news of their progress on this project. The Toronto Branch of OGS developed its own Electronic Search Service for a database of baptisms-marriages-burials in historic York County.

You can also check the catalogues of LAC and AO for previously deposited historic church register material. Their collections are closed to further acquisitions. Any offers they receive of more material are directed to an appropriate religious archives. LAC published *A Checklist of Parish Registers on Microfilm* any of which can be borrowed. The Church Records Collection at AO is likewise catalogued by town or township locations. Full lists of the collections can be consulted on their websites, with individual microfilm numbers when applicable. Extracts or abstracts of some historic church registers have been published in *Ontario History*, *The Ontario Register* and in the periodicals of various county or township historical societies. The "Early Ontario Records" section of Bill Martin's website incorporates dozens of published registers that need to be searched page by page.

When you must contact a local church, please remember that they seldom have full-time staff to answer queries or to search their registers. Some may stipulate written enquiries only. For postal correspondence, be sure to include the courtesy self-addressed envelope (SAE) and return postage in Canadian stamps or International Postal Coupons. A token money order should accompany your request as another courtesy. Some churches now charge a fee for service, but all of them always appreciate a donation. You are at the mercy of the person who answers your letter—whether he finds the right record, whether he transcribes it "as is" or makes his own interpretation of names. Some churches provide the requested information on a standard form, hand copied from the register and signed by the current priest. One hapless recipient of photocopies immediately noticed that although the day and month of a baptism were clear, the *year* was nowhere to be seen. Some clergy habitually wrote the year at the top of the register page, but did not repeat it in each individual entry. The church correspondent was protecting the privacy of others by shielding all surrounding entries from the photocopier, thus obliterating a critical piece of information.

As far as personal visits go, do not expect a minister or church secretary to welcome you if you have not made an appointment. They may not allow access to their registers, or they may only allow limited and supervised access. Policy may exclude the photocopying of register pages. If you do visit, it is wise to get a feel for the person you are dealing with. If they have no interest in local history or genealogy, you will not endear yourself by regaling them with your personal ancestry. Do not be surprised if the incumbent displays no knowledge of, or particular curiosity in, the history of that church. He or she may be on a rotation system of a few years here and a few years there, with more than enough pressing duties to occupy time.

Early Churches

The following churches are among the earliest established in the eighteenth century period of the province, with dates of first congregational meetings or establishment. Many have been published, transcribed or indexed.

RC = Roman Catholic; CE = Church of England

L'Assomption (RC) Detroit/Sandwich, 1760+

St Marks (CE) Newark (Niagara-on-the-Lake), 1793+

St. Andrews (Presbyterian) Newark 1795+

Pelham Meeting (Quaker) Niagara, 1800+

St James Cathedral (CE) Toronto, 1800+

Rev. Langhorn (CE) Midland District, 1787+

Rev. McDowall (Presbyterian) Midland District, 1800+

Friends (Quaker) Adolphustown, 1798+

Ebenezer (Lutheran) Midland District, 1791+

St George (CE) Kingston, 1785+

Zion (Lutheran) Dundas/Stormont Counties, 1790+

St Andrews (Presbyterian) Williamstown, 1779+

St John (CE) Sandwich/Windsor, c1796+

Other churches based in Quebec are relevant to some of the earliest Ontario settlers, particularly Loyalists who spent time there before moving west.

St. Gabriel Street (Presbyterian) Montreal, 1792+

Christ Church (CE) Montreal, 1766+

Notre-Dame-de-Montréal (RC), 1642+

Christ Church (CE) Sorel QC, 1784+

St Regis Mission (RC) south side St. Lawrence River, 1764+

Denominations and Archives

Some religious denominations have archival staff and departments on a national or widely self-imposed scale. Some have several of a regional nature, according to their internal organization or historical development. Current addresses are listed in Appendix III, but see also the websites on pages 103–04.

A few observations may be of assistance before you correspond with or plan a personal visit to an archives. The prime consideration to keep in mind is that these centres exist for purposes inherent to a particular religion and its own mandate for collection and conservation. They were *not* created to serve genealogists, although we may be their largest group of patrons. As when approaching an individual church, the genealogist must duly inform himself in advance as much as possible about the collections, check the open hours, make an appointment, if required, and respect whatever limitations of access or assistance he encounters. In some cases, requests by correspondence will be handled for a set fee.

Some of the paper records of genealogical interest generated by churches, and collected by religious archives, have already been mentioned. There are other collections of a more general nature to be found in these archives. You may find memoirs or diaries of clergymen; missionary society reports; administrative correspondence; histories of particular churches; church bulletins, newsletters or anniversary commemorations; minutes of meetings; manuscript or published biographical information on clergy; yearbooks of church and clergy addresses; and photographs and plans of church buildings.

Catholic

There are fourteen dioceses of the Roman Catholic Church in Ontario. Not all of them have archival facilities, but those that do are usually busy. The good news is that their awareness of preserving historical church material led most bishops to allow the Family History Library to microfilm the vital registers within their dioceses, up to 1910 or later. Thus, the diocese, as well as the FHL in Salt Lake City, have copies of these films. Microfilms can be borrowed through local FHL Family History Centers. Several Catholic archives recommend using microfilms at Family History Centers, as their own offices may have little staff or space to accommodate heavy genealogical usage. Exceptions to the microfilming program were the Diocese of Hamilton and parts of the Diocese of Alexandria-Cornwall. Addresses of diocesan archives are listed in Appendix III.

See the "Bishops and Dioceses" section of the Canadian Conference of Catholic Bishops website. There you can easily obtain diocesan addresses and information for Ontario by way of a map. Quintin Publications sells a booklet called *An Address Guide to the Catholic Parishes of Ontario*, arranged alphabetically by place name. Some, not all, listings show the date of establishment for the church. Their similar companion *Guide to the Catholic Parishes of the Province of Ontario* is more detailed.

To help with areas where registers may not have been microfilmed:

- Renie Rumpel of Ontario Indexing Services has created an alphabetical listing for all names and related information from Roman Catholic marriage registers available at AO in RG 80. The thirteen parishes are mainly in the Toronto and Home District area from 1828 to 1870, with a few from the Niagara Peninsula.

- Global Genealogy sells transcripts of the registers for many parishes in eastern Ontario, compiled by the MacDonald Research Centre, namely Stormont, Dundas and especially Glengarry County.

- The library collection of the Société franco-ontarienne d'histoire et de généalogie has many French parish registers for this province. Assomption (Windsor, 1700-1985), Penetanguishene (1835-1982), Belle-Rivière (1840-1985), St-Jean-Baptiste d'Amherstburg (1802-1985) and St-Jean-Baptiste (L'Orignal, 1835-1992) are only a few. The collection is housed in the North York Central Library's Canadiana Department in Toronto along with the OGS collection.

- Transcriptions of registers for the Alexandria diocesan area and parishes in the bordering Quebec counties of Vaudreuil and Soulanges are sold by Alex. W. Fraser, although it is not an easy website to navigate.

- "Genealogical Sources in the Catholic Archdiocese of Toronto You May Have Overlooked" by J.L. Bulger was published in *Families* Vol. 24, No. 1 (1985).

Anglican

The Anglican Church of Canada has become the official name for the Church of England in Canada. It also functions on an episcopal system, having seven dioceses throughout the province. The *ecclesiastical* province of Ontario coincides more or less with the geographical province of Ontario. Kenora, in the far northwest, comes under the territory of the Diocese of Keewatin in the ecclesiastical province of Rupert's Land. It could be confusing for novices that one of the seven dioceses in the province is also called Ontario, with its archives at Kingston.

Diocese locations and addresses can be found at the Anglican Church of Canada website. All Ontario dioceses also have websites for finding individual parishes or churches, varying in the amount of information about their history and their resource centres or archives. Published lists of diocesan parish records are frequently out of date now because ongoing acquisitions are more easily updated online. Some diocesan archives may only have in-house inventories. And a few historical records of some churches or parishes still remain at the church where they were created.

Because the Diocese of Toronto was the first created in what became Ontario, its territory covered all of the first parishes from east to west and, for some time, its archives housed many of those old registers. However, early parish registers have been "repatriated" to the appropriate diocese within whose boundaries they now fall. Some collections may be restricted, and most archives have part-time or changing hours, so a call ahead is most wise. Additional finding aids, publications and pamphlets can be found there.

The LAC has copies from archives in Britain of Anglican missionary records for the Society for the Propagation of the Gospel in Foreign Parts, the Church Missionary Society and the Colonial and Continental Society.

Methodist

Methodism was a very large denomination in nineteenth-century Ontario, its growth influenced by immigrants from both England and the United States. Various types of Methodism were popular—Wesleyan, Episcopal, Primitive, New Connexion and Bible Christian—and generally, the smaller sects are easier to locate in community pockets or clusters. On the whole, however, searching out records for a Methodist ancestor is a challenge for diverse reasons:

- The initial clergymen covered vast distances at irregular intervals.

- After circuits had been created to link congregations, chapels and churches increased. The names and territory of circuits could frequently shift.

- Many registers kept by the early clergy and circuit riders are lost to us. They may have disappeared to church superiors in another country, they may have gone into retirement with the man himself and later been disposed of or destroyed or they may still exist privately among descendants or manuscript collectors or dealers in old books.
- The United Church of Canada union in 1925 reduced Methodism as a separate movement to a minor role.

In 1843, the Wesleyan Methodists resolved that a general registry of births and baptisms be kept for the whole church at the conference establishment in Toronto. Ministers were given a book in which they recorded the baptisms they had performed, and submitted it yearly to the general registrar acting as book steward. The registrar then copied the returns into a general registry book. Those register books are available up until the 1890s. Their arrangement is by town and township but not in strict chronological order, since later records were entered on previously blank pages. The great majority are for Ontario, with a few from nearby Quebec areas.

These unique Wesleyan Methodist baptismal registers are at the United Church of Canada Archives (UCA), comprising a set of four volumes on four microfilm reels. Usually the records show the name of the child, date and place of birth and baptism, names and residence of parents and the minister's name. The films can be viewed at the United Church Archives or the Family History Library, or borrowed through either institution. A prepared finding aid for place names and page numbers is available. The OGS completed nominal indexing of the registers, thus a master list of names is available. The master list, as well as the entire transcribed set, can be purchased in microfiche form from UCA or OGS. The OGS website also offers contact and price information for individual county abstracts published by OGS branches. Online transcripts are available at the Wesleyan section of Bill Martin's website, listed alphabetically by surname.

It is believed that most other Methodists did not follow this practice of a central registry. However, a baptismal register does exist for the Niagara Conference of the Methodist Episcopal Church, dating mainly between 1857 and 1886. This series is a single volume, without pagination. The entries contain the name of the child, date and place of birth, date of baptism and names of parents. OGS member Louise Hope has extracted the information and sorted the entire list alphabetically in *Index to Niagara Conference Methodist Episcopal Church Baptismal Register,*

1849-1886. The introduction includes information about the Niagara Conference and its circuits or charges during that time period. Please note that entries range far and wide, and are not restricted to the Niagara Peninsula.

Steve Marshall extracted Primitive Methodist baptisms for the Markham Circuit in *Families* Vol. 28, Nos. 2 and 4 (1989) and Vol. 29, No. 2 (1990), and other similar extractions can be found among local OGS branch publications. *The Lord's Dominion* by Neil Semple is the comprehensive book to consult on Canadian Methodism. Sherrell Leetooze has written extensively about the Bible Christian group. LAC has copies of archival material for the Methodist Missionary Society in London, England.

United Church of Canada

The United Church Archives (UCA) in Toronto is the central repository for church-related material from its five Ontario Conferences (Bay of Quinte, Hamilton, London, Manitou, Toronto) as well as records for the Church on a national basis. The UCA moved from its long-time location at Victoria University in downtown Toronto but remains within the city. Genealogically speaking, this means that UCA collects material from United Churches created after the 1925 union, and from the churches that amalgamated into the union—Methodists, Congregationalists, the majority of Presbyterian churches and, later, Evangelical United Brethren. All of these merging members had had their own historic divisions and amalgamations. For tracing Ontario ancestry, the eastern counties of Grenville, Carleton, Prescott, Russell, Stormont, Dundas and Glengarry are in the United Church Conference of Montreal-Ottawa; the Manitoba-Northwestern Ontario Conference takes in communities in the far northwestern part of this province. United Church policy is for congregations to send their inactive records to the Archives.

If a church or minister's register is in their holdings, you will find it by consulting their online or on-site catalogues. Descriptions of its church records are searchable by place name at their website through the ARCHEION search engine. The fonds description indicates the record's original denomination. Place names can be villages, towns, townships, cities, circuits and charges. So, again, a map of your area plays a key role. For example, catalogued under "Belleville" is a Methodist Episcopal circuit register (1805–1853) that covered an area from Smiths Creek (Port Hope) to Napanee, including Prince Edward County. This particular register has been transcribed and published by the Bay of Quinte Branch UEL Association. Circuit or charge names are usually cross-referenced. One of the effects of the union was the change of name by some churches that date from the nineteenth century. Examples are an original (and common) name like First Presbyterian Church may now be called Main Street (or what-have-you street) United Church; Morriston Evangelical Brethren Church became Zion Mount Carmel United Church.

The Congregational church did not have a large historical presence in Ontario and was seen mainly in some urban areas. It was absorbed into the United Church of Canada union in 1925.

Archives staff can only answer inquiries regarding material that is *not* available through their interlibrary loan. A personal visit is a must to fully explore more finding aids and reading room shelves. There are a number of additional card catalogues to other collections, such as Methodist, Presbyterian and Congregational newspapers and periodicals. Among the administrative records and correspondence there are also personal papers of clergy and missionaries, as well as historical sketches. All archival collections are retrieved by the staff at the Reading Room reference counter.

Regarding denominations that later joined the United Church union, see *The Canada Conference of the Evangelical United Brethren Church, 1864-1964* by Getz and Spaetzel. An article of interest is "The Beginnings of the Evangelical United Brethren Church in Upper Canada" by Harold Brix in *Canadian Methodist Historical Society* Vol. 10 (1993). The original Brethren in Christ were known as Tunkers or Dunkards. George Cober wrote *Historical Sketch of the Brethren in Christ Church*. "The Archives of the Brethren in Christ and Messiah College" by Morris Sider in *Families* Vol. 30, No. 4 (1991) and Sider's article "The Early Years of the Tunkers in Canada" in *Ontario History* Vol. 51, No. 2 (1959) are also relevant.

Presbyterian

The Presbyterian Church in Canada Archives and Record Offices in Toronto is the national repository for all those churches that did not enter the United Church union in 1925. Prior to 1925, various schisms in Presbyterian doctrine and practice some of them inherited from events in Scotland—saw splits and unions evolving in Canada. Some of the names were Church of Scotland, Canada Presbyterian, Kirk of Scotland, Reformed Presbyterian and other smaller groups. The archives encourages individual congregations to send their valuable paper records, including clergy registers, to the archives for microfilming. Originals are returned to the church, and the archives keeps the filmed copy.

The Presbyterian Archives has about 450 original or microfilmed registers (remember that certain Presbyterian records may be found at UCA). These are described at their website, which also shares the ARCHEION search engine. More is available in the way of private papers and biographical material. All must be consulted on-site in their Reading Room. The archives has a good collection of individual church histories, which it encourages each church to undertake and publish. You can request research by staff for set fees.

LAC and UCA have copies of material from the Glasgow Colonial Society. Ancestors who served as ordained Church of Scotland clergy can be found in the multi-volume *Fasti Ecclesiae Scoticanae*, a series of biographies. Clergy who served overseas in Ontario and Quebec are in the original volume VII, published in 1928. See articles such as Peter Russell's "Church of Scotland Clergy in Upper Canada: Culture Shock and Conservatism on the Frontier" in *Ontario History* Vol. 73, No. 2 (1981) and "American Presbyterians in the Niagara Peninsula, 1800-1841" by John Banks in *Ontario History* Vol. 57 (1965).

Lutheran

The Eastern Synod of the Evangelical Lutheran Church in Canada covers Ontario and all provinces easterly except Newfoundland and Labrador. Eastern Synod collections of church-related material are in their archives at Wilfrid Laurier University Library's Special Collections in Waterloo, Ontario. Some historic church registers are there, some of them microfilmed. Noteworthy are the old Lutheran congregations of the Eastern and Midland Districts, serving the needs of German-speaking ex-soldiers and settlers of Palatine and Dutch Reform background. Few others pre-date Canadian Confederation. As with most church archives, a great deal of other material exists in the form of original papers; church administration records; and related committees, books and publications. A detailed finding aid is online at the website.

The microfilms for the Eastern and Midland District registers, and some for Waterloo County, are also available at LAC and AO.

Baptist

Today there are still a number of variations of the Baptist faith in Canada. Our ancestors may have belonged to a Regular Baptist,

Close Communion Baptist, Free Will Baptist or Union Baptist church. The Canadian Baptist Archives at McMaster University Divinity College in Hamilton collects records from the Canadian Baptist Federation, including a few from the different traditions. The records of genealogical interest are mainly marriages. Historical records will not include infant baptisms. Believers are baptized as adults, and thus their names are on membership rolls. Material in the archival collection comes from early congregations in the Toronto area, Norfolk County, Oxford County and the towns of Dundas, Kingston and Brockville. Some nineteenth-century Plymouth Brethren records are within their holdings, as well as many theses from student graduates.

An online finding aid, "Genealogical Research Information Page," tells family historians what they can expect from the collection in addition to a large library of related books. Research in their material is on-site only. Visiting hours are quite limited and an appointment must be made. The archivists will deal with written inquiries of a concise nature for set fees. The microfilmed "Canadian Baptist Historical Collection" of biographical files is available at AO as well.

Mennonite

Mennonites are a group that produced divergent streams of practice and worship, rather than the doctrinal differences that occurred in some other faiths. Their agriculturally oriented, pacifist communities separate them from the world at large. Conferences have been formed of the most numerous like-minded congregations, like the Mennonite Conference of Eastern Canada and Mennonite Brethren. The Mennonite Archives at Conrad Grebel College at the University of Waterloo actively collects records of congregations, institutions and leaders. Located within the college library, the archives requires an advance appointment for a personal visit.

Online, you will find a list of congregational records in their holdings from various conferences, with historical dates and descriptions. Mennonites too did not practise baptism of small children. The archives' collection of bishops' books is important for the recording of marriages and adult baptisms. The archives also has many, many family history records and a wide range of manuscripts. Historically, Mennonites have had some similarities with various Brethren groups and Tunker traditions. *Trail of the Black Walnut* is a history of Pennsylvania Mennonite families coming to Upper Canada. Ezra Eby's original *Biographical History of Waterloo County* was a large undertaking about the descendants and ancestors of pioneer Mennonite families, and continues to be revised and updated.

Further reading is available in the articles "Mennonite History" by Peter Bartels in *OGS Seminar Annual, 1986* and "Niagara Mennonite Settlers Along the River and Lake Erie" by Harold Nigh in *OGS Seminar Annual, 1987*.

Quaker

Numbers in the Society of Friends, commonly called Quakers, may have dwindled over the past 200 years, although there are still a dozen or so meetings in the province today. The Canadian Friends Historical Association is an active organization. Schisms among the Friends occurred in 1812 when the Children of Peace separated and 1828 when the Orthodox and Hicksites disagreed. Quaker marriages traditionally took place before the entire congregation, who witnessed with their signatures. The names and residence of the parents of both bride and groom are normally recorded. Monthly meeting minutes also regularly contain references to the wayward and the members delegated to approach them.

The Quaker Archives and Library located at Pickering College in Newmarket has a collection that starts with very early material from different locations of meeting minutes, marriages and family registers. The facility includes the non-circulating Arthur Garratt Dorland Reference Library and the archival collection of the Sharon Temple Museum Society. Children of Peace, also known as Davidites, constructed their temple at the village of Sharon beginning in 1825. It is now a national historic site.

In the last few years, volunteers have been transcribing the original minute books of meetings, and developing genealogical indexes and finding aids. The first nominal index was for the seminal Yonge Street Meeting, which was recognized by 1804, published in print format. Transcripts of names from minutes and vital events registers of Yonge Street, Pelham (Niagara area), Adolphustown (Bay of Quinte area) and others are posted on the website. The *Canadian Quaker Genealogical Index* is searchable there for names from these records.

Friends who married out of the faith are often noted in meeting minutes. Many such marriages were performed by magistrates whose records have disappeared. The couple's subsequent "adoption" of a different religion could mean a loss of the ancestral connection for a family historian. Usually the names of the disowned are included in the above indexing of meeting minutes, but often without reference to the name of the intended spouse. An article by William Britnell in *Families* Vol. 15, No. 2 (1976) called "Irregular Marriages of the Yonge Street Friends, 1806–1828" is an excellent finding aid that connects straying Quakers to their parents. Britnell researched cemetery stones, census, church records and other records to provide extra identifying information whenever possible.

The Quaker Archives library catalogue is also available online. Volunteer staff can only deal with quite straightforward written inquiries. Researchers are encouraged to plan personal visits but make a necessary appointment. The historic collection on microfilm is also available in London at D. B. Weldon Library, University of Western Ontario, at AO and LAC. Dorland's *The Quakers in Canada: A History* remains the classic book on that subject. Other relevant articles are "The Use of Quaker Records for Genealogical Research in Ontario" by Jane Zavitz in *Families* Vol. 19, No. 1 (1980) and "Where the Friends Were/Are" by Harold Zavitz in the OGS *Bulletin* Vol. 9, No. 3 (1970) with a wonderful map of Quaker settlement and cemetery locations.

Disciples

Officially known now as Christian Church, Disciples or Disciples in Christ were not a large denomination. Nonetheless it had and has adherents in several parts of Ontario. Immersion baptism is one of their fundamental practices. Historically, record keeping by the congregations was not of standard practice and older records may be difficult to find or non-existent. The Reuben Butchart fonds at Victoria University in Toronto probably has the most information about their history and locations within the province.

Jews

People of Jewish faith have been present in Ontario for a considerable time, since at least the early part of the nineteenth century. Synagogues are the focus for religious rites that include the expected marriage and burial or funeral records. In addition, look for *bar mitzvah* and *bat mitzvah* records, the formal coming of age ceremonies for boys at age 13 and girls at age 12 or 13.

There may be *mohel* records of male circumcision, or the naming of a female child, both traditionally taking place eight days after birth. Such records bear genealogical importance especially if they exist prior to civil registration. Children may be given a Hebrew or Yiddish forename that is used at marriage or other religious occasions.

Most synagogue records are retained by individual congregations. Older, no longer existing congregations normally deposited their records with a newer congregation. A 100-year restriction is not unusual for requests of birth records. The Ontario Jewish Archives is a repository for many different types of sources, but not specifically for vital records, although it has some synagogue records and family histories (see Chapter 8).

Mormons

The Church of Jesus Christ of Latter-day Saints are also known as Mormons. They have had a historic presence in Ontario since the 1830s as the Mormons began a long migration westward. In *Families* Vol. 43 No. 1 (2004), Ken Sisler's article "Early Ontario Mormons," gives some biographical information on early church members who were born, or settled, in Ontario.

There were other nineteenth-century religious denominations with smaller numbers or less visibility, which by now have either grown dramatically or virtually disappeared. There are often books about them, historical societies formed for them, or private archival collections started, for such groups as Brethren, Amish, Jews, Latter-day Saints, Seventh Day Adventists and others. Those that are most active are listed in Appendix III. Certain Moravian records from archives in England and Pennsylvania can be seen at LAC.

District and County Marriage Registers

District Marriage Registers

The government of Upper Canada's first attempt to gather statistics on marriages, and who were performing them, resulted in a series of registers created by district clerks of the peace who expected all "nonconformist" clergy to send in yearly details. But submissions to a district clerk prior to 1831 were few and far between. The series of district marriage registers that do survive have the great majority of entries after 1831 due to legislation at that time, although the established Anglican and Catholic clergy were exempt. Even then, the registers are not comprehensive since some ministers did not always comply. Marriage information from this period and in these district registers is minimal: names of the parties, place and date of marriage, denomination or minister and witnesses.

District registers continued up until 1858 when newer legislation was enacted. To find an appropriate register, you must know the general location for your ancestor and which district covered that area at the time. The maps at the front of this book will help you compare county boundaries with the shifting district outlines as new ones were added. Remember, the registers are *copies* of papers turned in to district clerks but in most cases are the only extant form. Registers have survived for the following districts.

Bathurst	London
Brock	Newcastle
Colborne	Ottawa
Eastern	Prince Edward
Gore	Simcoe
Home	Talbot
Huron	Victoria
Johnstown	Wellington
Western	

A few districts are not available at all—registers for the districts of Niagara, Midland and Dalhousie are missing. Most of the original books are at AO and are microfilmed alphabetically by district name. The FHL also has the microfilms. The AO on-site finding aid and website list microfilm numbers for both facilities. A few of the registers contain returns for baptisms or burials.

Microfilm users beware: some aberrations are noted in the microfilmed series. Some district marriage returns that were available at the time of microfilming appear in the finding aid and on the microfilms as *county* returns. They are as follows, with the district name preceding the county name under which they are labelled.

Colborne 1843–1858	Peterborough County
Simcoe 1842–1858	Simcoe County
London 1851–1857	Elgin, Middlesex Counties

Most (but not all) of the registers were nominally indexed by hand at or about the time they were created. The existing

Ontario County Marriage Register, 1858-1869, RG 80-27-2, vol. 45, p. 136; AO microfilm MS 248 reel 12

handwritten indexes appear on the AO microfilm along with the registers. They can be time-consuming to read because of cramped handwriting or faded pages, and indexing for one surname initial may overflow to resume on other pages under a different alphabet letter. An index that begins at the front of a volume may continue at the back. Once in a while only the groom's name is indexed. From 1968 to 1990 a number of these registers were abstracted and indexed in *The Ontario Register*.

In 1994 Dan Walker of NorSim Publishing began the systematic abstraction and indexing of the original registers and all available loose returns. The publishing was continued by Global Heritage Press, resulting in at least eighteen volumes (some in multiple parts) of *The Marriage Registers of Upper Canada/Canada West*. Walker and his team went further to compile the *Vital Records of Upper Canada/Canada West* series from individual church registers for this pre-1869 period. Some of the old church registers are difficult for the average researcher to access, thus the publications are a great boon in filling gaps and providing missing material for the old district registers. Maps and good introductions are provided.

Filed 4th January 1862.   No 1862

	BRIDE.			WITNESS.		DATE OF
RESIDENCE.	PLACE OF BIRTH.	NAMES OF PARENTS.		NAME.	RESIDENCE.	MARRIAGE.
ooklin	Whitby	William	Jane	John W Gard, Mary A Huntington	Brooklin	Jany 2
hitby	Toronto	Fredk	Catherine	John Gall, Phebe Park	Whitby	March 21
ckering	Pickering	—	—	Jas H Redman, Jas Mackie	Pickering, Harmony	May 1
ilrough	Scarborough	—	—	John Whaler, Eliza Mckline	Scarborough	May 2
umbus	Toronto	Stephen	Thomasina	Buck S Whittee, Eliz Michael		May 13
liarra	England	Elijah	Catherine	Daniel Cherry, Fanny Dickson		May 16
ckering	Cornwall UC	John Boddy	Eliza	Geo Stephenson, Fanny Dickson	Oshawa	May 29
whitby	E to hitby	Geo	Margt	Lewis T Pascoe, Sarah T Leo	E to hitby	June 29

Some clergy returns of this period had not been forwarded from district clerks to a provincial registration board. Some were left as loose returns without being copied into registers, or they were recorded and then stored away in a county office. The Justice portfolio at AO now holds such older files of clerks of the peace, those that have been discovered. Some included baptism or burial returns. Even a few Catholic and Anglican records have turned up. You can find their listings in section 2.2 of the online AO guide *Sources of Family History*, which is also a print handout.

Among clergy records that pre-date or overlap with the county marriage register period, Walker has also produced a few additional volumes relevant to the above. Some came from then-uncatalogued material at AO or from individual churches of the areas. They are:

- Haldimand County Marriage & Burial Registers, 1851–1865
- Middlesex County Marriages and Baptisms, 1848–1858
- Perth County Baptism, Marriage & Burial Register, 1852–1859

County Marriage Registers

Beginning in 1858, and continuing until civil registration was instituted in 1869, county marriage registers succeeded the district marriage volumes. The newer registers were intended to include marriages of *all* denominations. Much more information was requested here: names and ages of the couple, residences, birthplaces, names of parents, quite often the birth surname of the mother, date and place of marriage, denomination, name and residence of witnesses. Again, they were microfilmed alphabetically by name of the county and films can be borrowed through AO and FHL.

Glengarry County marriages 1858-1869 are not available in the AO series. The original register is available at LAC. However, Donald McKenzie has indexed and abstracted the details in a Global Heritage Press publication. Global also acquired publishing rights to the collection of the MacDonald Research Centre, which produced many local church transcripts and family histories.

Very few of the county registers have an index on the actual microfilms. Generation Press produced 37 volumes of indexes, not all in the same format. Some volumes merely give names and reference numbers to the county volume. Others are extracts, but sometimes do not cite volume and page numbers. Second editions of the series have been published by Global Heritage Press. Remember that all these registers were *copies* created by clerks. Their rendition of spellings or place names from a minister's returns can be erratic. Modern indexers could have had an equally difficult time with a clerk's handwriting or the general quality of the microfilm.

The AO guide "Sources of Family History" will give you the microfilm reel numbers you need for borrowing or on-site usage. Again, the FHL has both the district and county series, with their own distinct microfilm numbers, also posted on the AO website. *Genealogy.com* has produced, apparently from independent indexing, a searchable CD-ROM for the county marriage register series.

Other marriage records and/or parish registers are listed in LAC's *Checklist of Parish Registers on Microfilm* and in AO's Church Records Collection. The lists can also be consulted online through their search engines. The collections have a wide spread of date ranges at both repositories. AO often has copies of the LAC microfilms, as does the FHL.

Reading and Reference

Briggs, Elizabeth and Colin J. Briggs. *Before Modern Medicine: Diseases and Yesterday's Remedies.* Winnipeg, MB: Westgarth Publishing, 1998.

Britnell, William and/or Elizabeth Hancocks, compilers and indexers. *County Marriage Registers of Ontario, Canada, 1858-1869.* 37 volumes. Second editions. Campbellville, ON: Global Heritage Press, 2005.

Burrows, Sandra and Franceen Gaudet, compilers. *Checklist of Indexes to Canadian Newspapers.* Ottawa, ON: National Library of Canada, 1987.

Butchart, Reuben. *The Disciples of Christ in Canada Since 1930.* Toronto, ON: Canadian Headquarters' Publications, Churches of Christ (Disciples), 1949. See also Reuben Butchart fonds at Victoria University, library.vicu.utoronto.ca/special/butchart.htm.

Cober, George. *Historical Sketch of the Brethren in Christ Church: Known as Tunkers in Canada.* Gormley, ON: n.p., 1953.

Cronmiller, Carl R. *A History of the Lutheran Church in Canada.* Kitchener, ON: Evangelical Lutheran Synod of Canada, 1961.

Dorland, Arthur G. *The Quakers in Canada: A History.* Second edition. Toronto, ON: Canadian Friends Historical Association/Ryerson Press,1968.

Eby, Ezra E. *A Biographical History of Waterloo Township.* 2 volumes. Berlin, ON: Ezra E. Eby, 1895-1896. See ourroots.ca for the text of the book and also www.ezraeby.com.

Epp, Frank H. *Mennonites in Canada 1786-1920: The History of a Separate People.* Toronto, ON: Macmillan of Canada, 1974.

Fasti Ecclesiae Scoticanae. Volume VII. Scotland: Bannatyne Club, 1928.

Getz, J. Henry and George C. Spaetzel. *The Canada Conference of the Evangelical United Brethren Church, 1864-1964: A Century in Canada.* Kitchener, ON: Canada Conference of the United Evangelical Brethren, 1964.

Gilchrist, Brian J., compiler. *Inventory of Ontario Newspapers, 1793-1986.* Toronto, ON: Micromedia, 1987.

Grant, John Webster. *A Profusion of Spires: Religion in Nineteenth-Century Ontario.* Toronto, ON: University of Toronto Press, 1988.

Hope, Louise I., compiler. *Index to Niagara Conference Methodist Episcopal Church Baptismal Register, 1849-1886.* 2 volumes, A-K, L-Z. Toronto, ON: Ontario Genealogical Society, 1994.

Ivison, Stuart and Fred Rosser. *The Baptists in Upper and Lower Canada Before 1820.* Toronto, ON: University of Toronto, 1956.

Jewitt, Allen E., compiler. *Early Canadian Marriages in Erie County, New York, 1840-1890.* Hamburg, NY: Allen E. Jewitt, 1982-.

Leetooze, Sherrill Branton. *Bible Christian Chapels of the Canadian Conference.* Bowmanville, ON: Lynn Michael-John Associates, 2005.

McKenzie, Donald A., compiler. *Death Notices from the Christian Guardian, 1836-1850.* Lambertville, NJ: Hunterdon House, 1982.

_____. *Glengarry County Marriage Register 1858-1869.* Campbellville, ON: Global Heritage Press, 2008.

_____. *Death Notices from the Christian Guardian, 1851-1860.* Lambertville, NJ: Hunterdon House, 1984.

_____. *Obituaries from Ontario's Christian Guardian, 1861-1870.* Lambertville, NJ: Hunterdon House, 1988.

_____. *Obituaries from Ontario's Christian Guardian, 1873-1880.* Lambertville, NJ: Hunterdon House, 1996.

_____. *Obituaries from the Christian Guardian, 1884-1890.* Campbellville, ON: Global Heritage Press, 2005.

_____. *Death Notices from the Canada Christian Advocate, 1858-1872.* Lambertville, NJ: Hunterdon House, 1992.

_____. *Obituaries from the Canada Christian Advocate, 1873-1884.* Ottawa, ON: Donald A. McKenzie, 1998.

_____. *More Notices from Methodist Newspapers of Ontario, 1830-1857.* Lambertville, NJ: Hunterdon House, 1986.

_____. *More Notices from Ontario's Methodist Newspapers, 1858-1872.* Ottawa, ON: Donald A. McKenzie, 1993.

_____. *More Obituaries from Ontario's Methodist Newspapers, 1873-1884.* Ottawa, ON: Donald A. McKenzie, 2001.

McNeill, John T. *The Presbyterian Church in Canada, 1875-1925.* Toronto, ON: General Board of the Presbyterian Church in Canada, 1925.

National Council of Churches. *Yearbook of American and Canadian Churches.* Annual. New York, NY: National Council of Churches in Christ in the U.S.A., 1973-.

Quintin, Robert J., editor. *An Address Guide to the Catholic Parishes of Ontario.* Pawtucket, RI: Quintin Publications, 1994.

Reaman, G. Elmore. *The Trail of the Black Walnut.* 1957. Reprint. Toronto, ON: McClelland and Stewart Limited, 1979.

Reid, William D., compiler. *Death Notices of Ontario.* Lambertville, NJ: Hunterdon House, 1980.

_____. compiler. *Marriage Notices of Ontario.* Lambertville, NJ: Hunterdon House, 1980.

Rumpel, Renie A., compiler. *Roman Catholic Marriage Registers in Ontario, Canada, 1828-1870.* Waterloo, ON: Ontario Indexing Services, 1997.

Semple, Neil. *The Lord's Dominion: The Story of Canadian Methodism.* Montreal, QC/Kingston, ON: McGill-Queen's University Press, 1996.

Stratford-Devai, Fawne and Ruth Burkholder. *Vital Records in Ontario Before 1969.* Campbellville, ON: Global Heritage Press, 2003.

Walker, Dan and Fawne Stratford-Devai, Robert W. Calder, et. al., compilers and indexers. *The Marriage Records of Upper Canada/ Canada West, District Marriage Registers.* 18 volumes. Some revised editions. Campbellville, ON: Global Heritage Press 199-. Formerly from Nor-Sim Publishing in Delhi.

_____, compilers and indexers. *Vital Records of Upper Canada/Canada West.* Campbellville, ON: Global Heritage Press, c1999-.

Wilson, Thomas B., compiler. *Marriage Bonds of Ontario, 1803-1834.* Lambertville, NJ: Hunterdon House, 1985.

_____, compiler. *Ontario Marriage Notices.* Lambertville, NJ: Hunterdon House, 1982.

_____, editor. *The Ontario Register.* 8 volumes. Lambertville, NJ: Hunterdon House, 1969-1990.

Alex. W. Fraser. www.glengarrycounty.com/awfrrbks.html

Ancestry.ca. www.ancestry.ca

The Anglican Church of Canada. www.anglican.ca/index.htm

Baptist Archives. www.macdiv.ca/students/baptistarchives.php

Bill Martin's Early Ontario Records. my.tbaytel.net/bmartin/

Canadian Conference of Catholic Bishops. www.cccb.ca/site/index.php?/lang=eng

Find A Grave. www.findagrave.com

Genealogy.com. www.genealogy.com

Global Heritage Press. www.globalgenealogy.com

Interment.Net. www.interment.net

Jewish Genealogical Society of Canada (Toronto). www.jgstoronto.ca

Ontario Jewish Archives. www.ontariojewisharchives.org/research.html

Lutheran Archives. library.wlu.ca/archives

Mennonite Archives. grebel.uwaterloo.ca/mao

Mount Pleasant Group of Cemeteries. www.mountpleasantgroupofcemeteries.ca

Northern Ontario Gravemarker Gallery. freepages.genealogy.rootsweb.com/~murrayp

The Ontario Association of Cemetery and Funeral Professionals. www.oacfp.com

Ontario Cemeteries Resources. www.wightman.ca/~dkaufman

Ontario Cemetery Finding Aid. www.islandnet.com

Ontario Genealogical Society. www.ogs.on.ca

Ontario GenWeb. www.geneofun.on.ca/ongenweb

Ontario Historical Society. www.ontariohistoricalsociety.org

Ontario Jewish Archives. www.ontariojewisharchives.org

Presbyterian Church in Canada Archives. www.presbyterian.ca

Region of Peel Archives. www.peelregion.ca/heritage/archives.htm

Quaker Archives.
www.archives-library.quaker.ca/en/introduction.html

Quintin Publications. www.quintinpublications.com

Saving Graves. www.savinggraves.org

Société franco-ontarienne d'histoire et généalogie. www.sfohg.com

United Church of Canada Archives. www.unitedchurcharchives.ca

Wesleyan Methodist Baptismal Registers.
freepages.genealogy.rootsweb.com/~wjmartin/wesleyan.htm

5

Census Returns

Reference Dates

1842	Province-wide census of the Canadas, heads of households only
1851	First census to name all household members, enumerated 12 January 1852
1861	Census enumeration date 14 January 1861
1871	First Dominion census, enumeration date 2 April 1871
1881	Census enumeration date 4 April 1881
1891	Census enumeration date of 6 April 1891
1901	Census enumeration date 31 March 1901
1911	Census enumeration date 1 June 1911

Census returns are a staple source for family research. Finding ancestors in a census return gives you a look at household composition and details of the inhabitants. Finding them over an extended period of returns will show how a family changed as it grew and aged. From the beginning of population enumerations, information was requested about household statistics and work production. The oldest returns have minimal information, if they survive, placing a man in a particular place in a given year.

Like many other sources used in genealogical research, Canadian census returns are conveniently accessible in microfilm form. Historically, most of the original paper enumeration sheets from 1851 onward have been routinely destroyed after microfilming took place. Thus many originals do not remain for consulting, even if archival conditions allowed access to fragile paper documents. When the words "surviving" or "existing" describe census returns, we mean the microfilm version. Chapter 1 gives a brief reference to original sources versus image copies. Sometimes the census filming quality leaves much to be desired, so we want to be aware of the medium's condition as well as the information offered by the source.

Family historians find the most rewards in the increasingly more detailed census returns from 1851 onward when all members of a household or family are named. The personal schedules, also referred to as population schedules, provide valuable genealogical information. There you will learn, among other pieces of information, a family's religious affiliation that will help in seeking potential church records. Separate schedules for additional types of information were created later but again have not always survived. Agricultural schedules and others, such as deaths, industry and livestock, are important for a capsule economic portrait of a family. Only the 1871 census exists with all its schedules intact.

It is vital to remember that we do not know who gave the family or household information to the enumerator (census-taker). The informant may not have been the most knowledgeable family member, so some guessing and misinformation occurred. Enumerators of nineteenth-century censuses were invariably from the more literate of the community, but even they could not always cope with back-roads travel, fatigue, unfamiliarity with some names and a certain amount of hostility towards government intrusion.

Occasional "double" enumerations happened, despite enumeration instructions, when someone was away from home. Such occurrences happened in the case of students, domestic servants, itinerant workers, travellers or just plain overnight visitors. Sometimes a parent or spouse enumerated the person at home, while the same person was also recorded at his or her temporary location. If discrepancies are noted between two enumerations, we need to evaluate which record might be more reliable.

LAC's *Catalogue of Census Returns on Microfilm, 1666–1891*and the addendum *Catalogue of Census Returns on Microfilm, 1901* are the principal finding aids, with references for the microfilm reel numbers. They should be available at the resource centre where you view the films, or can be consulted online at the Canadian Genealogy Centre. See page 119 for the 1911 census and finding aids.

Early Censuses

Before 1842, the law provided for an annual census by township assessors, which was filed with the district clerk of the peace. Relatively few of these returns have been preserved. The very earliest may only establish a residence for a head of household at a certain date and a household profile of males and females in broad age categories. Returns that connect an individual to a lot and concession number are genealogically significant. Sometimes the early censuses were combined with property assessment rates, for local tax collection purposes. Official maps of early enumeration districts have not survived, although census-takers occasionally drew maps of their particular boundaries on the census return itself.

Sporadic surviving returns exist for townships in the districts of Gore, Niagara, Newcastle, Midland, Johnstown and Ottawa. Most are listed in the LAC's *Catalogue of Census Returns on Microfilm*. Most can also be viewed at AO. Because these district records include assessment or collector rolls as well as census information, they are also mentioned in the Municipal Records section of Chapter 9. Halton-Peel Branch OGS has indexed the districts of Gore, Newcastle and Ottawa. Niagara Peninsula Branch extracted and indexed the surviving 1828 returns for its area.

1842

Collecting statistics for 1842 was one of the first major projects of the newly combined government of Canada East and West. Over 100 columns of information were requested on the 1842 census. It names the heads of households only, but contains details for household members—age range, country of birth and religion. Agricultural data is given for the property of the head of household. Some enumerators arbitrarily entered the concession and lot numbers on the left hand side for rural areas. "Number of years each person has been in the province when not natives thereof" and "Number of aliens not naturalized" can be meaningful columns for estimating an emigration or settlement year. Not all the townships were then settled or organized enough to take this census, and not every census that was originally recorded has survived. The database on *Ancestry.ca* called "Ontario and Nova Scotia Census, 1800-1842" is extremely limited in scope for Ontario. It is based on a transcribed compilation of a few selected townships.

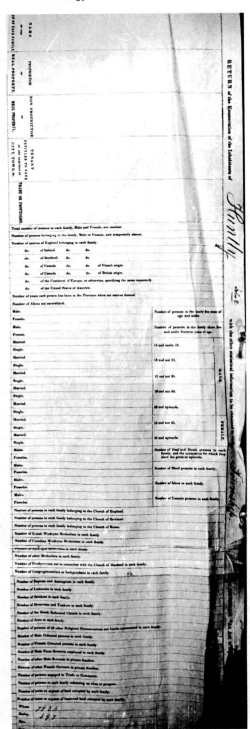

1842 Census Upper Canada, Bathurst District, Huntley Township, column headings; Library and Archives Canada microfilm C-1344

Again, many OGS Branches have nominally indexed or transcribed the surviving 1842 census returns for towns and townships within their regions. The format of the enumerators' sheets was long and wide, making microfilming awkward. Viewers must carefully examine the sheets to follow the ancestor's line under each column heading amidst the cramped handwriting of most enumerators.

1848 and 1850

Census returns for these two years survive *for only three districts*— Huron, Johnstown and Newcastle— of the nineteen districts in existence in the province at that time. A few fragments have survived for other areas outside these districts. A nominal index compiled by Brian Lee Dilts is available at many institutions in print or microfiche form. It is essential that researchers are not misled and understand the coverage is limited. The introduction to his index is full of useful information.

In 1848 and 1850, again just the family or household head is named. He or she appears on one line with information continuing across eight pages and more than 140 columns. Forms and columns for the two years are very similar. Household members are given choices for many religions and places of birth, several groupings in which to place children's ages, questions regarding school or college attendance, and the presence of farm servants, among many other columns. Sifting through the extensive agricultural and additional information can build quite a full picture of a family's contemporary economic position. The enumerations were likely undertaken in the spring of the year, but researchers should study a particular return to see if the enumerator dated it or noted when he filed it.

The returns for Johnstown and Newcastle Districts are included in LAC's *Catalogue of Census Returns on Microfilm, 1666-1891* with microfilm numbers. The original material for

1848 Census Canada West, Newcastle District, Northumberland County, Hamilton Township, p. 129; Library and Archives Canada microfilm M-5911

Huron District is at D.B. Weldon Library, University of Western Ontario, in London. Some returns have survived for parts of the London District and are in the holdings of the Norfolk Historical Society. Scattered returns for other areas may have been located by and preserved in a regional repository.

1851

This census was the first enumeration to name every individual in each household. It also has provision for separate sheets of agricultural information. By 1851, many towns and townships had enough population to warrant dividing them into enumeration districts with different enumerators for each. Unfortunately, the 1851 census too is not available for some areas—one example is the entire city of Toronto (see Alternatives below). Furthermore, some districts within a township may be missing. For instance, the personal schedule for one district out of the original four is all that survives for Darlington township in the former Durham County. Be sure to record this kind of negative information whenever you are searching. A "missing" ancestor may simply mean he was enumerated on paper that no longer exists.

The enumerators for this census year carried out their duties in early 1852. The foremost items of genealogical interest are occupation, place of birth, religious denomination, "age next birthday" and marital status. Deaths during 1851, including cause and age, were requested in a column on the personal schedule. Other columns referred to a person's residence "if out of limits," basic literacy status, children attending school and "infirmities" (deafness, blindness or unsound mind).

Agricultural schedules follow each district's personal census schedule, giving the important information of lot and concession location for the head of household, whether the person was an owner or tenant, the number of acres farmed and annual produce. Occasionally the population schedule for a place no longer exists, but the agricultural schedule does—at least providing evidence of residence. Sometimes the agricultural schedules are also totally or partially missing. As an example, Chingacousy township in Peel County has only one surviving agricultural schedule out of five districts.

Legibility of handwriting can be a problem, but this is true for most census returns. A different problem is the occasional non-sequence of pages in the microfilming procedure, even though they have been stamp-numbered in seemingly right order. When a family begins near the bottom of a page and does not continue logically at the top of the next page, you will have to hunt for the correct following page, which could appear a few pages farther ahead or even a few pages back.

Space was provided for the enumerators to make general remarks but most confined themselves to observations on the

1851 Census Canada West, Huron County, Usborne Township, p. 21; Library and Archives Canada microfilm C-11728

dominant industries, the quality of agricultural conditions and, perhaps, the variety of churches or eminent buildings in their districts. To their great chagrin, some enumerators failed to receive an adequate supply of government forms and had to improvise their own. Robert E. Paterson of North Easthope Township was not the only one to observe: "I have no remarks to make but if ever you should make me enumerator again I hope you will send me more paper." Another census-taker was so fed up with severe weather conditions and his recalcitrant neighbours that he complained it took an hour or two to record six or seven names and was never sure whether the informant was telling the truth, especially regarding the agricultural census.

Digital images of the 1851 census pages from Library and Archives Canada are online at the Canadian Genealogy Centre. The CGC does not have a nominal index, so searching is done by place name. However, the subscription-based website *Ancestry.ca* has a nominally searchable database linked to the images of pages. The same cautions about questionably indexed spellings apply to this database as to others. The website *AutomatedGenealogy* also is also in the process of indexing the 1851 census. Ontario Indexing Services has created every name indexes to the 1851 census for four county areas: Wellington, Bruce and Grey, Lennox and Addington, and Wentworth-Hamilton.

1861

The format of the census page was continued from 1851 with 50 names on a page, for townships. The basic questions or columns scarcely changed. A column for "Married within the year" referred to the preceding twelve months. Happily for genealogists, a number of enumerators interpreted this as "in which year were you married?" Different enumeration forms were issued in the cities, one per household, requiring the head to fill it in and sign it. The microfilming of the forms resulted in often tiny handwriting for today's family historians to decipher, but many do offer the ancestor's signature as a benefit. City householders were formally advised that the forms would be collected on 14 January, to show who had slept in the house the previous night.

The 1861 returns also had more than one page for the personal schedule. The additional pages and columns continue after the personal page of names. They show the type of dwelling place and how many families were in each, and business and employment information. Many of these extra pages are missing on the microfilms. Deaths during 1860 are requested. Make a note about which *enumeration district* of a township your family was found in, to find the appropriate agricultural schedule. In 1861 those schedules are grouped together at the end of all the town/township personal schedules in one county. Quite often this will involve viewing a different microfilm reel. Agricultural schedules will not necessarily be in the same township order as the personal schedules. The name of a township is sometimes omitted at the top of the pages, so you may have to search the unnamed pages as well.

Look for enumerators' remarks, which could have been added wherever space was available throughout the personal schedules. Some enumerators have added notes about a specific business or noteworthy building. Some have even singled out individuals in their districts. In St. Lawrence Ward of the 1861 return for Toronto, the enumerator was so impressed with Mr. Edward Leary, "the oldest man in my division," that he wrote a long note about the man's age, birthplace, emigration date and various occupations, ending with, "He retains all his mental faculties save a little want of hearing, and can walk four to five miles daily at a smart pace."

A province-wide nominal index to the 1861 census does not yet exist. Local OGS branches or Ontario GenWeb volunteers have indexed selected parts of it. Ontario GenWeb's *Census Project* is another place to search for local returns that have been indexed.

1871

In 1871, the first federal census was taken for the new Dominion of Canada, including Ontario. It had nine separate schedules, all of which have been preserved on microfilm. Schedule 1 is "Nominal return of the living." Schedule 2 is "Nominal return of the deaths within the last twelve months." Schedule 3 is "Return of public institutions, real estate, vehicles and implements" and Schedule 4 is "Return of cultivated land, of field products and of plants and fruits." This last is in fact the agricultural schedule, with the key information of lot and concession number for each household. This schedule gives figures for crops and food that help a descendant grasp a family's production and consumption, especially in rural areas. Schedule 5 is "Return of live stock, animal products, home-made fabrics and furs," which also has much interest for the family historian. Schedule 6 is "Return of industrial establishments," which notes manufacturing and related businesses, giving an idea of the neighbourhood. The remaining schedules relate to forestry, shipping and fisheries, and mining, which were in specific parts of the province at that time.

By carefully noting the page number and *line number* on the nominal return for the head of household, you can find his information on subsequent schedules, which all follow each Schedule 1. Only Schedule 2 (deaths) and Schedule 6 (industrial) do not correspond to a line number in the personal schedule.

A new format with 25 names to a page and a few new columns were introduced in the 1871 personal return. Besides "Married within last twelve months" we find "Born within last twelve months," the latter often providing the month of birth of a child less than one year old. This is the first time we see the column "Origin." It refers to the country of origin for the paternal emigrant ancestor of each person. Thus we know that a person born in Ontario, whose origin is stated as Irish, had an ancestor from Ireland in his male lineage. Children in the census should have the origin of their father. As an example of how this column can help to identify people, in one family the husband's origin was English, the wife's Irish, the two oldest children French, and the remaining children English. Although they were all listed with the same surname, this supported family tradition that the wife had children by a previous marriage to a French Canadian.

The 1871 census was also the first that did not conform to all the contemporary county boundaries. Three artificial counties were created for census enumeration purposes only and also continued during later census returns. Each artificial county took towns and townships from more than one real county. This could be confusing to a researcher because the artificial counties do not exist on a geographical map. Under its census section, the Canadian Genealogy Centre provides a link to "Electoral Atlas of the Dominion of Canada (1895)" that shows the boundaries and townships included in the new creations.

The townships and towns assigned to the three artificial counties are as follows, with their real county locations in brackets.

Bothwell

Bothwell (Kent)   Orford (Kent)
Camden (Kent)   Ridgetown (Kent)
Dawn (Lambton)   Sombra (Lambton)
Dresden (Kent)   Thamesville (Kent)
Euphemia (Lambton)   Zone (Kent)
Howard (Kent)

Cardwell

Adjala (Simcoe)   Caledon (Peel)

Albion (Peel)   Mono (Simcoe, later Dufferin)

Bolton (Peel)

Monck

Caistor (Lincoln)   Moulton (Haldimand)

Canborough (Haldimand) Pelham (Welland)

Dunn (Haldimand)   Sherbrooke(Haldimand)

Dunnville (Haldimand)   Wainfleet (Welland)

Gainsborough (Lincoln)

The *Index to the 1871 Census of Ontario* was a partnership project between OGS and LAC, and the first major census tool to be computerized. The *Index* can be searched in a database at the Canadian Genealogy Centre by surname, given name, occupation, ethnic origin and key word, which could include a religious denomination. A database entry will give the town or township, division and page number to take you to the original record. The 30 print volumes can be found on library shelves.

Please note that the *Index* (and the database) is only for heads of households and "strays," that is, anyone in a household with a different surname from the head. It is not an every name index. In a household that includes extended family with the same surname as the head, like grandparents or adult brothers, the latter will not be in the *Index*. A full transcription of all names is planned for the Family History Library's *FamilySearch* website.

1881

The 1881 census is quite similar to 1871 in format. Columns were added here for the birthplaces of each individual's parents. Originally it had eight schedules but only the personal returns were microfilmed by Statistics Canada. Great dismay was expressed after the release of these records to LAC and the public domain, because of the generally poor microfilming quality. Whole divisions of a town or township may be overexposed or illegible. Thomas Hillman's restrained comment in *Catalogue of Census Returns on Microfilm* is that the 1881 census (and others filmed during the same period) "is not of a consistent quality, not all images are decipherable."

The FHL transcribed the 1881 Canadian census and created a searchable database from it, freely available on its *FamilySearch* website. Again, the transcribing has its flaws with

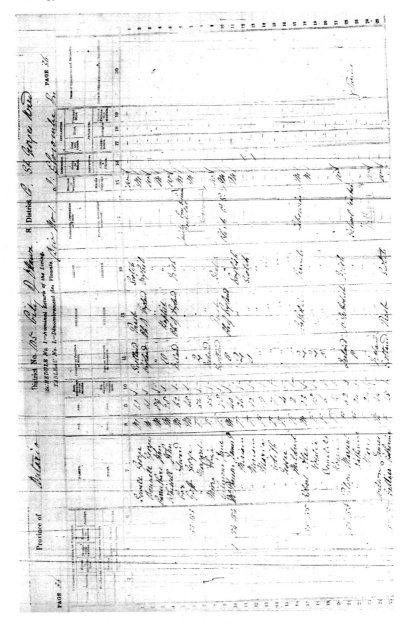

1881 Census Ontario, district 105, City of Ottawa, sub-district C, St. George Ward, division 1, p.36; Library and Archives Canada microfilm C-13230

the spelling and interpretation of names, so the indexing is not perfect. Nevertheless, the results for each entry will show an entire household with references to both FHL and LAC microfilm numbers.

1891

In the next decennial census of 1891 there were genealogically significant additions. A new column asked for each person's relationship to the head of the household. The predictable responses were "W" for wife, "S" for son and "D" for daughter. The initial "L" means lodger or non-family member, but in some instances can refer to relatives beyond the immediate family nucleus. Other relationships might be written out in full, like "mother" and "grandson" and so on. Another addition was the provision for the birthplace of each parent of a person, meaning country of birth. Some pages in this census may also be found out of sequence, and unfortunately the returns for a few places are partially or wholly missing, especially in Wellington County. Indexes for the 1891 census have been compiled at local levels, such as OGS branches and the *Ontario GenWeb*.

1901

By 1901, the census boundaries corresponded more closely to electoral divisions, and this trend continued in the twentieth century. When enumerated, this census had eleven schedules, of which only two now survive on microfilm. The population schedule is of greatest interest. The other extant schedule, "Return of buildings and lands, churches and schools," is usually placed at the beginning of each new subdistrict or ward. It shows rural property descriptions as the earlier agricultural schedules did, or street addresses for urban areas. The catalogue *Census Returns 1901* advises that random samples of additional schedules may be inserted here and there.

Without question, census returns after the turn of the twentieth century provide the greatest wealth of information for the genealogist. In addition to new columns in 1901 for employment and earnings data, the basic questions from past census years have been supplemented with:

- Colour. A person with any degree of "red" or "black" or "yellow" heritage was required to identify with that colour.
- Month, day and year of birth.
- Place of birth was to be designated "R" for rural or "U" for urban.
- Racial or tribal origin, "the line of descent being traced through the father in the white races." Enumerators were instructed that such terms as "Japanese" and "negro" were

Automated Genealogy 1901 Census Transcription Project   http://automatedgenealogy.com/census/SurnameList.jsp?surname=Tic.

Site Home Linking Message Boards Help**Automated Genealogy** Census Indices: 1901 1906 1911 1852CA 1851NB

1901 Census of Canada
Records with Surname Tickner

The soundex code for Tickner is T256.
Below are other surnames with the same soundex code. Click on a surname to see the listing for that
name, or click on the checkbox next to one or more names and then click the merge button to produce one
listing including all the checked names.
☐ Taschemor ☐ Tichner ☐ Tichnor ☐ Tigner ☐ Tsinrman ? ☐ Tucner ☐ Tushnier?

If you want to include a name with a different soundex enter it here: [   ]
Merge

There are surname notes with suggested surname of Tickner. Help

Givens begins with: A B C D E F G H I J K L M N O P Q R S T U V W X Y Z ?

Filters:
Givens contains: [   ]   Gender: [   ]   Age/Year: [   ] +- 1   Month: [   ]
[   ] **Filter**

Surname **Tickner** occurs in the following provinces: MB (6) ON (15) All (21)

There are 15 matching records.

Sort by geographic location

Surname	Givens	Age	Province	District	Subdistrict	Enum. District	Page	Line
Tickner	Albert	27	ON	ESSEX (North/Nord)	Windsor (City/Cité)	l-16	3	49
Tickner	Allice	30	ON	KENT	Chatham (City/Cité)	b-2	14	39
Tickner	Almena?	50	ON	KENT	Chatham (City/Cité)	b-2	14	38
Tickner	Austin	29	ON	KENT	Chatham (City/Cité)	b-2	14	35
Tickner	Bertha	24	ON	KENT	Chatham (City/Cité)	b-2	14	36
Tickner	Bessie	28	ON	LINCOLN & NIAGARA	Niagara	g-1	4	30
Tickner	Clarence	18	ON	KENT	Chatham (City/Cité)	b-2	14	40
Tickner	Clark	50	ON	KENT	Chatham (City/Cité)	b-2	14	37
Tickner	Ethel	15	ON	KENT	Chatham (City/Cité)	b-2	14	41
Tickner	Francis	5/12	ON	ESSEX (North/Nord)	Windsor (City/Cité)	l-16	4	2
Tickner	Laura	11	ON	KENT	Chatham (City/Cité)	b-2	14	43
Tickner	Lesley	14	ON	KENT	Chatham (City/Cité)	b-2	14	42
Tickner	Lillian	27	ON	ESSEX (North/Nord)	Windsor (City/Cité)	l-16	3	50
Tickner	Morley	10	ON	KENT	Chatham (City/Cité)	b-2	14	44
Tickner	Wolfred	1	ON	ESSEX (North/Nord)	Windsor (City/Cité)	l-16	4	1

Sort by geographic location

1 of 1   3/9/2008 9:02 AM

*Search screen results for Tickner, 1901 Census Ontario, database, AutomatedGenealogy.com
(http://www.automatedgenealogy.com : accessed 9 March 2008). Used with permission.*

races, but terms like Canadian and American were not. On
the other hand, "Scotch" and "Irish" and other nationalities
were clearly entered in this column. Very specific instructions
were also given for a mix of native blood with other races
("breeds"), thus researchers working to prove native ancestry
will find this column very helpful.

- Nationality.
- Mother tongue.

Library and Archives Canada's digital images of 1901 census pages can be seen at the Canadian Genealogy Centre website. They are searchable, but only by geographic locations. CGC does not have a nominal index. However, the *Automated Genealogy* website provides a free searchable database for all provinces in the 1901 census. Search results will connect to transcriptions of census pages, and from there to the LAC digital images. The quality of indexing at this site is commendable. *Ancestry.ca* also has a comprehensive database for all of Canada also linked to LAC images. Ancestry's search options can be used in a variety of ways to good effect, although the user may need to apply a variety of spellings for some surnames. At both sites the images can be manipulated for enhanced reading, downloading or printing.

1911

The 1911 census, like earlier ones, is divided into geographic districts and subdistricts. It was composed of thirteen schedules but only the population schedule was microfilmed before the paper records were destroyed. The household location, whether rural or urban, was recorded on this surviving schedule. Age, month and year of birth, marital status, religion, occupation, infirmities and commonly spoken language are among the now familiar questions. New information included whether an individual had life insurance, or accident and sickness insurance and its value. This is the first time divorce appears in the marital status column.

A few notes regarding the enumerators' instructions:

- Household or family members were to be enumerated in their *usual* residence, even if they were absent on census day.

- Place of birth referred to country, or province if within Canada. Ancestors of East European origin may have "Russia" as their birthplace. Descendants must be aware of how much territory and nationalities were controlled by the Russian Empire when the ancestor was born. The "Nationality" column may clarify this.

- In the column "Racial or tribal origin" aboriginals were required to state the name of their mother's First Nation.

- Children of a mixed marriage with one white parent were required to classify themselves as of the other race.

- Column 18 represents employment in addition to one's chief occupation. Codes were used to describe the types of jobs,

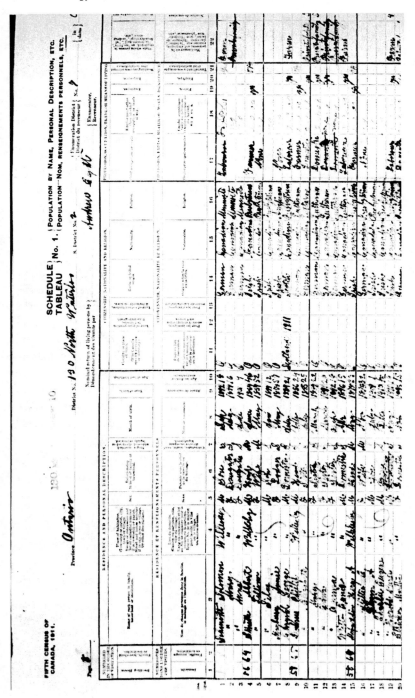

1911 Census Ontario, district 130, Waterloo North, sub-district 10, Wellesley Township, enumeration district 7, p. 8, digital image, Library and Archives Canada, Canadian Genealogy Centre (http://www.collectionscanada.ca/ : accessed 21 February 2008); LAC microfilm T-20407

and can be seen on charts at the Canadian Genealogy Centre's website in its census section.

Digital images of LAC's 1911 census pages can be viewed online at the Canadian Genealogy Centre. There, the database can be searched by geographic location only, with no nominal indexes. Both *Automated Genealogy* and *Ancestry.ca* offer indexed databases, as above with the 1901 census. LAC has no plans at present to publish a finding aid for the 1911 census. An in-house guide and the CGC website offer detailed information.

Later Census Returns

Canadian census enumerators were sworn to confidentiality in the performance of their duties after 1901. The federal government understood this to mean no access to future census information. After considerable public and legal debate about the interpretation of this issue, parliamentary legislation was amended in June 2005. It had two very important consequences for family historians and other researchers. It allowed for timely access to further census returns up to 2001—Statistics Canada will release a census 92 years after it was enumerated, into the keeping of Library and Archives Canada and thus the public domain. As for censuses in the twenty-first century, an "informed consent" compromise was enacted. From 2005 onward, each resident who fills out the questionnaire is asked for specific consent to allow future access to the household information. Negative answers, or no answers at all, will seal that information forever. However, that compromise stipulation is subject to parliamentary review by 2011.

For an outline of information that was enumerated from 1911 to 1951, see "The History of the Canadian Census" by Stephen Deller in *Families* Vol. 27, No. 3 (1988). In 1956 the traditional ten-year gap between censuses was shortened to five years.

Reminders and extra tips for census searches:

- Boundaries for the wards in large towns and cities in later census returns may be ascertained from contemporary directories. AO has handy large-scale maps of major cities with ward boundaries.

- Paul McGrath's "Toronto Street Finder" for census years is a valuable tool on the *OntarioRoots* website.

- When you find your family on a census sheet, do not stop reading at their entry on that page. Always finish searching the entire town or township for other occurrences of the same surname. Potential relationships among families may not be apparent at first reading, but your notes could save future back-tracking.

• When seeking ancestors in a village or town that was named as the family residence, you might not find this place listed in the earliest returns, like 1851 and 1861. In many cases, the town or village was included within its surrounding township, perhaps as one of the sub-districts. In 1871, 1881 or later it may have merited a separate enumeration.

• Some miscellaneous entries in the finding aids could easily be overlooked. Under "Institutions" in the 1891 census there are sub-headings for various counties. These returns are mainly for charitable homes and hospitals, and facilities for the needy, aged and homeless. The difficulty in trying to identify an ancestor in these institutions is that surnames may not always be shown. Other miscellaneous headings are Indian Reserves (Lambton County in 1861), Ojibwa Indian (Middlesex County in 1851) and Grand River Tract (Haldimand and Brant Counties 1816-1832).

So far, the discussion has been about the original *sources*. The following observations and cautions may be useful regarding the *information* in the sources. We can't know how vigilant an enumerator was in his duties of explaining the rules to each household, especially if he was weary, cold or impatient. Even more, we can rarely, if ever, be certain who gave information to the census-taker. The head of household, or family father, could have been away working. The busy mother of small children could have been distracted with domestic chores. An older child might have been uncertain about ages and other details. A lodger, visiting relative or neighbour could have known even fewer specifics. Such scenarios could lead an informant to guess or give unintentionally incorrect answers. Misunderstanding, ignorance or carelessness in responding to questions could be problematic in any census information. Being alert to the deeper issues of a source like this reminds us to not only critically examine the information, but also to seek other sources for more evidence.

Names

We expect names on a census to be quite reliable. The points to keep in mind have been mentioned before, but bear repeating. Surnames often vary from the spelling you expect, and indeed from one census year to another. The enumerator's variations are not so odd when you consider that names were normally spoken to him, not written, so phonetics play a major part in the recording of an unfamiliar name. Imagine the consequences when an Englishman was enumerating a district of Germanic immigrants, or an Irishman was given a neighbourhood of French-speaking Canadians! By comparing the names of spouse and children, ages, birthplaces and so on with an earlier or later census return, you may be able to make convincing identifications.

Identification can also be a problem when nicknames have been used for first names, for example, Nancy for Ann, Minnie for Melinda or Wilhelmina, Sally for Sarah, Polly for Mary, Peggy for Margaret, Harry for Henry, Fred for Frederick or Alfred, Dan for Donald, and countless other variations. A child known by one of his forenames in childhood may have used a second name in later years, or perhaps assumed a name more to his liking.

Ages

The discussion in this category presents several anomalies that every family historian needs to consider. Ages are frequently wrong on a census return—at times only slightly off, at other times very off-kilter. Family historians are accustomed to using ages to calculate a year of birth. An ancestor's age, year or precise date of birth needs strong support from other records.

Personal vanity in adulthood could cause an individual to revise his or her age, usually to appear younger or to narrow an age gap between spouses. Elderly people who were born in large families during pioneer times may have lost track of their age. In some instances, pride in a well-functioning advanced age has added a few years! On the other hand, genealogical experience often tells us that the younger a person is in a census, the more reliable his age may be. The assumption is a parent would have little or no reason to knowingly alter a child's age.

Most of the slight differences in age are likely the result of misunderstanding the question. The enumerators were supposed to record information for the household as it existed on the official date of enumeration. Rural census-takers normally took several days to cover local territory, and sometimes there were delays of up to several weeks. The 1851 and 1861 recordings, when the census question was age *at next birthday*, took place in winter amidst dreadful conditions for many enumerators. Residents with birthdays between the official date and the day the enumerator appeared at the door could simply have responded with their current age, if the enumerator failed to remind them of the rules. Some census returns for 1861 were not being returned until mid-February, as shown in examples from the counties of Bruce and Lanark. Despite awareness of such possible occurrences, we tend to presume the great majority of people were giving their ages for the 1852 calendar year, because the 1851 census was taken early in January of 1852.

The same possibility of mis-stating age could occur in any later census. To pose an example, remember the official enumeration date for the 1871 Canadian census was 2 April 1871. Age at the specific census date was expected. If a person reached her 40th birthday on 4 April 1871 and the census-taker showed up on 9 April 1871, that person might automatically say she was 40, when in fact she was still 39 on the census date. A precise date of birth was asked in twentieth century returns. Although the latter is definitely exciting information, in many cases it is proving erroneous. We don't know why the day, month or year may be incorrect. Perhaps the informant was uncertain about his or her own date, or those of other household members, but felt pressured to respond to the question.

Birthplace

The informant may not have known the exact place of birth for some members of the family or household, so sometimes this information could also be dubious. Some of the abbreviations used for an Ontario birthplace are

O. (Ontario)   U.C.   (Upper Canada)
C.W. (Canada West)   E.C.   (English Canada)

Birthplace marked as "F" in the 1851 census was often used with different meanings, despite instructions to the enumerators to apply it to individuals *born of Canadian parents*. The "F" has been interpreted in some families for "French" birth, meaning French-Canadian. Some enumerators went astray on their own initiative. In Camden East a census-taker reported that his "F" referred to a person of British-born parents, while another man in Richmond used the designation for "foreign-born" parentage. It pays to look for enumerators' remarks!

The extravagant use of ditto marks by many enumerators—those "Do." entries on line after line—can be misleading. The writer's fatigue or carelessness could result in all children or household members being shown with the same place of birth as the head of family or his spouse. Examine children's birthplaces with those of the parents for reasonable sequence. A husband born in Canada and a wife born in Germany were unlikely to have had children born in Germany.

When the first child or children of several in a family were born outside Canada, you might infer two things. The parents' marriage probably took place where those children were born, not in Canada. The time period between the last child born outside Canada and the first child born here likely indicates the interval when the family immigrated.

Religion

Religious affiliation may be more accurate than most data in a census. Watch for a wife's religion differing from that of her husband. To find the couple's church marriage record, you should look for sources in both denominations. The marriage venue was often favoured by the wife's choice of parish or minister. You may notice a family's change in denomination from one census year to another. That could have an impact on a search for the baptisms of the couple's children. Most frustrating is the head of family who lists "no creed" or "none" in the religion column. The only hope is to locate the same family in an earlier census, or perhaps an older generation of parents who are still affiliated with an organized religion. If they resided in the same area for some time prior, you can investigate local histories and narrow down the possibilities from then existing churches.

Most entries in the religion column are self-evident, but the more common abbreviations for some Christian denominations are listed below. Other denominations flourished in small pockets here and there. By 1911 more than 203 religions were tabulated in Canada.

BC	Bible Christian, a Methodist offshoot
C	Christian, Congregational
CE or EC	Church of England, English Church (Anglican)
CONG	Congregational
CP	Canada Presbyterian
CS or KS	Church or Kirk of Scotland
D or T	Dunkard, Tunker
EL	Evangelical Lutheran

EM or ME	Episcopal Methodist
EP	Episcopalian (Anglican)
EU or EV	Evangelical
EUB	Evangelical United Brethren
FRIENDS	Quaker
FWB	Free Will Baptist
MENN	Mennonite, Mennonist
NC	(Methodist) New Connexion
PM	Primitive Methodist
RB	Regular Baptist
RC	Roman Catholic
RP	Reform Presbyterian
UP	United Presbyterian
WM	Wesleyan Methodist

Alternatives

The phrase "census substitute" is sometimes used to describe a source that lists names associated with a time and place, similar to the early censuses. We do need to be aware of the limitations or omissions in any such source. Extant tax assessment and collection rolls are one option. The eventual publication of city and county directories becomes very useful this way later on. Some options are mentioned here.

- Early congregations of various religious persuasions often petitioned the government for a small grant of land to build their first church, chapel or meeting house. Such petitions are frequently in the Upper Canada land petitions series (see Chapter 6), indexed under the name of a town or township or occasionally by the name of the denomination. Each and every adherent may not necessarily be included, but the collected signatures form a type of local census for heads of families *of that religion*. The name or signature of your ancestor may be one of the earliest pieces of evidence for him.

- Elliott, Walker and Stratford-Devai in *Men of Upper Canada* compiled a nominal index after surveying militia lists for the province in the 1828-1829 time period. Great effort was made to find substitute lists for the few areas where militia lists did not survive. The result is a very valuable resource for adult males who were in the 19 to 39 age category. Some areas also had later lists of their second battalions, which add men in the 40 to 60 age bracket. Men who were exempt from militia training will not appear on these lists. Those exclusions were mainly for officials in key government positions, or for religious faiths that forbade the bearing of arms. Recognized Quakers, Mennonites, and Tunkers were released from militia duty upon payment of token fines.

- Toronto Branch OGS volunteers created the *City of Toronto Tax Transcription Project* as a substitute for the lost 1851 census. The project is a database of the city's 1853 tax assessment rolls, linked to digital images. Access is available at the websites of *OntarioRoots* or City of Toronto Archives. Plans are to expand this project to the neighbouring townships.

- The Department of Agriculture created a questionnaire in 1853 that constituted, in effect, a type of census. It is not known how many questionnaires were originally distributed, nor how many were returned, but 41 have survived. They were intended for farmers who had immigrated within the past 45 to 50 years, potentially a large portion of the population. The information gives the man's religion; his country, county and parish of origin; year of arrival in Canada; his age at that time; whether immigration was independent or assisted; his financial position then; how and where he acquired his property; and so on. The questionnaires are at LAC in the Immigration Branch of the Department of Agriculture, RG 17, Vol. 2325. You can obtain copies of the documents by reference to the following names, identified by their township location.

Farmer	Township
Henry Airth	Horton
Thomas Alton	Nelson
Joseph Barnard	Monaghan
Walter Beatty	Yonge
John Blake	Goderich
John Breckon	Nelson
John Brill	Bagot
Thomas Cairns	Plympton
Samuel Cole	Sarnia
Thomas Corrigan	Clarendon
Robert Cromar	Woolwich
Thomas Earl	Blandford
Thomas Fee	Emily

William Filliter	Bagot
William Hamilton	Ramsay
William Jenkins	Goderich
Thomas Jowsey	Eardley
Patrick Kelley	Elizabethtown
Thomas Lamb	Usborne
John Lightfoot	Cavan
Joseph Mathewson	Blandford
Edward McCrea	Bagot
Donald McLean	Eardley
Ewen McLean	Brock/Kincardine
James McQueen	Esquesing/Pilkington
John Munro	Horton
Richard Richardson	Goulbourn/Clarendon
Charles Robertson	Windham
James Rowan	Kincardine
Henry Rowlings	Plympton
James Shaw	Clarendon
Simpson Shepherd	Plympton
Alexander Smart	Clarendon
Joseph Stewart	Elizabethtown/Clarendon
James Sutton	Hamilton/Cavan
Robert Syme	North Sherbrooke
Philip VanKoughnet	Cornwall
James Wagar	Harwich
John Wallon	Bagot
John Wilson	Guelph
John Windle	Bagot

- Canada was at war in 1940 when a compulsory national registration of all Canadian adults over the age of 16 was enacted. The federal government had assumed broad powers under the War Measures Act and the National Resources Mobilization Act. Registration gave the government the potential to mobilize certain people or resources for national defence or security purposes. To that end, the population was to give information about education, health status, occupation, employment, training and skills and previous military experience. The questionnaires also asked for the personal information we customarily expect on a census return—name, address, age, date of birth, marital status, place and country of birth (for the individual's parents as well), year of arrival in Canada if applicable, and nationality. Aliens in Canada in 1940 were also required to fill and submit the form.

The registration forms are in the custody of Statistics Canada (Appendix II) governed by privacy legislation. It is possible to obtain copies by meeting certain conditions. The individual whose form you request must have died a minimum of twenty years ago and you must provide proof of this. Furthermore, you must be able to identify the individual by full name and address in 1940. A directory for that year should assist you. The order form can be found by searching "1940 national registration" on Statistics Canada's website.

Reading and Reference

Dilts, Brian Lee. *1848 and 1850 Canada West (Ontario) Census Index.* Salt Lake City, UT: Index Publishing, 1984.

Elliott, Bruce S., editor. *Index to the 1871 Census of Ontario.* 30 volumes. Toronto, ON: Ontario Genealogical Society, 1986-1992.

_____, Dan Walker and Fawne Stratford-Devai, compilers. *Men of Upper Canada: Militia Nominal Rolls, 1828-1829.* Toronto, ON: Ontario Genealogical Society, 1995.

Hillman, Thomas A. *Catalogue of Census Returns on Microfilm, 1666-1891.* Ottawa, ON: Supply and Services Canada, 1987.

_____. *Census Returns 1901.* Ottawa, ON: Minister of Supply and Services Canada, 1993.

Rumpel, Renie A., compiler and editor. *Index to the 1851 Census of Canada West (Ontario).* Waterloo, ON: Ontario Indexing Services. *Lennox and Addington Counties,* 2000. *Wellington County,* 2000. *Bruce and Grey Counties,* 2001. *Wentworth County and Hamilton,* 2003.

Ancestry. www.ancestry.ca

Automated Genealogy. www.automatedgenealogy.com

Canadian Genealogy Centre. www.collectionscanada.ca/genealogy/index-e.html

City of Toronto Archives. www.toronto.ca/archives

Family Search (FHL). www.familysearch.org

Norfolk Historical Society. www.norfolklore.com

Ontario GenWeb. www.geneofun.on.ca/ongenweb

Ontario GenWeb Census Project. ontariocensus.rootsweb.com

Ontario Roots. www.ontarioroots.com

Statistics Canada. "1940 National Registration." http:www.statcan.ca/.

6

Land and Property Ownership Records

Reference Dates

1784	Land grant to Six Nations Indians, Grand River Valley
1788	Land boards were formed for the four original districts (see maps)
1795	Land registry system was established
1819	Legislation authorized land grants to 1812 War veterans
1824	The Canada (Land) Company was incorporated to colonize the Huron Tract and Crown reserve lands
1827	Free land grants ended for all but military and Loyalist claimants; open land market began
1847	County registry offices began keeping separate copybooks for township and town property transactions
1859	Married women were given limited rights to dispose of inherited property
1865	Abstract Indexes to Deeds were created; full copies of memorials recorded in new copybooks
1901	Veterans Land Act; grants for military service in Fenian Raids and South African (Boer) War
1917	Soldier Settlement Act; World War I soldiers eligible for land grants

Locating Property Descriptions

The importance and relevance of land records in family history are not always given due attention. As in most of North America, so in Ontario, land records reflect the people who were constantly pushing frontiers. In pioneer societies, farming some land to sustain a family was of prime consideration for the settlers. In Upper Canada, the great variety of land occupation and ownership documentation preceded all other types of records of interest to genealogists. Chapter 2 has some suggestions for locating an ancestral family whose whereabouts within the province are unknown. In order to make the best use of land records, you will need to narrow a general location to an exact description of the property they resided on.

A rural property description involves the name of a township, a concession number and a lot number. That information is the way to access many different series of land records. When hamlets and villages increased in size to overtake surrounding agricultural communities, subdivisions of the original 100 or 200 acre lots were developed. The subdivision plan was registered on the lot where it was formed. County and district land registry offices hold any number of maps and plans created over the years for localities within their jurisdictions. Registered subdivision plans had their own lot numbers that eventually became integrated into overall urban planning. The house numbers on a street were sometimes changed. Street names occasionally changed. If you find that a town or city is the location of your ancestors, a series of directories would be the main source for an exact address.

Using some of these suggestions to find a property description may also help you locate an ancestor even if he did *not* own land:

- the Ontario Land Records Index, in case a Crown grant was involved
- the agricultural schedule of census returns (1851–1871 and 1901)
- nineteenth-century historical atlases and their township maps
- county or town/city directories
- wills and estate files
- local histories of towns and townships
- tax assessment rolls, although before 1850 their availability is sporadic
- documents found in county, town or township indexes to deeds, when such indexes are available

Townships, Concessions, Lots

The majority of townships are rectangular because the first surveyors set a general pattern of nine miles in width (east-west) and twelve miles in depth (north-south). Of course there were always exceptions when natural geographic features interfered with neat planning. Lake shorelines made "broken fronts," and meandering river courses caused irregular patterns. Smaller remnants between regular surveys were known as gores. Some of the earliest townships, for instance Charlottenburg or Etobicoke, resemble a patchwork of mini-surveys. Occasionally an exceptionally large land grant in one or more townships resulted in a special survey, such as the German Company Tract in Waterloo County.

With an appropriate map, you can study your ancestor's location in proximity to geographic attributes and amenities such as roads, railroads, villages and towns. Of further interest, the Archives of Ontario has a collection of surveyors' reports, including their orders, instructions and field diaries.

Allowances were made from the beginning for reserved township lands for the future support of government and the Protestant clergy and the establishment of schools. Sales of these Crown, clergy and school reserves began in the late 1820s.

Township land was divided into a number of concessions, fourteen being the original norm. BF refers to a broken front concession. Mysterious initials may appear with a concession in a property description, which actually give additional directions, for example, NTR = North of Talbot Road, WSYS = West Side of Yonge Street, EHS = East of Hurontario Street, SSRR = South Side of Raisin River. Many other examples can be found where a major road or river was a surveyor's landmark or baseline. Usually they can be deciphered by studying the township map or its history. In some townships on the Great Lakes you will see a concession described as number *xx* "from the lake" or "from the bay."

Concessions were traditionally separated by road allowances, so that each 100-acre property on the concession strip would have access to at least one road. Every road allowance was not necessarily opened for usage. Roman numerals customarily designate a concession number on maps. The term range rather than concession is occasionally used.

The division of concession strips into lots usually generated 200- or 100-acre pieces of property. Arabic numbers were used to mark the lots. Rural grants for farmers were seldom fewer than 50 acres. Descriptions like "the north-west quarter" or "the front half" appear when division of a property occurred, perhaps for conveyance to heirs or for sale to buyers. The severance of a piece of property off the initial 100- or 200-acre lot is described in legal instruments in *metes and bounds* measurements, that is, by the surveyor's measure of distances, angles and directions related to the original boundaries. See John Becker's article "Early Land Surveys in Southern Ontario" in OGS *Families* Vol. 46, No. 1 (February 2007).

Crown Land Records

The initial distribution of lands for the first settlers of what was to become Upper Canada was influenced by several factors. First and foremost, the British Crown was responsible for the acquisition of lands from aboriginal tribes in the upper part of the province. The Crown was the sole authority controlling land allotment through appointed representatives. Other factors included main access to an area by water transport, strategic planning for settlements near existing military forts and how quickly the surveyors could work. Certificates for occupation of a certain piece of property were originally issued to the Loyalists and other very early settlers. With the Constitutional Act of 1791, the government made a significant switch from the original seigneurial tenure system of old Quebec to a freehold system of land ownership. The former certificates became redeemable for deeds or Crown patents of freehold ownership.

Land Granting Process

There were always a number of procedural steps in the granting of Crown land up to 1827, the period when land itself was freely available. Each step involved the creation of documents in various government departments. Regulations governing the general process changed from time to time. Special types of grants required certain qualifications on the applicant's part. Thus, the wide array of records and references can cause some bewilderment for a new researcher.

Some of the documents that were created, not necessarily all for each applicant:

- a Land Board certificate
- a petition requesting land
- an order-in-council authorizing the grant

- a warrant from the council to the surveyor general
- a receipt for fees paid to the receiver general
- a fiat from the attorney general authorizing the surveyor general to act
- a location ticket or description from the surveyor general
- a Crown patent (first title deed)

Library and Archives Canada has retained custody of some original records for Upper Canada, but most of these have been microfilmed and made available at other institutions, such as Upper Canada land petitions. The great majority of land records that pertain to Upper Canada, Canada West and Ontario can be found at AO in their RG 1, Crown Lands. See the Land Records section of the AO Research Guide 299 (online and paper handout), "Sources of Family History."

Ontario Land Records Index

The major finding aid for Crown land grants is the Ontario Land Records Index (OLRI), compiled and computerized by the Archives of Ontario, and deserves detailed discussion. This Index, on microfiche, was distributed to libraries throughout the province. Genealogical society libraries, FHL Family History Centers and other institutions with an interest in Canadian genealogy have copies. This is the only province-wide index that dates from the first years of settlement. It summarizes the original grants from the Crown as derived from the surveyor general's Crown lands papers. In addition, it includes some of the holdings administered by the Canada Company, and the smaller volume of records in the Peter Robinson fonds. All sources are in AO holdings. Subsequent transactions and conveyances after the grants, between individuals, do not appear in the OLRI. Section 3 of this chapter treats land transfers after land was granted by the Crown.

The OLRI was prepared in two sets: an alphabetical surname index and an alphabetical town/township name index. The former is more popularly used by genealogists, and you are advised to investigate alternate surname spellings. What it will tell you, whenever the information was available from the original source, is a property description, the date and type of grant, the type of transaction and, if it was a free grant, to which category it conformed. Reference is also given to the original source for double-checking.

The OLRI is only a *tool*, and its prime value, beyond that

all-important property description, is in leading you to original sources for further research. The individual's name appearing on the Index was called the *nominee* or grantee, sometimes the locatee. See the illustration for the comments that follow.

First Columns   Columns for the nominee's name, the township, concession and lot numbers are straightforward although the property description is sometimes not available. In some cases a *residence* is given which differs from the location of the grant. This residence may actually be where the person was living, and intended to remain. On the other hand, it may have been a temporary location while awaiting the outcome of his request for land, or it may have been the town where his petition was submitted. Being approved for, and in receipt of, a grant of Crown land did not automatically imply that the nominee went to live on that property, or had any intention of doing so. Early nominees were known to sell their rights for ready cash. You can't assume that the person became the official title-holder of the property unless a Crown patent was ultimately issued to him.

Date Identity Code   The Date Identity Code column can be one of eight numbered documents.

NAME OF LOCATEE	TOWNSHIP / TOWN / CITY	LOT	CONC.	DATE IO.	ISSUE DATE	TRANS TYPE	TYPE FG	TYPE OF LEASE / SALE	ARCHIVAL REFERENCE RG SERIES VOL PG
ELLIOT MATHEW RESIDENCE	MALDEN			8	17970218	FG	OR DEED NO.		01 C13 013 069
ELLIOT MATHEW RESIDENCE				8	17930711	FG	OR DEED NO.		01 C13 014 254
ELLIOT MATTHEW RESIDENCE	PUSLINCH	F1/2 35	9	2	18420305	A	DEED NO.		01 C15 003 200
ELLIOT MATTHEW RESIDENCE	LOGAN	10	5	4	18470605	L	DEED NO.		CC 83 030 375
ELLIOT MATW. RESIDENCE				8	17950620	FG	OR DEED NO.		01 C13 013 068
ELLIOT MICHAEL RESIDENCE	DOURO	E1/2 9	3	1	182nC	FG	PR DEED NO.		01 C14 020 031
ELLIOT MOSES RESIDENCE ELIZABETHTOWN	MARA	N1/2 28 & 29	12	8	18170326	FG	SUE DEED NO.		01 C13 081 109
ELLIOT MOSES RESIDENCE ELIZABETHTOWN	ELIZABETHTOWN	E1/2 6	7	2	18340702	FG	COMM DEED NO.		01 C13 091 016
ELLIOT ROBERT RESIDENCE BURGESS	BURGESS	SW 1/2 10	9	8	18211114	FG	ME DEED NO.		01 C13 096 027
ELLIOT ROBERT RESIDENCE WHITCHURCH	WHITCHURCH	15	7	8	18310602	L	CL DEED NO.		01 C13 152 111
ELLIOT ROBERT RESIDENCE	SEYMOUR	SE PT 16	7	1	18330221	S	CL DEED NO.		01 C14 020 221
ELLIOT ROBERT RESIDENCE	PUSLINCH	FT1/2 21	GORE	5	18480224	S		CL	01 C1113 002 231
ELLIOT ROBT RESIDENCE	SEYMOUR	SE1/2 16	7	5	18330221	S	CL DEED NO.		01 C1113 001 071
ELLIOT ROBT RESIDENCE	ELLICE	24	9	4	18451114	L	DEED NO.		CC 83 030 190
ELLIOT SAMUEL RESIDENCE	ELIZABETHTOWN	1/2 35	2	1	178vC	FG	OR DEED NO.		01 AIV 004 103
ELLIOT THOMAS RESIDENCE EMILY	EMILY	NE1/4 7	2	1	18200830	FG	LA DEED NO.		01 C14 132 144
ELLIOT THOS RESIDENCE	WINGHAM (T)	28 W ARTHUR ST		5	18710224	S	SCH DEED NO.		01 AIV 003 105

Alphabetical listings by surname, Ontario Land Records Index; microfiche, Archives of Ontario

1 location ticket	5 sale
2 assignment	6 Canada Company contract
3 patent	7 Canada Company deed
4 lease	8 Order-in-Council (OC)

Location tickets normally give the exact property description of the grant. In effect, they were certificates of occupation. They are dated and show the authority from which they originated. Their purpose was to allow the nominee to take physical possession of a property, whether by himself or a designated agent, and begin to meet whatever settlement obligations might have been stipulated. Clearing a certain portion of land and/or erection of buildings for habitation and livestock were commonly expected.

Assignment means that the grant recipient was not the original nominee in the records of the Surveyor General. The nominee could have assigned his right or claim and obligations to a second party. Some properties have a history of several

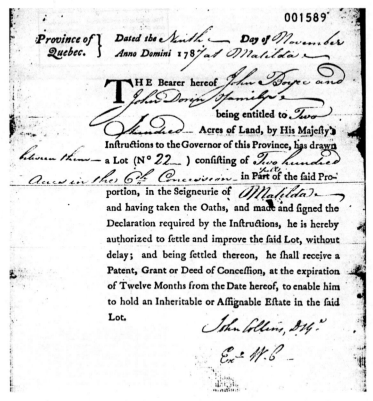

John Boyce and John Dorin certificate (1787), Township Papers, RG 1-58, Matilda, p. 1589; AO microfilm MS 658 reel 292

assignments before one person met the requisite settlement duties or fees, or both.

A *patent* was the first ownership title. Elsewhere known as a title deed, we use the word patent as a short form for Crown patent. From this point forward, a chronological record of most subsequent transactions on a property can be traced in land registry office records.

A *lease* from the Crown was for certain reserved properties it was not yet prepared to sell. Crown, clergy and school reserves were held as investments. See more below about Canada Company leases.

A *sale* indicates a straight purchase by the individual from the Crown at the going price per acre. Sales of Crown lands became a source for government funds from 1827 on.

Order-in-council was one of the first documents for approval for a grant, from the ruling executive council. It authorized the next bureaucrats in the chain to implement action.

In most cases, you should be able to search out the original document or source that is indicated in the OLRI's Date Identity Code column. They are not kept in one convenient collection (except for Canada Company records), but are scattered in such other series sources as Township Papers, Heir and Devisee Commission records, Orders-in-Council and others.

Canada Company   A *contract* on the OLRI indicates an individual who agreed to lease or purchase a property, for a fixed price, from the Canada (Land) Company. At its formation in 1824, the Canada Company acquired the outstanding Crown reserve lands that had not then been leased or applied for. The Canada Company also developed the Huron Tract, un-surveyed bush country that covered a vast area in what became the Huron District, parts of the present counties of Huron, Perth and Middlesex. The Canada Company records used in the OLRI were their registers of leases and sales. Therefore "contract" could refer to either type, as per the code in the "Trans[action] Type" column.

Deeds were awarded by the Canada Company when a purchaser had made his final payment. This explains any discrepancies in dates between (6) and (7) on the OLRI. Often several years would pass between the first and final payments. If the individual was able to make the total payment upfront, the same date will be shown for both documents. There are other records in this fonds of interest to the genealogist (but not on the OLRI), like Canada Company applications for deeds 1827-1949, registers of wills 1826-1920, burial certificates 1842-1923, and remittance books 1843-1847. The company performed various functions for settlers in remote or frontier locations. The remittance books are a record of those who sent money to destinations in the British Isles through the company's services. The overseas addresses can be good clues to the settler's family relationships and/or place of birth. See Holt and Williams in the Reading and Reference section below for an index to the remittance books.

Issue Date   The date of issue is keyed numerically to year-month-day. A precise date appears if it was on the original source. Many of the earliest entries simply say "1789C" meaning *circa* 1789, and were probably location descriptions from the first land boards.

Trans[action] Type

| FG Free Grant | S Sale |
| L Lease | A Assignment |

Three of these are a repeat of the above Date Identity column. *Free Grant* is one of the most important findings. It means the settler was here when land itself was still free, or he had a special qualification, and will be categorized by a code under Type of Free Grant.

Type Of Free Grant   This column provides the most rewarding clues if it applies to your ancestor. Some free grants were dispensed without the payment of all administrative costs and fees, while others required reduced or full fees. After 1826, free land grants were discontinued to all but Loyalist and military or militia claimants. Later immigrants had to buy their land from the Crown, or perhaps from another individual, at the market rate.

OR	Old Regulations
COMM	Heir & Devisee Commission
NR	New Regulations
MC	Military Claimant

1819 Regulations

| M | Militia grant |

1820 Regulations

| ME | Military Emigrant |

1825 Regulations

SE	Scotch Emigrant
FF	Full Fees
PR	Peter Robinson settler
UE	Loyalist grant
LB	Land Board

DUE	Daughter of Loyalist
AA	Gratuitous/hardship grant
SUE	Son of Loyalist
V	Veteran, Fenian or South African
CR, CL, SCH	Crown, Clergy and School Reserves

Regulations made by government are reflected in the first few designations as they were amended. The main concern gradually shifted from ensuring that settlers would actually occupy their land to the collecting of fees. Grants given under old regulations preceded the creation of Upper Canada and generally have "1789C" or "1790C" rather than a specific date. By 1825 fees had sharply increased in the effort to generate revenue for the Crown.

Paying *Full Fees* indicates a "common" settler who did not qualify for one of the privileged or special status categories. Chapter 11 gives more information on the three types of *Loyalist* grants. *Heir and Devisee Commission* records are discussed later in this chapter.

Military Claimant was a disbanded soldier of the British Army who was entitled to a grant for his service, the size of the grant determined by his rank at the time of discharge. The same applied to those Loyalists who saw active service in a provincial corps during the American Revolution. *Militia* grants were made in early periods: in 1816–1817 to strategically locate ex-soldiers for potential defence purposes, and in 1819–1820 to reward militia veterans who took part in the War of 1812. Further information on men in these two groups should be available in their petitions for land.

Military Emigrant refers to specific groups who had financial assistance to emigrate from Scotland and settle in the Bathurst District. There, the Perth and Rideau settlements of Lanark County were administered by the Quarter Master General's department of the British military. The reference does not mean the immigrant himself was involved with the military. *Scotch Emigrant* was a grant offered to sons of these Military Emigrants, for one year only in 1815, to induce more immigration. Reports made by the administrators of these two groups can be found in a variety of Crown land papers. Many of the administration returns and schedules, with property locations, or lists of settlers receiving government provisions on their arrival, are available at AO.

Peter Robinson settlers from Ireland were subsidized from 1823to 1825 to settle in Lanark County and the Peterborough area. The Peter Robinson fonds at AO contains a number of ships' passenger lists and returns of settlers' locations.

Land Board indicates one of the original four district land boards given the power to assign lots. It was a decentralization measure to speed up land granting and get people settled. The mandate of these first-appointed bodies, to hear petitions and issue certificates of occupation, lasted from 1788 to 1794. Certificates are frequently found in the Township Papers series. See Corupe's *And Your Petitioner Will Ever Pray* for transcribed records of the Mecklenburg (soon changed to Midland) District. Her detailed Introduction and Foreword are thoroughly explanatory about this source seldom-used by genealogists.

A second appointment of Land Boards from 1819 to 1825 was created for the same purpose, but their records are *not* included on the OLRI. Fawne Stratford-Devai and Bruce S. Elliott have brought the second series to light in a series of co-authored articles, starting with "Upper Canada Land Settlement Records: The Second District Land Boards, 1819-1825" in *Families* Vol. 34, No. 3 (1995) and continuing through Vol. 35, No. 3 (1996). They provide alphabetical lists of recipients.

Gratuitous grants were accorded after government review to certain indigent settlers already living on their lands at a bare subsistence level, unable to pay fees, which were then waived. Further information about *Veterans* grants in the early 1900s can be obtained from the land grant files at AO or from military records at LAC.

Type of Lease/Sale

CR Crown Reserve   CL Clergy Reserve

SCH School Reserve   I Indian Land

The first three categories in this column apply to lands that had initially been reserved or held back for the future support of government, religion and education. The reserving of 1/7 of all land for clergy and Crown in 1791 resulted in checkerboard patterns of reserved lots in some townships, and sometimes entire townships were set aside. Reserves became one of the contentious issues in the Reform movement of the 1830s because they impeded settlement. Indian land is a less frequent note on the OLRI for an area not yet resolved by Crown appropriation or survey.

Archival Reference   The final columns on the OLRI give the source reference. Most come from AO's RG 1, Crown Lands records and several sub-groups within it. "CC" is the abbreviation for Canada

Company. Both the Peter Robinson fonds and Canada Company fonds at AO have more extensive material besides that shown on the OLRI.

See the AO online and paper Research Guide 205 "How to Use the Ontario Land Records Index ca. 1780-ca. 1920" and especially the Research Guide 215 "From Grant to Patent: A Guide to Early Land Settlement, ca. 1790 to ca. 1850."

Some articles are suggested for more understanding of the land granting system.

"Records of the Land Granting Process: Pre-Confederation" by Patricia Kennedy in *Families* Vol.16, No. 4 (1977).

"Crown Grants in the Home District: The System and the Existing Records" by John Mezaks in *Families* Vol. 14, No. 4 (1975).

"Military Land Granting in Upper Canada Following the War of 1812" by Eric Jarvis, in *Ontario History* Vol. 67 (1975).

Petitions

A petition to the Lieutenant Governor in Council was the beginning of the process to acquire land from the Crown. The collection called Upper Canada land petitions is at LAC, but AO and FHL as well as other resource centres have microfilm copies. LAC created and later microfilmed a nominal card index as the alphabetical surname guide to finding the petitions. A supplementary index was also microfilmed for omissions from the first index. Since the indexes derive from a variety of old handwriting on documents that are often difficult to read, surname searching may require some creative imagination. Microfilm reel numbers are on the Canadian Genealogy Centre website for interlibrary borrowing. The CGC plans to have the indexes online in 2008.

A name, place, date and reference number are on the index. The place name in the index is not necessarily where the petitioner was living, or planned to live. He may have gone to the nearest town to find someone to pen the petition for him. The index shows many petitions with the place names "Newark" or "York" because the individual or his agent applied directly at the seat of government.

Upper Canada petitions are typically arranged in chronological "bundles" of one surname initial. Once you have the date, bundle, and petition number from the index, you can find the right microfilm to view the petition itself. LAC and AO have on-site finding aids for this purpose, but also the CGC website provides the information.

Some petitions are very straightforward with little personal information about the petitioner other than his presence in the province at that date. Others may give his arrival date in Canada, previous residence or place of birth, age, marital status, the number of family members accompanying him or qualifications for a special type of free grant. When sons and daughters of a Loyalist petitioned for their free grants, they named their fathers to demonstrate their eligibility. Oaths of allegiance to the Crown or character affidavits are often included with the petition papers.

You will rarely find a property description on these petitions. If the petition was "recommended" or approved by the Executive Council, the dated notations on the back of it can often be cross-referenced to an entry on the OLRI. It is extremely important to see those inter-government notes because they tell you if the person qualified for what he was asking. If he was turned down, there might be an explanatory note or a request for additional information.

Men petitioning for military or militia grants will state the name of their regiment or company with dates of service. Supporting documents, such as discharge papers or a commanding officer's sworn statement, were filed with the petition, but not all the supplementary papers were microfilmed. When British Army service was involved, it is a perfect lead to War Office records in the National Archives at Kew, England, or possibly to the British Military "C Series" (see Chapter 10).

Land Books

On the same index to Upper Canada land petitions, you will find references to land book numbers and pages, recording the receipt of petitions in Executive Council minutes. Normally the extracts in these books will add no new information to what was in the petition itself. However, if an original petition has not survived, which occasionally happens, the land book entry confirms its erstwhile existence. OGS has produced the very thorough *Index to the Upper Canada Land Books* in nine volumes from 1787 to 1841. It is more complete than the extracts previously published in *Reports of the Department of Public Records and Archives of Ontario* in various years from 1928. A true gem in each volume is the introduction to the land granting process and records by Patricia Kennedy. The OGS *Index* is also available on a CD-ROM searchable by name or place.

To his Excellency John Graves Simcoe, Esquire, Lieute-

nant Governor, and commander in Chief of the Province

of Upper Canada, &c. &c. &c.

IN COUNCIL.

The Petition of *David Jones of the Township*
of Barton, who came into the Province in the Year
1787 with a wife & five children — has received
lands for himself, but not any for his family —

Respectfully shews,

THAT your petitioner is desirous to settle on the lands of the Crown in this Province, being
in a condition to cultivate and improve the same.   That he is ready to take the usual oaths,
and to subscribe the declaration, that he professes the Christian Religion, and obedience to the
laws, and has lived inoffensively in the country which he has left.   Prays your Excellency,
would be pleased to grant him *300 acres of land for his family* upon the
terms and conditions expressed in your Excellency's proclamation bearing date the 7th day of
February, 1792, or such other quantity of land as to your Excellency in your wisdom may think
meet.   And your petitioner as in duty bound will ever pray.

Niagara
6 May
9 April 1796

David Jones (1796), Upper Canada Land Petitions, RG 1, L 3, vol. 254, J bundle 2, petition 31;
Library and Archives Canada microfilm C-2108

While Upper Canada land petitions are still the most often consulted group, there are other series of petitions at the Archives of Ontario. Petitions to the Commissioner of Crown Lands from 1827 are arranged alphabetically and microfilmed. There are petitions from 1901 to 1922 for grants for militia and military service during the Fenian raids of the 1860s and the South African War. Petitions also appear scattered through the Township Papers collection and the correspondence of the Civil Secretary, 1766–1841, better known as Upper Canada Sundries. There is a chronological calendar to the Sundries on several reels of microfilm at both LAC and AO that mentions all names appearing in the documents. At LAC there is a card index specifically for names of land petitioners in the Sundries. See Leo A. Johnson's "The Upper Canada Sundries: An Important Source for Family History" in *Families* Vol. 31, No. 4 (1992). Extracts from the Sundries form a large part of *Pioneers of Upper Canada, 1783-1839* by Doris Bourrie, although not all are from petitions.

Orders-in-council, fiats, and warrants were some of the various documents created by different departments during the land granting process. If a petition for land is missing, these kinds of documents are original sources providing direct evidence of participation in the land granting process. Records of the district land boards, 1788–1794, may also be useful in that evolving period. See AO's online series of sources included in first district land boards, or Research Guide 215, for the desired microfilm reel. Also at AO is a card catalogue of selected correspondence to the surveyor general and the commissioner of Crown lands, indexed alphabetically by correspondents' names.

Heir and Devisee Commission

The two groups of records in this series are the First Commission 1797–1804 and the Second Commission 1805–1911. The job of both commissions was to clarify land titles before patents were issued. Much of their work dwelt on claims stemming from the eighteenth century when Crown nominees had settled a lot but had neglected to exchange their original certificates or location tickets for a patent. To complicate matters, some Crown nominees had left the province by 1795 when the issuance of patents commenced. Some had died on their properties leaving little or no documentation, so the eldest son or legal heir would have to ask the commission for a hearing. Some had assigned their rights to unrelated parties as "assignees" or "devisees," which could have happened several times within a few years. Without a nominal index and the existence of individual case files, the records of the first commission are not easy to use. They are generally arranged in reports from the districts. Genealogical information is usually sparse, but they do contain commission decisions and occasionally some documents or letters.

The individual case files of the second commission have been indexed alphabetically by the surname of the *claimant*. The code COMM on the OLRI alerts you to a file for that particular name. This works well for a researcher seeking information on an ancestor acting as the claimant. But it does not work well for finding information on the ancestor when the claim or title passed away from the family surname. The way to get around this problem is to know the description of the property involved, and search the Abstract Index to Deeds (see below) to learn who did receive the patent. If a file exists, it will likely be indexed under this person's name, but should have some reference in it to your ancestor's original claim.

Some of the supporting documents given in evidence to the commission could include old land certificates or location tickets, assignments, copies of wills, receipts, sworn affidavits, and correspondence. The files are rich in genealogical rewards because, when applicable, they refer to family relationships. Occasionally a file consists of conflicting claims from two or more people for the same property. A patent would finally be issued to the appropriate party when the commission had weighed all the evidence, and the surveyor general had confirmed the validity of the original nominee.

LAC holds the first commission records and some of the second. AO has records of the second commission and select parts of the first. Consult the Canadian Genealogy Centre website for more details or AO Research Guide 215 for their online name index to the second commission files.

Excellent background articles are John Mezaks' "Records of the Heir and Devisee Commission" in *Families* Vol. 16, No. 4 (1977) and H. Pearson Gundy's "The Family Compact at Work: The Second Heir and Devisee Commission of Upper Canada, 1805-1841" in *Ontario History* Vol. 66, No. 3 (1974).

Township Papers

This group of records is arranged at AO by township, and then by concession number and lot number, so knowing a property description is essential for accessing them. They contain miscellaneous papers referring to a specific piece of property before the date of the patent. For some properties there are no papers at all. This is usually the case when an entire township or vast holdings had been granted to one person or company for subsequent disposition.

All manner of documentation may turn up here, such as leases, assignments, old location tickets or certificates, survey descriptions, maps of lot boundaries, receipts for payments, correspondence complaining about survey lines, prices of land, quality of land, settlement duties, disputes with neighbours or squatters, and so on. This can be one of the few sources of information for an ancestor who left Ontario or disappeared before obtaining a patent, during a period for which census returns and other records are not available.

Patents

The patent was the ultimate document of ownership sought by most Crown land applicants. Some fulfilled the contemporary settlement requirements and paid any necessary fees soon after their occupation of the land. For those who had to buy land after 1826, many years could lapse between the petition that began the process and receiving a patent. Variables affecting the length of time could include the health of the nominee, weather or soil conditions, the amount of labour he could perform or hire and the difficulty in raising cash for fees or payments. Extensions were often requested for making payments, or to complete the clearing of a specified portion of land or road allowance.

Land patent books at AO contain copies of these documents, indexed by township, 1793–1852. Another index, of names, 1826–1967, is also available on microfilm. Should a certified copy of a patent be required, it can only be obtained from the Ministry of Natural Resources, Crown Land Registry (Appendix II). You need to supply the name of the township, and concession and lot numbers, with the name on the patent and its date.

Not to be overlooked are the interesting patent plans that were created when each new township was surveyed. The names of the nominees were usually written on them and many have later add-on information to assist the surveyors and other departments. More than one plan can exist for a township, with information or names that vary. Some names on the maps may have been for leases that were not followed through with a patent. The titles of individual plans are listed in AO's Crown Lands inventory. The maps can only be viewed in the AO Special Collections Reading Room.

Portion of Robert Campbell Crown patent (1852), Upper Canada Land Petitions, RG 1, L 3, vol. 143 Part II, C bundle 8, petition 73; Library and Archives Canada microfilm C-1739

Land Registration

To this point we have been discussing the process that climaxed with a patent: ownership or title to a piece of land. The property registration system was in place by 1795. From that point on when Crown patents could be issued, a different system regulated and recorded the conveyance of real property. A land registry office (LRO) is located in each county, with sometimes more than one for large counties. Land titles offices were established in districts of the northern areas as they developed. Many of the historic records can be consulted at AO and FHL on microfilm.

Access to property registration records is based on the township name, concession and lot numbers for rural properties, or a lot number on a registered plan of subdivision for urban parcels. Learning the latter for a large urban centre means converting a street address into the required lot and plan numbers, usually with the assistance of the registry office. Smaller towns or villages can be more easily followed through the original 100- or 200-acre parcel from which the town grew, into a registered plan.

The procedure for property transactions—buying, selling, mortgaging and so on—involved a signed and witnessed agreement or contract between two or more parties. The document would be taken to the local county registrar of deeds for official registration on the property record. A witness would also be present. The salient points were extracted to make a new record called a memorial. Usually one copy of the memorial was deposited with the registrar for safekeeping, and the main contracting party would retain his original document. The memorial was copied into a book, and these are known as the copybooks of deeds.

Copybooks Of Deeds

From 1795 to 1847 copybooks were first generated by designated district; then county registrars recorded township deeds in the order of receipt. "Alphabetical Indexes" were prepared, and have survived for most areas, listing the relevant townships alphabetically, with deed numbers and names as they were received and entered. This type of index was a convenience for the clerk to find a specific memorial within the copybook relating to a certain township and piece of land. *Nominal* indexes to the older county copybooks are not always apparent. If available, such indexes were sometimes made within each copybook, but others were created separately. Copybook series are usually denoted with letters, as in Copybook B or Copybook G. The oldest copybooks, created before 1847, are arranged by county names.

Until 1846, registration of a deed was a voluntary act. This explains why there may be an odd gap in the early history of a property. Sometimes a person who registered a purchase is not recorded as disposing of it later, and the next registered transaction involves a new owner whose purchase was not recorded. During the period of this basic system, the memorials were not necessarily recorded in uniform fashion by all registrars. In some places and times, the county registrar position was conjunctive with the function of clerk of the peace or clerk of the surrogate court.

In 1846 new legislation required a separate copybook for each township. Record keeping was standardized with government-issued register volumes. Nominal indexes to the memorials and copybooks were prepared alphabetically by surnames of grantors and grantees, and are usually referred to as grantor/grantee indexes. A law in 1851 made registration of all land documents mandatory. As the population increased and spread into inland areas, new administrative jurisdictions were created. Some townships were figuratively "shifted" into new geographic boundaries. Township copybooks, or occasionally copies of copybooks, were then transferred to the keeping of the newer jurisdiction.

In 1865 more changes came. The practice of memorializing was abolished. Instead, the full text of the deed was copied by the registrar for his office, and the full text was written into the copybook. A new Abstract Index to Deeds was to be created for each original piece of Crown land in every town and township. Modern technology eventually did away with copybook practice late in the twentieth century.

Abstract Index to Deeds

The chronological history of transactions on each piece of property is called the Abstract Index to Deeds. They were created in 1865 retroactively to the date of the patent. This means that pre-1865 entries were copied into new books, with occasional omissions or errors. As a snapshot history, the Abstract Index shows the date of each document, the number it was given, the date it was registered, the type of transaction or conveyance, the names of the grantor and grantee, the size or description of the piece of land, the consideration or money involved and perhaps some additional remarks. Abstract Index books can continue in several volumes as time went on.

The number in the Abstract Index will take you to a source document, but make note of a possible variation in date between the document itself and its registration. The date of registration may affect your search for the deed itself or the relevant copybook. Some people did not bother to have their ownership recorded until much later when they wished to mortgage it or sell it.

Instruments and Deeds

The word "instrument" was commonly used to describe any document of conveyance or transaction concerning real property, including deeds. Terminology for different types of instruments typically appear on an Abstract Index:

- sales (B & S for bargain and sale)
- mortgages (M)
- quit claims or releases (QC or Rel)
- assignments and discharges of mortgages (A of M, D/M)
- indentures
- agreements
- deed polls
- wills
- life lease or annuity (LL or LA)
- orders or vesting orders (VO)
- sheriff's deeds
  - While copybooks may be somewhat easier to access on

microfilm at AO or FHL, remember the original paper documents were deposited with the relevant LRO. The documents themselves have been microfilmed by the LROs and are only accessible on-site. You can visit an office or contact it with precise information from the Abstract Index to request copies.

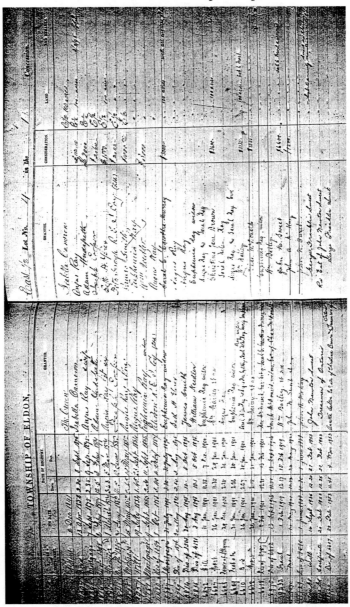

Eldon Township, Abstract Index to Deeds, Book A, pp. 4-5, Peterborough County Land Registry Office; Archives of Ontario microfilm GSU 202214

A mortgage, or a number of sequential mortgages, can be a telling feature in the history of a property. Quite often this signals the building of the family home as opposed to the original, temporary shanties or log houses most pioneers began with.

Wills were frequently registered against a property without being probated in the Surrogate Court. Court and legal expenses were thus avoided, especially when the inheritance of property was clear-cut with no complications of detailed trust arrangements or converting real property to cash for heirs. These wills number in the thousands in the nineteenth century. Some of them have been recorded in both the registry office and the surrogate court.

The assent of a wife was required by common law in certain transactions the husband undertook, that is, barring her dower right to a standard portion of his real property. Finding the name of the wife—almost always only her first name—might be a new point of identification. On a few occasions a relationship might be specified in a deed, such "eldest son and heir" or a woman described as the wife or widow "of _____."

Some of the most revealing documents, in the genealogical sense, are the quit claims, also called releases. They result when a deceased property owner left several heirs. A quit claim was required from the next of kin to release their heritable claims and clear the property title for a new owner. These releases can be a genealogical bonus when they come from married daughters, children living in distant places, a widow who may have remarried or siblings.

Appearing less often are vesting orders issued by chancery court and sheriff's deeds. Vesting orders were entered on an Abstract Index to indicate that chancery court resolved a conflict among heirs, or between an heir and the executors or administrators of an estate. The related court documents are not filed at the registry office, so further investigation along that line must turn to chancery court records under the Quieting Titles Act. There are two sub-series of these records at AO. A sheriff's deed indicates that the previous owner had lapsed so far in tax arrears, or some other offence, that the municipality had seized the property and authorized the sheriff to sell it. Such sales are often featured in the advertisement section of local newspapers.

If you had information about your ancestor's property description and his name does not appear in the Abstract Index or any available nominal indexes, it likely means he was renting the property from the owner. These rental agreements between individuals are seldom if ever registered. You may be able to confirm his status by investigating the agricultural schedule of a census, a county directory that shows rural locations by townships or township assessment/collectors' rolls for taxes.

General Registers

Legislation that took effect in 1866 required that counties keep a separate General Register to record unprobated wills and other miscellaneous documents. The other documents might include bankruptcy assignments, insolvencies, powers of attorney and diverse legal papers—all land-related but without precise property descriptions or perhaps too indefinite to file in a particular township category.

Again, many of the above-mentioned documents and registers can be searched on microfilm at AO and FHL or in person at a county land registry office. Similar records for northern and northwestern Ontario areas, which were settled much later than southern Ontario, were created at district land titles offices. Their records are not available at AO. So LTOs should be personally contacted or visited. LRO and LTO addresses are listed in Stratford-Devai and Burkholder's *A Guide to Ontario Land Registry Records*. They can also be found through the government of Ontario website by putting "land registry" into the search engine. Most LROs and LTOs now offer a combination of government services, but they still have the most extensive collections of microfilmed land documents. Photocopies of Abstract Index pages or deeds can be obtained from them in person or by mail if the lot-concession-township description is provided with the deed number, date of registration and name of grantor.

Since the 1880s, private and municipal interests have deposited non-land-related registrations and loose documents for safekeeping and storage at LROs . Among them could be such items as railway debentures, civil court judgments, partnership registrations or school board documents. Even the occasional marital separation agreement has been found. Most of these items remain at the local offices.

Tips

The main value of a document involving your ancestor is evidence of his residence at an exact date, and the types or variety of his transactions that reflect his economic circumstances. In fact, his occupation is usually stated. "Yeoman" is a very common term, meaning "farmer" to all intents and purposes. If you can access one of the first documents submitted to the land registrar, you may find your ancestor's signature, assuming it was not an "X." Apart from the personal value of such a memento, the signature can be an important factor if or when identification problems arise. Comparing signatures on various documents can help to distinguish among several men with the same name.

Some land records can be a unique source for revealing family relationships. The researcher needs perseverance to find all the appropriate records, and certainly some background of contemporary legal application is useful. Following the ancestor and his family name in the Abstract Index and its corresponding documents might outline for you when he officially took possession, when he disposed of it by sale or inheritance and/or how long his descendants remained there. In a minority of auspicious cases, the ancestor acquired the land while still at his former place of residence—this may be your only tip to his previous whereabouts. At the other side of the equation, the ancestor may have established himself in a new place of residence before selling his former property. These are wonderful clues, found in the simple description accompanying the man's name, "of _____ " [a town or township name], when it differs from the place of the immediate transaction.

Here are a few additional tips.

- Genealogists want to remember that sometimes more than one degree of copying was undertaken in earlier periods. The usual warning applies about the possibilities of transcribing errors and the need to examine related sources.
- Copybooks do not carry the signatures of participating parties.
- Abstract Indexes for every incorporated village were not necessarily microfilmed.
- The word "index" does not always refer to *name* indexes.
- Note whether a numbering system refers to a page number or an instrument number.
- The registration date of a document will normally determine whether it is located in a county (pre-1847) or a township copybook.
- When using the AO and FHL microfilms, one must be especially careful to note the title/name of the register or series as seen on the film itself. Cataloguing information or labels on microfilm boxes do not always totally describe their contents. For instance, the microfilm boxes for copybooks were first labelled as "Deeds" by the GSU microfilmers.

- When using the FHL catalogue, search for land records by the county name; click on "view film notes" to see the list of townships and towns.

APOLROD

The Association for the Preservation of Ontario Land Registry Office Documents was spearheaded in 1996 by dedicated genealogists in cooperation with other heritage stakeholders. A government steering committee was created in response to the early work of APOLROD. The resulting Land Records Steering Committee included APOLROD, the government's Real Property Registration Branch and the Archives of Ontario. APOLROD coordinated volunteers who performed heroic work to inventory pre-1955 holdings in land registry office holdings. Lack of storage space and repeated policy reviews threatened the loss of many historical records. During the lengthy negotiation and inventory process, even more material was uncovered in the LROs. Different repositories were sought and persuaded to accept collections of regional and local interest. Most such records have been successfully dispersed to other centres, including AO. See APOLROD articles by Fawne Stratford-Devai on the *Global Gazette* website, especially "Where Have the Ontario Land Records Gone?" for records placement. There is also an article listing all LROs and LTOs. The full inventories are available at individual LROs and LTOs and at AO.

POLARIS

The modern automation of the land registry system is called the Province of Ontario Land Registration And Information System (POLARIS). The millions of parcels of land in the province are being entered into the new electronic system. At the same time, a massive reform of land registration is being effected by conversion to the Land Titles system and parcel registers. As each parcel of land is entered into the electronic database, it is assigned a unique property identification number (PIN). You can use the computers at LROs to search for the geographic address of a property and obtain the necessary PIN as a key to further documentary research. That is the main benefit for genealogists, since the history of each property on the database is incomplete and may only extend to the past forty years or so.

John S. Hagopian's article, "The Use of Land Registry Offices for Historical Research" in *Ontario History* Vol 87, No 1

(Spring 1995) is a good synopsis, although he mistakenly credits the Ontario Genealogical Society with microfilming historic land records actually done by the Genealogical Society of Utah. For practical information see Janet Globe's *Title Searching in Ontario*.

Reading and Reference

Bourrie, Doris. *Pioneers of Upper Canada, 1783-1839*. Thornhill, ON: Doris Bourrie, 1991.

Coleman, Thelma. *The Canada Land Company*. Stratford, ON: Perth County Historical Board/Cumming Publishers, 1978.

Corupe, Linda, transcriber and indexer. *And Your Petitioner Will Ever Pray: The Papers of the First Land Board of the Mecklenburg/Midland District, 1789-1794*. Bolton, ON: Linda Corupe, 2006.

Gates, Lillian F. *Land Policies of Upper Canada*. Toronto, ON: University of Toronto Press, 1968.

Globe, Janet M. *Title Searching in Ontario: A Procedural Guide*. Third edition. Toronto, ON: Butterworths, 1991.

Gunnell, Art. *Index to Land Settlement in Thunder Bay District*. Toronto, ON: Ontario Genealogical Society, 2005.

Holt, Ruth and Margaret Williams. *Genealogical Extraction and Index of the Canada Company Remittance Books, 1843-1847*. Weston, ON: Ruth Holt, 1990.

Lee, Robert Charles. *The Canada Company and the Huron Tract, 1826-1853: Personalities, Profits and Politics*. Toronto, ON: Dundurn Press, 2004.

McFall, A. David and Jean McFall. *Land Records in Ontario Land Registry Offices*. Third edition. Toronto, ON: Ontario Genealogical Society, 1987.

Smart, Susan, editor. *Index to the Upper Canada Land Books*. 9 volumes. Toronto, ON: The Ontario Genealogical Society, 2001-2005. Also CD-ROM, 2007.

Stratford-Devai, Fawne and Ruth Burkholder. *Ontario Land Registry Office Records: A Guide*. Campbellville, ON: Global Heritage Press, 2003.

Winearls, Joan. *Mapping Upper Canada, 1780-1867*. Toronto, ON: University of Toronto Press, 1991.

APOLROD.
   www.globalgenealogy.com/globalgazette/APOLROD/index.htm
Global Gazette. www.globalgazette.com
Government of Ontario. www.gov.on.ca
Linda Corupe. home.ica.net/~corupegla

7

Court and Related Records

Reference Dates

1793	Establishment of Court of Probate and District Surrogate Courts
1827	Probate and Surrogate Court jurisdiction extended to guardianships
1850	Surrogate Courts became county rather than district jurisdictions
1858	Court of Probate was abolished
1884	Married Women's Property Act; allowed to dispose of real property and earnings, e.g. through execution of a will
1892	Provincial Succession Duty Act, limited application
1914	Succession Duty Act was applied to all estates
1979	Succession Duty tax was abolished

The Archives of Ontario is the custodian of court records for the province. Estate files, including wills, are perhaps the most significant part of the collection for family historians, but are by no means all of the interesting and informative sources. Courts for handling civil matters and criminal offenses originally had some overlapping jurisdictions. The lesser courts sat at the district's administrative town/centre and convened quarterly. Higher courts were represented by senior judges who visited on a regular basis. There is a comprehensive finding aid for using all these records in the AO Reading Room, RG 22, Court Records. You can find descriptions of many series online through the Archives Descriptive Database.

Wills and Estate Files

Beginners should understand that a will is only one document in an estate file. Other papers in the same file can contain important information and clues about family relationships, the financial position of the deceased, business operations and the distribution of assets. We become accustomed to referring to Surrogate or Probate Court material as estate files, or estates, unless the discussion narrows to one document within the file.

Prerogative Courts

Until 1793, Prerogative Courts, similar to those of the same name in England, dealt with estate matters. Almost nothing is available from this period with the exception of a few records of the Hesse (later Western) District and Lunenburg (later Eastern) District. A copy of the Hesse District register, 1789–1791, is the most informative of these earliest records, and contains estate material for 20 men:

James Bennett	Nicholas Lorrain
Jacques Campau	George McDougall
John Casety	John McPherson
Charles Desforges	Michel Roy
Philip Dejeane	Thomas Shephard
Gabriel Gene	Joseph Socia
Nicholas Goyeaux	Garret Teller
Garret Greverat	Augustin Thebault
Samuel Judah	Thomas Williams
Joseph Labreche	Peter Younge

A few loose pages of Court minutes survive from the Lunenburg District, 1790–1791, referring to four estates. Just the names of the petitioners and of the deceased are given, without details:

Adam Cline	Alexander McPherson
Capt. Peter Everett	Barnaby Spencer

In Leeds and Grenville Surrogate Court, a handful of documents refer back to this pre-1793 period, for Timothy Buell, Adam Cline, Christian Sheek and Abijah Wead. One estate file survives in the Western District Surrogate Court, for Colin Andrews.

The above lists were compiled by Catherine Shepard and published in her booklet *Surrogate Court Records at the Archives of Ontario,* which includes enlightening background facts on different court periods.

From 1793 to 1858, the two courts involved in probate and administration of estates were the Court of Probate and the District Surrogate Courts.

Court of Probate

The Probate Court had exclusive jurisdiction over estates valued at £5 or more, with landed property in more than one district. This comprised a minority among the population, often considered the wealthy elite, which was not always the case. The number of files that resulted was relatively low compared to the concurrent Surrogate Courts. The nominal index prepared by AO is available on-site and online as Appendix A1 of the Court Records finding aid. It was also published by OGS as *Court of Probate: Registers and Estate Files at the Archives of Ontario (1793–1859),* now out of print. The index gives the name of the deceased, his residence, his occupation or status, the date of the file and microfilm numbers. The filmed files do not always include all the original papers and may not show a date of death. You can infer that the death occurred between the date of the will (if there is one) and the date of the petition for probate (if there is one) or the date of filing with the court. Files have been microfilmed in one alphabetical series. Backup registers usually exist, with abstracts of the grants of probate or administration. They may contain reference to files that no longer exist.

Surrogate Courts

The District Surrogate Courts were initially responsible for probate matters with real property in one district only. They existed during the same period as the Court of Probate and collectively handled many more cases. The system for filing and keeping these records varied slightly from place to place, which explains how much or how little material you may find.

Pre-1859 Surrogate files have been microfilmed in county arrangement at AO. When districts vanished in 1850, Surrogate Courts continued in each county, thus the records are not found in one master series. Fortunately, there is one nominal index to all files province-wide up to 1858. No matter in which district an individual died before 1859, the index leads you to the relevant county of filing and the microfilm number. The index gives the person's name, the year of the file, the county of residence and a file number if there was one. AO has placed the index online and on-site as Appendix A25 of RG 22. When searching the Probate and Surrogate Court indexes and making notes, be sure to distinguish between them.

In some instances, the original file either no longer exists or was not microfilmed. There may be backup registers—a type of copybook—available for abstracts of the basic information. Some districts or counties kept separate copybook registers for grants of probates (estates with wills) and administrations (estates with no wills).

In 1859, when the County Surrogate Courts assumed sole administration of probate and estates, the new legislation required more detailed and standard recording practice. New numerical series of files were begun. Access to the files from 1859 is by the county index, which gives you a number with an individual's name. Normally there will be several index books for one county. Usually the index number refers to the actual estate file, but occasionally access to the file is by another indexing method. Some County Surrogate Clerks also recorded reference numbers to all the various registers they kept—grant books, non-contentious business books and register books—one of which may be the right key to the estate file you want. So it is essential that you note all numbers in any index. Both the AO court records finding aid and Shepard's *Surrogate Court Records* explain which is the correct number to locate a file.

The microfilmed indexes, alphabetical by surname, are available at AO up to the 1960s in most cases. It can be helpful to know that occasionally a county decided to be especially efficient by organizing its indexes, or some of them, by the main letters following the surname initial. For example, under "B" you might find separate indexes for names beginning with Ba, Be, Bi, Bo and Bu, with possible variations for Bl, Br and so on. If you are not aware this random system occurs, you might search the first "Ba" section without realizing there is more.

Estate files have been microfilmed to 1930 and can be borrowed through AO interlibrary loan and the FHL. Only York County files are on microfilm up to 1967. Because the later non-microfilmed files in AO custody are in an off-site storage centre, you must allow for a few days' retrieval time. The most recent files stay at the county courthouses, along with their matching indexes, up to about forty years past. Courthouse addresses are on the AO pathfinder called Wills and Estate Files. The courts are now known as Superior Courts of Justice – Estates Division.

County indexes 1859 to 1900 have been published by Generation Press with 36 counties represented in 27 volumes. These indexes were created from the microfilmed files, rather than repeating the handwritten indexes. In this way some "fugitive" files were located, and some noted as missing on the microfilm were checked against the original AO file holdings. Some OGS Branches have also published indexes to Surrogate records, extending beyond 1900.

Note that in the Generation Press series, the AO microfilm reference numbers given in the introduction to volumes 1 to 25 are for a self-service retrieval system *no longer in use* at AO. AO has since reverted to the original GS numbers to correspond with the Genealogical Society of Utah filming.

Estate Files

The creation of an estate file, whether Probate Court or Surrogate Court, whether the deceased was testate or not, entailed a number of documents, even if they have not all survived or were microfilmed. *Testate* describes a person who died with a proper will; *intestate* refers to someone without a will or with an improperly executed will. Some discussion follows on these various documents and their genealogical value. In general terms, the earlier the file, the fewer documents have been created or preserved.

Almost everyone is familiar with the general form and intent of a will. According to English common law, the provisions of a will regarding property, both land and personal, come into effect upon the death of the testator. A valid will names at least one executor. When the will has been duly processed through a court, and the judge has issued *letters of probate*, the executor is bound to its terms regarding distribution and settlement.

Early wills traditionally begin with "In the Name of God, Amen … " which captures the essence of a society that held religious observance in high regard. Some wills stipulate burial wishes, perhaps naming a particular cemetery or church. Or a clause in the will might direct a gift of cash or land to a local church or clergyman. Sometimes the testator will mention whether he is in good physical condition, or perhaps "frail in body" or words to that effect. Occasionally he might mention his age.

An ancestor's signature on a will is a unique souvenir. There are times when a signature is very useful for identification comparison with other documents. Also, a researcher may detect in it visual evidence that the testator is elderly or ill. An "X" for a signature does not necessarily indicate an illiterate individual. Depending on his health at the time, often mentioned in the will's preamble, he may have been too weak to make more than "his mark." There are cases where a sworn affidavit was included from a witness to the will, stating that the testator, although sound of mind, was too feeble to execute the signature.

Codicils to a will take place when the testator has changed his mind about one or several provisions in his will and/or distribution of his estate. Codicils can reflect the maturity, death or estrangement of children, as well as changing circumstances in the assets of the estate.

A will may mention several children, *but not all children may be named.* Sometimes only one child is mentioned, for the inheritance of land. Perhaps this legal direction was to avoid any potential conflict with the old common law custom of the eldest son inheriting all property. In our pioneer societies and later, it was often the youngest child or children who stayed at the family home to care for aging parents. Frequently they were recognized as caretakers in a will. When families were large and spaced over a 20- or 30-year span, the eldest were normally well-established in their own lives when a parent died. Benefits to older children in the form of property, cash or loans may have been gifted in advance of the execution of the will, and the will might allude to an arrangement like this. A one dollar bequest to a son or daughter is usually not a sign of disowning them, as is sometimes interpreted. Rather, the token was included in recognition of children who had received an inheritance before the testator died. A will may direct the division of land among designated heirs and describe the portions exactly.

A bonus in a will is a reference to married daughters or the full names of grandchildren or other relations. Ambiguous language carried into the nineteenth century from earlier times might use such terms as "daughter" for daughter-in-law or "nephew" for the child of a cousin or step-sibling. The testator may refer to children from an earlier marriage of his spouse without distinguishing them as step-children. A witness to the will or an appointed executor might have the same surname as the testator, implying a relationship that the will does not specify.

If the wife is not mentioned in a husband's will, chances are high that she predeceased the testator. "My now wife" is a common phrase, not to be interpreted as the sign of a second or later marriage for the testator. He may indeed have had one or more previous marriages, but the phrase is familiarly used for a one and only wife. Before 1859, married women did not have the right to dispose of property, whether they brought it into the marriage or acquired it later. Until then, women had no separate identity from that of their husband, another long-standing tradition of English common law. Legislation in Upper Canada in 1859 gave a woman limited rights to dispose of inherited property, and to do so by executing a will. Augmented legislation in 1884 gave her much more freedom in the disposition of property during her lifetime or by designating heirs in a will.

Remember that probate and court records are not the only source for locating a will. In Chapter 6 of this book, the occurrence of non-probated wills as land conveyances was mentioned. It has been estimated that as many as 50 percent of existing wills in the nineteenth century were not probated. Wills can also be found among Heir and Devisee Commission Records and Canada Company Papers.

Administration

When a person died without executing a will but with enough assets to warrant the probate process, *letters of administration* were required. One person, or occasionally more than one, would petition the court to serve as administrator. That person was often a surviving next of kin or, less often, a significant creditor. By the English tradition of primogeniture, the eldest son stood to inherit from the father when no will was executed or located. In 1851, Canada West and East officially abolished this custom in favour of equal disposition among all children.

In the first days of the province, an administration file does not yield as much information as a probate file with a will. An administrator of an estate was required to sign a bond of surety with the court to ensure performance of his duties. Usually two other people would provide financial support on the bond by declaring their financial worth equal to that of the estate in question. The administrator was obliged to fulfil certain court conditions such as providing an inventory of the estate assets, making distribution to heirs or creditors, and itemizing the administrative accounts. In later years, we see releases from next of kin, relinquishing their rights to administration of the estate. They may reveal the residence of a previously unknown or missing son or daughter.

Administration *with will annexed* happens when a will failed to appoint an executor. Administration *de bonis non* involves some change from the executorship originally appointed in a will. The appointed executor may have died in the meantime, or renounced his duties in favour of someone else.

Petitions

It is the petition for application from an executor or administrator that gives the official date of death of the deceased. In intestate cases for administration of an estate, it is often the widow or eldest son who applies for the right to administer although creditors too had a right to apply. When the petitioner for administration was not a next of kin to the deceased, the judge would issue a public citation for the next of kin to appear before him if he or she wished to exercise his or her own rights. This kind of notice would be inserted in a local newspaper. Thus, if there is no citation in the file, one might assume that the petitioner had a relationship to the deceased.

Petitions usually state the date and place of death of the deceased, place of residence and occupation. This is primary information coming from an original source. The standard legal phrase for the date of death is "on or about" the day, month and year. In the case of properly appointed executors, you may find a document of renunciation of responsibilities by one or more executors. Whether this person was related to the deceased or not, the name, residence, occupation, and perhaps relationship will be stated. Poor health or relocation to an inconveniently distant place are the most common reasons for renunciations.

A *caveat* is an occasional document in an estate file to show that an heir, or potential heir, contested either the petitioner's application or some provisions of the will. The estate file might have some documentation in it to show the outcome. Then again, the problem may or may not have been tried as a separate court action, perhaps in Chancery Court (see below). If there is no official judgment document about this in the estate file, the status quo of the will's provisions would have been upheld. The file will also indicate to whom probate was granted.

Inventories

An inventory was generally made of the deceased's real and personal property. Making an inventory was one of the obligations of the executor or administrator who did it alone or called upon local appraisers. Inventories give a welcome view of the ancestor's

Executor's petition (1881), Elizabeth Parkes estate, Leeds and Grenville Counties Surrogate Court, RG 22-179, file 959; AO microfilm GS1-463

lifestyle and/or economic circumstances, with values placed on household goods, farm stock and crops, agricultural equipment or occupational tools. Cash in the bank, insurance policies and even promissory notes can be listed.

Succession duty schedule B (1910), Almira Franklin estate, Norfolk County Surrogate Court, RG 22-228, file 31; AO microfilm MS 887 reel 1507

Not every estate file will have an inventory. On the microfilmed records, they are more common in estate files before 1850 and after 1880. The latter date shows a distinct shift from detailed items to rather broad categories of personal property. An interesting article for background reading is Brian Osborne's "Wills and Inventories: Records of Life and Death in a Developing Society" in *Families* Vol. 19, No. 4 (1980).

From 1914, for taxation purposes, the Ontario Succession Duty Act required every estate to show the various types of property owned. Serving as a type of inventory, several standard form pages in the file will show assets and their values. In Succession Duty forms there is also a schedule to show the residence or address of the beneficiaries and their relationship to the deceased. This particular type of taxation in Ontario was abolished in 1979.

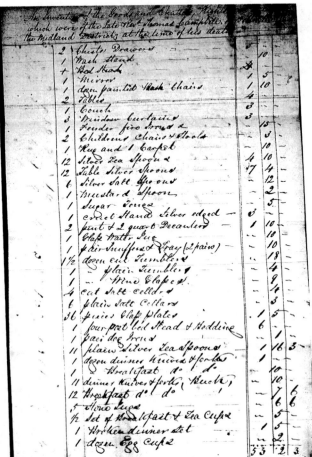

Inventory, Rev. Thomas
Campbell estate file (1835),
Upper Canada Court of
Probate, RG 22-155; AO
microfilm MS 638 reel 42

Guardianship

Since 1827, guardianship papers and files have been included with estate files and their indexes. They are indexed by the surname of the children, not the applicant. Later a few counties developed guardianship indexes separate from estate files. The files can be a good source of family information, but they are not common. When a man executed his will, knowing his children were underage, he could include a clause commending them to the mother's care, or name an additional guardian for specific educational or financial plans on their behalf. If such provision was made in the will, it is unlikely that a formal guardianship application would be made.

A widow was normally recognized as the guardian of her own infant or minor (under the age of 21) children. The scenario for the creation of a guardianship file generally occurred if minor children stood to inherit something substantial from their father upon reaching the age of majority and their widowed mother remarried. The applicant for legal guardianship might be her new husband, or a paternal relative of the children. A guardianship file can tell you the name of the deceased father, the names and, quite often, the ages of the children, the name of the mother and the applicant for guardianship. Occasionally there are cases where both parents have died, leaving young children, and an uncle or grandfather might be the applicant. Certainly there were far more cases of informal "adoption" of children by stepfathers or next of kin than were processed in the Surrogate Courts.

Registers

County Surrogate Clerks kept register books into which they copied the main facts of a file. Initially, this consisted only of the grant (letters) of probate or administration and, perhaps, a summary of the will and the petition. After 1858, the copy of the grant included the deceased's date and place of death. Depending on the type of grant, a full copy of the will was included, or else the letters of administration show the relationship (if there was one) of the administrator to the deceased. In the absence of an original file, the registers are definitely of value. The registers normally have name indexes.

If an estate file or register reference for an ancestor cannot be found in the county where he is known to have died, it could mean that he did not own any land, that is, real property. His personal property may not have been extensive enough, and/or was not in dispute, to warrant the expense of the court procedure. Then again, if he owned land and died testate, his will might simply have been registered in order to transfer title, in a land registry office. These wills are treated under land documents in Chapter 6.

Application to Probate

When you are sure that an ancestor died in this province, but you do not know *where*, there is a major index to aid you. From 1859 on, a central register was kept of every application for grants made in all the county Surrogate Courts. This was the responsibility of the Surrogate Clerk of Ontario. County courts were required to first notify the surrogate clerk's office in Toronto of any application that came to them. Keeping the application books ensured that no other application had been made for the same estate.

There is a two-fold procedure for searching these records up to 1968. You must first use the master nominal indexes that were created alphabetically by surname initial, in chronological order. The index gives merely a name and a number. The number refers to the application book entry and not to an estate file. As with all large indexes, you might find several candidates with the same name as your ancestor. The second step is to search the correct application book *for the year in which the name appeared in the index*, and find the numbered entry. Among other things, each entry line for a name will tell you in which county the actual file is located. This sequence is outlined in AO's online and paper guide, "Wills and Estate Files – A Pathfinder," to provide microfilm numbers.

The application books are quite informative and, if you end up with several possibilities, you may be able to identify the ancestor at this stage. After the reference number and the name of the deceased, the book entry shows the residence at the time of death (city, town, village or township), occupation or status, date of death, date the notice was received, name of the applicant (executor or administrator), his residence and occupation, whether it was for probate or administration and the county where the application was made. The applicant might be the widow or one of the children or another name you recognize. In other cases, you may have to search through many estate files to make the right identification.

The name of the county is the key to the next steps. Now you continue as outlined earlier, by searching the county Surrogate Court index for the file number of the name you are seeking, and then you proceed to the file itself.

At the present, the indexes and application books are microfilmed from 1859 to 1982. After 1964 the application books are in alphabetical, rather than numerical, order. From 1983, the original index books and application books must be consulted on-site at the former Surrogate Clerk's Office, now located in offices of the Ontario Court (General Division – Estates) in Toronto (Appendix II).

Civil and Criminal Justice

Quarter Sessions

Courts of General Quarter Sessions of the Peace, commonly called Quarter Sessions, were responsible for adjudicating on a variety of civil matters and criminal proceedings to a point. These were lower, or inferior courts, presided over by justices of the peace, also known as magistrates. Justices of the peace had additional functions that are discussed in the Municipal Records section of Chapter 9. Until 1841 Quarter Sessions were also responsible for local administration related to road and bridge improvements, bylaws for public safety, licensing for taverns and other public facilities, issuing certificates for performing marriages, the upkeep of the courthouse and jail, taxation rates and collection, petitions from the destitute or needy for social assistance and many such necessities for the public good. The courts appointed justices of the peace, sheriffs, constables, pathmasters, tax collectors and other district or county officials. Quarter Sessions continued throughout the nineteenth century (changed to Court of General Sessions of the Peace in 1868) and most of the twentieth, while its functions were gradually reduced in nature.

The early judicial work of these courts involved settling civil suits or offences for misdemeanours in disturbing the peace. However, cases involving assault, theft, forgery, fraud, arson, larceny, rape, and murder were also heard. Grand juries were regularly called for deliberation. The most serious crimes would be held over for a superior court sitting. The names of district officials and magistrates often appear in these records, along with anyone who became a juryman, plaintiff or defendant. The minutes of the court are the best source for

---

UPPER CANADA COURT RECORDS.   65

New York currency, per pound. The action is continued for the Court to consider.

The parties appeared, by their respective attorneys, and on motion of Mr. Smyth, the plaintiff's attorney, by procuration, the action stands over for eight days for the testimony of William Monforton.
William Groesbeck vs. Joseph Gamelin.

This cause is continued for eight days at the instance of Mr. Roe.
OLD CAUSES UNDER TEN POUNDS STERLING. Thomas Cox vs. Jordan Ivory.

The parties appeared and on motion of Mr. Roe, the plaintiff's attorney, the action is continued for fourteen days for further testimony.
James Fraser, Curator to the Succession of Samuel Judah, of New York, deceased, vs. Joseph Malet, of the Parish of St. Anne, Yeomen.

Continued for eight days for further proof of the delivery of the articles in question stated in the plaintiff's account and declaration.
James Fraser, Curator to the Succession of Thomas Williams & Company, of Detroit, Merchant, deceased, vs. J. B. Rheaume, of St. Anne, Yeoman.

Court adjourned to the 17th of September, 1789. T. S.

Court of Common Pleas, Thursday, the 17th day of September, 1789.
Province of Quebec. District of Hesse. 17 Sept. 1789. T.S.

Present: The Honourable William Dummer Powell, Esquire, first Judge of said Court, etc.

Walter Roe, attorney for the plaintiff, filed his contract of marriage and the defendant appeared. On motion of Mr. Roe (the plaintiff's said attorney) William Monforton was called as evidence, of full age and not interested, and duly sworn, says: "That he saw the plaintiff, Catharine Desriviere Lamoinodiers Dequindre sign her name to the exhibit A, filed in Court the tenth day of September instant."
Catharine Desriviere LaMoinodiers Dequindre vs. Her husband, Antoine Dagnis Dequindre.

(Signed) WM MONFORTON, Notary Public.

Called as evidence, Francois Perthuir, who is produced by Mr. Roe, the plaintiff's attorney, being of full age and not interested, and duly sworn.
Question 1st by Mr. Roe, the plaintiff's attorney: "Si le temoin connoit Antoine Dagnio Dequindre le defendant dans cette cause?" Answer: "Oui!"

6A

Court of Common Pleas, District of Hesse, 1789-1794, 14th Report of the Bureau of Archives, Province of Ontario (1918; reprint, Upper Canada Court Records, *Pawtucket, RI: Quintin Publications, n.d.) p. 65*

personal information, especially if an ancestor was an offender. Unfortunately, the minutes from the old districts have survived only in scattered fashion before the turn of the nineteenth century.

A clerk of the peace for the district, and later for a county, assisted the justices' preparations for court business and kept records of convictions, judgments, fines, pardons and jurors. The clerks issued writs and subpoenas, summoned jurors, notified sheriffs and handled payments for public officials. The clerks would also publish court returns in a local newspaper. Many of the judicial items, as well as district or county administration duties, were recorded in separate dedicated books but the survival rate is very mixed from one jurisdiction to another.

Newspapers usually gave extensive coverage while the courts were sitting and then, as now, they preferred to elaborate on the most scandalous or shocking items. If you find an ancestor in the court records, you may find even more details in a newspaper from the town where the court was in session.

Descriptions of extant historical records from these courts are in Court Records finding aid in the AO Reading Room. They are arranged alphabetically by names of the towns where the local district or county court held session, from Brockville to Woodstock. Some have a wide variety of material, while others consist only of roads and bridges reports. Lists of the historical material can be viewed online in AO's Archives Descriptive Database by searching for "quarter sessions." Adding the name of a district or county is also recommended. Some of the oldest extant court minutes have been published—see the Reading and Reference section for this chapter. "Records of the Courts of the Quarter Sessions of the Peace" by Ruth Burkholder in *Families* Vol. 32, No. 1 (1993) gives a good introduction to these courts and to the AO finding aid.

Superior Courts

The Court of King's Bench was the highest court in Upper Canada, presided over by the chief justice. King's Bench sessions were called by the Lieutenant Governor. Judges would travel to the districts for trials. Both civil and criminal matters were within its jurisdiction, although serious criminal trials were often passed to the District Assizes—the Court of Oyer and Terminer and General Gaol Delivery refers to criminal trials, and Nisi Prius to the civil trials they heard. Judgment docket books from the

Court of King's Bench 1796–1849 at AO provide the names of plaintiffs and defendants, their occupations and residences, the district where the action took place and the details and date of the judgment.

Historical bench books of many judges have been preserved at AO and microfilmed. While actual trial proceedings have seldom survived, the judges' notes on hearing case evidence fill many gaps. The records cover a chronological range of chief justices from James Buchanan Macaulay in 1815 up into the twentieth century, arranged by the name of the judge. "Judge Willis and the Court of King's Bench in Upper Canada" by Robert Hett in *Ontario History* Vol. 65 (1973) makes interesting reading. Linda Corupe's *Upper Canadian Justice* is highly recommended for its introduction and appendixes, including court structure and a glossary of terms.

The names and jurisdictions of several courts have changed slightly from time to time. For example, in 1881 King's/Queen's Bench became one division of the High Court of Justice, which was a branch of the newly established Supreme Court. For genealogical application to an ancestor, it is quite essential to examine the Court Records finding aids in depth. Consulting with the AO Justice portfolio archivist may be required because some records may not be processed or described online yet.

Jail and Prison

Jail may be defined as a place of incarceration for minor offenses or lawful custody while awaiting trial, while prison is where convicted offenders served their sentences. Each of the early districts, and then counties, had at least one "common gaol" and a sheriff. "Lockup houses" also existed for the least offenders. Before the establishment of a social welfare system, jails often housed the destitute and the insane as well. Library and Archives Canada has intermittent returns of prisoners, sent from district or county sheriffs to the provincial secretary, 1823 to 1861.

A fair number of old jail registers have survived and were microfilmed by AO. Some of the oldest extant are those for Hamilton (1832), Cobourg (1834), Toronto (1838) and Guelph (1840). You can view what is available on the AO website by typing "jail registers" into the search engine and looking for the name of the county town. More than one type of register was kept for different purposes. There may be committal registers, punishment registers, dietary records and inmate case files. Evidence of civil

1874

No.	NAME OF PRISONER	NATIVITY	AGE	RESIDENCE	TRADE	RELIGION	MARRIED OR SINGLE	READ OR WRITE	TEMPERATE OR INTEMPERATE	
6	Mary Townsend	Ireland	47	Ottawa	Servant	English	M	no	Intempt	
	Joseph Gethier	Canada	55	"	Grocer	R C	M	yes	"	
7	Edward Wright	England	38	"	Labrer	English	"	"	"	
8	Thos Hanaghan	Ireland	37	"	Butcher	R C	S	"	"	
9	James Shorey	England	44	"	Labrer	English	"	no	"	
10	Timothy Coghlan	Ireland	36	"	"	R C	M	yes	"	
	John Welsh	Canada	18	"	"	"	S	no	"	
13	Peter Huston	"	22	"	Blacksmith	Presby	"	"	"	
14	Eugene Lamintague	"	18	"	Labrer	R C	"	yes	"	
15	John Curtis	England	41	"	Barber	English	M	"	"	
17	Thos Busk	Canada	24	"	Machinist	R C	S	"	Tempt	
	John Deake	England	25	"	Labrer	English	M	no	Intempt	
22	Margaret Woodrow	Canada	40	"	Housekeeper	Methodist	"	yes	Tempt	
23	John Grimes	Ireland	50	"	Labrer	R C	"	no	Intempt	
	Robert Burns	"	44	"		English	S	yes	"	
24	Elizabeth Rowe	"	36	"	Housekeeper		"	"	Tempt	
	Joseph Sabourin	Canada	54	"	Labrer	R C	"	no	Intempt	
	Jane McLeod	"	47	Lancaster	Housekeeper	Presby	"	yes	Tempt	
	William Latimer	"	28	Ottawa	Cooper	English	"	"	Intempt	
	Eugene Pape	Switzerland	25	do	Grocer	R C	"	"	"	
28	Davie McGibney	Canada	14	"	Schoolboy	Presby	S	no	"	
	Michael Corell	"	19	"	Butcher	R C	"	"	"	

Ottawa Gaol Blotter (1874), Administrative Records of the Ottawa-Carleton Detention Centre, RG 20-84-1-19; AO microfilm MS 5166

charges was kept in civil registers, mainly concerning unfortunate debtors who might spend as much as a month in jail until they settled with a creditor or paid bail.

By 1850, there were at least eight prisons in the province for major offenders. "Origins of the Penitentiary System in Upper Canada" by Rainer Baehre in *Ontario History* Vol. 64 (1977) describes the historical development. A few noteworthy milestones were the opening of the Kingston Penitentiary in 1835, the Ontario Reformatory for Boys at Penetanguishene in 1859 and the Andrew Mercer Reformatory for Women in Toronto in 1878. LAC has records dating from 1835 for Kingston Penitentiary because it became a federal responsibility. The records contain inmate history ledgers, punishment books, reports from guards, medical registers, journals of wardens and many other items. Only a few prisoners' record books have been microfilmed, and it's necessary to consult LAC on-site finding aids No. 73-28 and 73-29 for access.

The annual *Journals of the Legislative Assembly* had intermittent reports naming convicts such as "Return of Convicts at the Penitentiary 1st October 1847" in 1848. Besides the names, information may be given on ages, physical description, type of crime and where sentenced, length of term or date of release and convict number. Hugh Armstrong lists 605 convicts who died at the Kingston Penitentiary between 1835 and 1915, extracted from the *Assembly Journal*, in *Families* Vol. 38 No. 4 (1999). The lists are also on his website, showing the date and cause of death, the crime committed, place of conviction/sentencing and, if available, age and place of birth.

Other prison and prison-related records are available at either LAC or AO, depending on whether an institution became a provincial or federal responsibility. Certainly not all records have survived from the nineteenth century. More related material is at AO in the Preliminary Inventory of the Ministry of Correctional Services, including records for industrial schools, jails, detention centres and industrial farms. There is a standard thirty-year restriction on personal information, and some files may be closed altogether. Additional reading could be "Crime and Punishment in Early Upper Canada" by Elmes Henderson in *Ontario History* Vol. 26 (1926).

Criminal Justice

There is a well-prepared guide to criminal justice records at AO, RG 22-392. A feature of the on-site paper finding aid is a four-part index to criminal indictment case files, from 1853 to 1929.The file numbers can be accessed in three ways: by alphabetical indexes to the surnames of defendants, by county name or by the name of the offence. A fourth index relates solely to indicted female criminals. References to all the individual files, close to 11,000, are posted online at the AO website in the county arrangement— alphabetical by county name and chronological within each county. Unfortunately, there are a few gaps in the records for some of the counties.

The files themselves consist of reports about the prosecution's cases in the Assize Court sitting. Defence material is not included unless there is a transcript of the trial itself. There are various selected documents and summaries, such as the bill of indictment, police information and the jury's verdict. Some files may have a trial transcript, evidence from witnesses, a coroner's report, the Crown Attorney's notes and preparations and other material. See "Criminal Assize Clerk: Indictment Case Files 1853-1929" by Ruth Burkholder in *Families* Vol. 34, No. 1 (1995).

As a side note, convictions for a broad number of crimes

QUARTERLY RETURNS OF CONVICTIONS

"Quarterly Returns of Convictions," The Age (Strathroy, Ontario): The Age Supplement, 15 April 1886

from eighteenth century times those committed against property or person—were subject to capital punishment. In practice, many cases were commuted to banishment or transportation from the province, for a specified period. Banishment required the convict to exit the province within eight days. Failure to comply meant facing the death penalty by hanging. Transportation to a penal colony in Bermuda or Van Dieman's Land (Tasmania) incurred considerable expense for the government and was employed most notably after the 1837 Rebellion. Although hanging continued for a reduced number of crimes, the death penalty was not officially abolished in Canada until 1976.

Records of the provincial Ministry of the Attorney General, RG 4 at AO, and RG 20, Records Related to Correctional Services Functions, are additional sources of possible interest. The most complete finding aids are in the AO Reading Room.

Treason

Prosecution of traitors to the Crown occurred most noticeably after the War of 1812–1814 and the Rebellion of 1837. The proceedings took place in the Assize Courts, but few actual trial records exist as mentioned above. High Treason records for 1814 at AO contain extant material on the trials of six men, and Commissions and Inquisitions on the forfeited lands of 23 men. (The Alien Act passed in 1814 said the lands of American-born subjects who left Canada for the United States after 1 July 1814 would be forfeited.) *Register of Persons Connected with High Treason* (during the War of 1812–1814) was compiled many years ago and has been reproduced by Brant County Branch OGS. Unfortunately it consists only of names with no source references. "The Ancaster 'Bloody Assize' of 1814" by William R. Riddell in *Ontario History* Vol. 20 (1920), is a graphic account of trials in the Gore District.

At LAC and AO the calendar to Upper Canada Sundries leads into the correspondence of the civil secretary regarding the evidence collected and men incarcerated after the 1837 Rebellion (LAC finding aid 881). Most men who were under suspicion were captured within two weeks of the aftermath, in December 1837, and charged with treason or insurrection. A certain number were able to escape capture by fleeing into the United States, as the leading figure, William Lyon Mackenzie, did. But hundreds languished in district jails awaiting trial, and the Sundries contain a number of petitions signed by dozens of supporters for release of lesser transgressors. Many of them were ultimately set free or pardoned on security for good behaviour. Other convicts were transported to Van Dieman's Land for life or for specific periods. Some were transported to the penitentiary at Fort Henry (Kingston) and some were banished from the province for life. A number of death sentences were commuted to transportation, but three were executed: Samuel Lount, Peter Matthews and James Morrow.

AO has a slim collection of High Treason (1838) records. The names involved are Ebenezer Wilcox, John Stewart the Younger and William Ketchum. Toronto Branch of OGS published *Rebels Arrested in Upper Canada 1837-1838*, which is a reprint of the list of 884 prisoners first published in newspapers in 1838, and reproduced in Charles Lindsey's *The Life and Times of William Lyon Mackenzie*. The listing includes "fugitives under indictment," that is, the men who had escaped capture or prison. On the 150th anniversary of the Rebellion, the Ontario Historical

Society sponsored a conference, and the resulting papers were published as *1837 Rebellion Remembered*, covering many aspects of society and politics in Upper Canada of the time.

Some articles for extra reading are:

"A Trial for High Treason in 1838" by William R. Riddell in *Ontario History* Vol. 17 (1919).

James A. Gibson's "Political Prisoners, Transportation for Life, and Responsible Government in Canada" in *Ontario History* Vol. 47 (December 1975).

"The Books of the Political Prisoners and Exiles of 1838" by John D. Barnett in *Ontario History* Vol. 16 (1918). "John Beverley Robinson and the Trials for Treason in 1814" by Ernest A. Cruikshank, in *Ontario History* Vol. 25 (1929).

See also "The Fenian Trials in the Province of Canada, 1866-7: A Case Study of Law and Politics in Action" by W.S. Neidhardt in *Ontario History* Vol. 66 (March 1974), which treats the Fenian Raids of the 1860s.

Other Court Sources

Chancery Court

From 1837 to 1881, the Chancery Court dealt with matters of equity or trusts, as in the estates of minors or the mentally impaired, or certain civil disputes. The court ruled on division of assets, foreclosure of mortgages, partnership settlements and other business of a personal nature. This court's rulings were based on the principle of fairness case by case, rather than precedents of common law. As a genealogist, you may come across a reference to a vesting order in a land abstract index to deeds, which is a Chancery judgment registered on a piece of property. You can obtain a copy of the vesting order through the land registry office, but it may not yield much more information than the final ownership decision.

On the other hand, Quieting Titles case files 1866–1964 are held in the historical Chancery Court records at AO. The files include the petitions from the appealing parties and other documentation. Registers that recorded certificates of title issued by the court are available from 1871 to 1964. Certain parts of the series are indexed or alphabetically filed. More information is available through a search for "chancery" in the Archives Descriptive Database.

In 1881 Chancery Court was merged with the Court of Queen's Bench and others, as above, to form the Supreme Court of Ontario. Its function continued as Chancery division under the High Court of Justice.

Coroners' Inquests

The records of inquests into suspicious or unexplained deaths would be extremely interesting to some genealogists, but relatively little material is extant from the nineteenth century. In 1880, there were some 700 coroners in the province when new legislation was passed to define their duties. An inquest could be held either by a request from the County Crown Attorney or by a coroner's opinion that death was not the result of natural causes or "mere accident or mischance." A jury would be called to examine evidence and witnesses. Surviving inquest reports made by county coroners vary in number and time periods. Many records have undoubtedly been destroyed in intervening years, but some may still rest in a county courthouse.

Inquest records can be found at AO in finding aids for Court Records and the Ministry of the Solicitor General or by searching AO's Archives Descriptive Database for inquests. A few records are available as early as the 1820s for some of the former districts. A 100-year restriction applies to more modern records. Files saved by the Chief Coroner's Office are representative only, and are by no means all the files from that period. From 1949 to 1980 the Chief Coroner's files retained highly visible or publicized tragedies, like the 1949 *Noronic* ship fire and its victims in Toronto Harbour. Scattered coroners' returns are accessible on LAC microfilm for the year 1873 for the Counties of Oxford, Grey, Bruce, Wellington, Dufferin, Leeds & Grenville and Wentworth.

Inquests are yet another circumstance when newspaper coverage, if the date of death is known, may supply further information. Many inquests were reported locally to avid readers and give insight to contemporary social sensibilities.

Reading and Reference

Armstrong, Frederick H. *Upper Canada Justices of the Peace and Association.* Toronto, ON: Ontario Genealogical Society, 2007.

Bourrie, Doris. *Pioneers of Upper Canada, 1783-1839.* Thornhill, ON: Doris Bourrie, 1991.

Corupe, Linda, transcriber and indexer. *Minutes of the Courts of Quarter Sessions of the Peace, for the Mecklenburg/Midland District.* Vol. 1: 1789-1790, 1794-1804, 1807-1816. Bolton, ON: Linda Corupe, 2001.

_____, transcriber and indexer. *Upper Canadian Justice: Early Assize Court Records (Court of Oyer and Terminer) of Ontario.* Vol. 1, 1792-1809. Bolton, ON: Linda Corupe, 2004.

Duquemin, Colin K. *Niagara Rebels: The Niagara Frontier in the Upper Canada Rebellion 1837-1838.* St. Catharines, ON: Canadian Canal Society, 2001.

Gibson, June, compiler, Elizabeth Hancocks, indexer, and Shannon Hancocks. *Surrogate Court Index of Ontario, Canada, 1859-1900.* 27 volumes. 1988-1994. Second edition. Campbellville, ON: Global Heritage Press, 2005.

Jones, James E. *Pioneer Crimes and Punishments in Toronto and the Home District.* Toronto, ON: George N. Morang, 1924.

Lindsey, Charles. *The Life and Times of William Lyon Mackenzie: With an Account of the Canadian Rebellion of 1837, and the Subsequent Frontier Disturbances, Chiefly from Unpublished Documents.* 2 volumes. Toronto, ON: P.R. Randall, 1862. Also reproduced in microform by Canadian Institute for Historical Microreproduction.

Kieran, Sheila. *The Family Matters: Two Centuries of Family Law and Life in Ontario.* Toronto, ON: Key Porter Books, 1986.

Oliver, Peter. *"Terror to Evil Doers": Prisons and Punishments in Nineteenth Century Ontario.* Toronto, ON: University of Toronto Press, 1998.

Rebels Arrested in Upper Canada, 1837-1838. Toronto, ON: Toronto Branch OGS, 1987.

Reports of the Department of Public Records and Archives of Ontario. Toronto, ON: King's Printer: 14th *Report* (1917): Hesse, Mecklenburg, Luneburg minute books, Court of Common Pleas, 1789-1794. 21st *Report* (1932): Home District 1800-1811. 22nd *Report* (1933): London District 1800-1809 and 1813-1818.

Shepard, Catherine. *Surrogate Court Records at the Archives of Ontario: A Genealogical Research Guide.* Toronto, ON: Ontario Genealogical Society, 1984.

Zufelt, Bill, editor. *Court of Probate: Registers and Estate Files at the Archives of Ontario (1793-1859).* Toronto, ON: Ontario Genealogical Society, 1986.

Hugh Armstrong. "Convict Deaths at Kingston Penitentiary, 1835-1915." Hugh Armstrong's Genealogy Site. www.cangenealogy.com/armstrong/index.htm.

Linda Corupe. *Genealogy Publications of Ontario and Quebec.* www.lindacorupe.com

Peter Vronsky. "History of Justice and Policing." *Crime and Punishment in Upper Canada 1790-1834.* www.russianbooks.org/crime/cp0.htm.

8

Settlement, Immigration, Naturalization

Reference Dates

1783	Opening of western Quebec to refugee Loyalists
1800	Large grant to Timothy Rogers for Quaker settlement in York County
1803	British Passenger Act; large grant to Col. Thomas Talbot for settlement extending from north shore of Lake Erie
1804	Lord Selkirk's short-lived Baldoon settlement
1805	German Company settlement in Waterloo County
1815	Military supervision began in Richmond and Perth settlements, Lanark County; majority of Selkirk settlers at Red River leave for Upper Canada
1823	Peter Robinson emigrants from Ireland begin to settle in Lanark and Peterborough Counties
1828	Naturalization registers began; Drummond Island migration to Penetanguishene
1852	Immigration became a Canadian rather than Imperial responsibility
1865	Passenger lists for ships arriving at the port of Quebec exist from this date
1869	First organized party of accompanied immigrant children arrived in Canada
1908	Border ports of entry established for Canadian customs and immigration
1947	Canadian Citizenship Act

This chapter will mention some of the pioneer settlement groups in Upper Canada and Canada West and the process that evolved to oversee increasing immigrant numbers. From Loyalist times, new settlement was managed by the British military and then by the Colonial Office until provincial officials necessarily played a larger role. Long before Confederation, the office of the provincial lieutenant governor was involved in assisting incoming immigrants. For a time in that early period, Crown land agents were expected to provide aid in settling newcomers in their areas. Then the provincial department of agriculture became responsible for immigration, and its correspondence registers from 1852 to 1893 are full of nominal references, with finding aids at Library and Archives Canada. *Families* Vol. 16, No. 4 (1977) contains Patricia Kennedy's "Records of the Immigration Process: Pre-Confederation." Later and into modern times, immigration to Canada was handled as a branch in a succession of federal departments.

Natives and Fur Traders

Native Ancestry

In spite of the misnomer, the term Indian has long been used in the classification of records pertaining to native Canadian and Ontario peoples. While "native" or "aboriginal" may be more appropriate, and First Nations is now widely used, the term Indian is used here for archival and historical sources. The British royal proclamation of 1763 is considered a landmark because the conquering British recognized native entitlement to the lands they occupied. Only the Crown could legitimately treat with the natives for the purchase of their lands. Some first recommendations for general reading are *Atlas of Great Lakes Indian History* and *Akwesasne to Wunnumin Lake, Profiles of Aboriginal Communities in Ontario.*

The current federal Department of Indian Affairs (DIA) was formerly the Department of Indian Affairs and Northern Development (DIAND). Its precursors date back to the eighteenth century colonial Indian Department under Sir William Johnson. A bureaucratic concept of paternalism evolved toward nearly all facets of native life. Therefore DIA contains a huge amount of historical material relevant to native status. Native reserves became common after British rule, financed in part by the original treaty lands, but with increasing expenses subsidized by the federal government. Reserves were and are collective property of the bands (First Nations) that inhabit them. Legal status of band membership became a matter outlined by successive federal

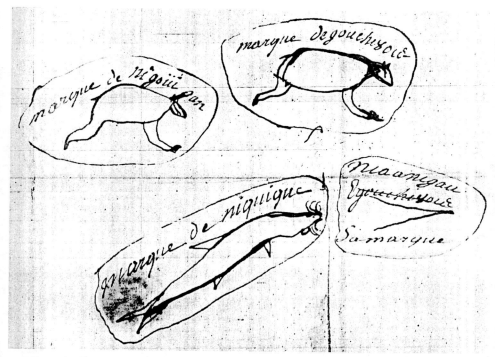

Ojibwa chiefs' signatures (1774), Alexis Maisonville petition (1790), Upper Canada Land Petitions, RG 1, L 3, vol. 327, M bundle 1, petition 202; Library and Archives Canada microfilm C-2191

legislation and ultimately determined by the local band councils.

In tracing native ancestry, the descendant must document a lineage back in time to an ancestor identified in contemporary sources as an Indian. However, finding a native ancestor several generations ago does not mean that a descendant can necessarily obtain First Nations status today. Depending on the tribe or the band, membership may be allowed simply through lineal descent no matter how many generations intervene, or it may be limited to "blood quantum." The latter usually means no less than one-fourth native blood, in other words, at least one full-blooded native grandparent. The quest for proving First Nations status diverges from regular genealogical research in that applications must meet both government and band approval. Most records created by band councils are restricted to their own use, but some historical material is included in Library and Archives Canada's RG 10 collection.

Highly recommended is the chapter called "Indian Status, Membership, and Family History" in Bennett McCardle's *Indian History and Claims: A Research Handbook*. Cecilia Carpenter's

How to Research American Indian Blood Lines: A Manual on Indian Genealogical Research is a practical handbook. Its emphasis on American Indians is still useful from a Canadian perspective. Natives living close to the international border were and are accustomed to crossing back and forth between mutual communities. Some knowledge of research in states like New York and Michigan will be helpful for certain families.

The Woodland Cultural Centre in Brantford is situated on Six Nations land, but its main focus is on the heritage of all Eastern Woodland First Nations. Housed in the former Mohawk Institute, the centre hosts a very fine museum, art gallery, language program and special events. To use the resources in its large research library, you must make an advance appointment (contact through its website or address in Appendix III).

LAC Sources

In its RG 10, LAC holds the largest source of material created by the federal government. Most of this record group is microfilmed on over 3,000 reels with records of the Indian superintendencies, agencies, administration, commissions, bands, schools, land records and more. Your research can start by consulting the several thematic guides on the Canadian Genealogy Centre website (Aboriginal Peoples), each of which leads to many descriptions, details and links, although the entire vast collection may not yet be completely described online. The guides "Researching Your Aboriginal Ancestors at Library and Archives Canada" and "Guide to the Records of the Government of Canada" complement Russell's *Indian Affairs Records at Library and Archives Canada*.

In using census returns, researchers are referred especially to those from 1891 onward, as in Chapter 5. Other census years may have specific sections for reserves and Indian lands.

AO Sources

For its share of resources, the Archives of Ontario published James Morrison's *Aboriginal Peoples in the Archives, a Guide to Sources in the Archives of Ontario*. First Nations tribes prominent in the history of this province are listed in the introduction. The book also lists the Indian reserves or communities recognized by successive governments over the years. A reference map shows all the treaty lands in Ontario. There are no fewer than 30 record groups at AO in which native information can be found. In addition, AO has select series of LAC's RG 10 and other helpful

LAC diffusion microfilms. To use the AO records, your first step should be the online and print guide "Aboriginal Sources at the Archives of Ontario: Their Use in Researching Native Ancestry and Status."

An important book published by OGS is *Understanding Ontario First Nations Genealogical Records* by David Faux. This is a thoroughly researched handbook for those groups of the Iroquois confederacy that removed to present-day Ontario after the American Revolutionary War—Cayuga, Mohawk, Oneida, Onondaga, Seneca and Tuscarora. Faux's notes and references alone make a complete list of source material. Copious examples of problem-solving techniques will encourage novices and also non-Six Nations researchers. Other books can be found using the tribal name as a key word in library catalogues. Some that may prove of interest for various tribes and other reservations are *Minishenhying Anishnaabe-aki or Walpole Island* by Nin.Da.Waab. Jig. See also publications by Fenton and Graham in the Reading and Reference section. *The Roll Call of the Iroquois Chiefs: A Study of a Mnemonic Cane from the Six Nations Reserve* was originally published by the Smithsonian Institution in Washington DC.

Historical mission and church registers for christianized natives and Métis are found in a variety of places or publications:

- The journals of Rev. Allen Salt, a Methodist missionary, with a few entries for Lac-la-Pluie in Rainy River District 1854-1855, Muncey Indian Mission in Middlesex County 1874, more coverage for Parry Island 1883-1899, and Christian and Beausoleil Islands in Georgian Bay 1875-1882; LAC microfilm C-15709.

- Records of the Moravian Mission among the Indians of North America from the Moravian Church Archives in Bethlehem, Pennsylvania are on 40 reels of microfilm and include some from southwestern Ontario.

- A transcript of Rev. Henry Barclay's register of baptisms, marriages, communicants and funerals among the Mohawks in New York 1735-1746 is available at the Montgomery County Archives in Fonda, NY.

- Baptisms from the LaPointe and Bayfield Indian Missions in upper Michigan ("Baptismal Records of Father Baraga") 1835-1887 were published serially. They began in *Lost in Canada?* Vol. 16, No. 4 (1992) and continued each following issue, including its successor *Canadian-American Journal of History and Genealogy for Canadian, French and Métis Study.*

The original register is at the State Historical Society of Wisconsin.

- Wesleyan Methodist vital records from the New Credit reserve in Brant County 1859-1881 are at the United Church Archives. AO has a microfilm copy.

- Transcripts of the registers of Her Majesty's Chapel of the Mohawks-Six Nations 1827-1877 can be purchased from Brant County Branch OGS.

- Original registers of St. Johns Church in Tuscarora Township are held at the Anglican Diocese of Huron. The FHL has a microfilm copy 1829-1866, while the Woodland Indian Cultural Educational Centre has photocopies 1867-1914.

See Appendix III for addresses and/or at the end of the chapter for websites.

The "Genealogy" page on the *Sneakers* website is of interest for Ojibway/Chippewa researchers. Numerous sources with information are given for natives of the Algoma District, Sault Ste. Marie area and Manitoulin Island. Links will also take you to even more sites.

Some articles to read:

"Documenting Six Nations Ancestry" by David Faux in *Families* Vol. 20, No. 1 (1981).

"The Tyendinaga Mohawks" by C.H. Torok in *Ontario History* Vol. 57 (1965).

"A List of Mixed-Blood Chippewa of Lake Superior, 1839" in *Lost in Canada?* Vol. 16, No. 1 (1991).

"The Sunegoos: A Nineteenth Century Mississauga Family" was the J. Richard Houston Memorial Lecture in *Families* Vol. 38, No. 3 (1999) by Donald B. Smith. It gives a very fine historical portrait of the New Credit First Nation.

"Catholic Missionary Labours on the Lake Superior Frontier" by Francis J. Nelligan in *Ontario History* Vol. 51 (1959).

The Trent University library has an online "First Nations Periodical Index" with links to newsletters and journals.

Fur Trade

Fur trading and exploration predated official settlement in the western part of Quebec. Some records from the fur trade era, such as those of the North West Company or the American Fur Company, and papers of individuals, for example, Simon Fraser, are held at LAC but they are not large collections. Fur Trade Papers c1812-1885 at AO include some private and some company papers. Under British rule from 1763, government licenses were required to trade with the Indians. The original licenses at LAC have been microfilmed. The business centre of the North West Company was Montreal, with posts along the routes within this province at Detroit, Michilimackinac and Fort William. French Canadians and Scots played a large role as working voyageurs. Some of them eventually settled in small clusters by the posts, but by and large they led an itinerant life. The best surviving collection of North West Company records can be found in the Hudson's Bay Company archives.

In a period before civil or church authority had been established, Montreal and Detroit are important locations for potential genealogical information about fur traders and their families. Marriages or baptisms could well have been solemnized or confirmed at those bases between lengthy trips. Some knowledge of the routes they used and the locations of military or trading posts is necessary for tracing records of military chaplains or travelling missionaries. See "Early Traders and Trade Routes in Ontario and the West" by E.A. Cruikshank in *Transactions of the Canadian Institute* (1891-1892). Hilda Beaty's article "Louis and Toussaint Charbonneau" in *Families* Vol. 26, No. 1 (1987) illustrates where some of these voyageurs travelled all over the continent and how vital records for them were found in Detroit. Useful publications by Donna Valley Stuart and others are in the Reading and Reference section.

Records created by military officials at forts along the travel routes, even those involving civilians, returned to England with the commanding officer. Missionary records likely devolved to superiors of the priest or minister's home base. Descendants of voyageurs in Ontario still live in pockets along the shores of lakes St. Clair and Huron. The Penetanguishene Centennial Museum and Archives is an excellent resource centre for French and native ancestors with fur trade and later connections. Its Georgian Bay Heritage League collection includes an impressive number of compiled family histories and church and mission records, especially marriage registers for Ontario and many parts of Quebec. Indexes to some of their many local cemetery transcripts are searchable online. Archives staff will provide research services if you can't arrange a personal visit.

Other articles are John Dulong's "Tracing Your Voyageur Ancestors" in *Proceedings of the OGS Seminar '95* and James Hansen's "Tracing the Voyageurs" in *OGS Seminar Annual 1986.*

The latter *Annual* also includes "The Draper Manuscripts" by Hansen who is the acknowledged expert on the large Draper Manuscript collection held at the State Historical Society of Wisconsin. The collection includes personal papers of many men directly involved in the fur business.

Hudson's Bay Company

The North West Company merged with the Hudson's Bay Company in 1821. The HBC had been involved in North American fur trading and exploration since 1670. In 1994 the company, based in London, donated its extensive archives and museum collections to the province of Manitoba. Thus, there are over 300 years of HBC holdings and records in the Archives of Manitoba in Winnipeg. In 2007 the Hudson's Bay Company Archives was officially recognized as a significant world heritage collection in the UNESCO Memory of the World Registry.

Employees of the company, or "servants" as they were known, came from both the British Isles and North America. The material also has references to native people and Métis. HBC servants worked at many trading posts within the boundaries of this province. In an appendix to her presentations on the HBC in OGS *Seminar Annual 1983*, Judith Beattie listed nineteen HBC posts in Ontario with the types and dates of records available. One of her articles, "The Hudson's Bay Company: A Presence in Northern Ontario," uses ten men as examples of what the records will reveal. Contract records can show name, age, home parish, occupation, wages and employment locations. Other types of records are employment ledgers, account books, inventories, pensions, wills and related papers, journals, maps and much more.

Copies of the HBC microfilmed finding aid are available at a number of Ontario locales, including LAC, the OGS Library, Lakehead University Library, Laurentian University Library and university archives at Queen's, Guelph and Trent. More to the point, there is much to explore on the HBC website. Archives staff have created biographical sheets, searchable alphabetically, for individual servants. Employment history is shown, wife and children, if known and reference to the archival documentation. Details for individual posts can also be found by using the search feature. Interlibrary loan is available for some microfilm. Otherwise, the archives will handle requests for document copies and provide a limited research service. LAC has copies of microfilmed HBC material.

Sponsored and Group Emigration

The governments of both Canada and Britain, as well as local authorities in the British Isles, arranged financially assisted emigration for unemployed or indigent labourers and their families. Emigration plans gave relief to over-burdened parish systems in England and provided Upper Canada with a loyal and dependable population. Emigration societies were a rather common phenomenon by which the socially conscientious could help their less fortunate citizens to more promising opportunities in the new world. Because there is a dearth of passenger arrival records in Canada before 1865, this chapter mentions some of the identified groups of emigrants to Ontario—those for which any kind of emigration, arrival, or settlement records are available. Many came on ships chartered for the purpose. Other groups, such as Quakers and Pennsylvania Germans, came overland from the United States.

A few Colonial Office records 1817–1831 regarding subsidized emigration plans are indexed by surname at LAC. For instance, they include ships' passenger lists for some of the Peter Robinson settlers and other groups that went to the Lanark County area. Those lists are also in the Peter Robinson fonds at AO. "Military Emigrants" and "Scotch Emigrants" were discussed in Chapter 5, under OLRI. In *Families* Vol. 25, No. 2 (1986), there is an article by Constance C. Dods called "A Selection of Lists from British Military Records, Series C" that lists names extracted from the records of various emigration societies in 1820.

Some of the leaders of early group migrations were Joseph Brant who led the Six Nations to the Grand River; Peter Robinson bringing Irish to Lanark and Peterborough counties; Timothy Rogers' Quakers; Berczy's German settlers; the Comte de Puisaye's French Royalists in York County; Allan McMillan's shiploads of Lochaber Highlanders to Glengarry County; Lord Selkirk's short-lived Baldoon experiment in Kent County; Lord Egremont's Petworth emigrants from Sussex, England; and Col. Thomas Talbot's settlements in western Ontario. The private papers or collections of some of these individuals can be seen at LAC or AO, and most have been the subjects of numerous books. Either their papers or the books may have names of emigrants in their groups. An association exists for the descendants of 1794 German pioneers in Markham Township, led by William Moll Berczy who was also instrumental in the development of early York.

Before and after the turn of the nineteenth century, a number of entrepreneurs applied for the grant of an entire township, on behalf of a group of associates. Whether they received such a grant depended on the stipulations and expectations of the Executive Council. Correspondence of this nature can be found in Upper Canada land petitions or Upper Canada Sundries. "Land Settlement in Upper Canada, 1783-1840" by Gilbert C. Anderson in the sixteenth *Report of the Department of Archives* (1920) gives the details of many settlement schemes.

Dozens of organized societies existed to promote the new waves of immigration throughout the nineteenth century and into the twentieth. Some had a short life span, others continued for some time. The Bytown and Ottawa Emigration Society was formed as Friends of Emigration as early as 1841. The British Colonial Emigration Society was established in London, England, in 1869. Others were created by religious groups. Whether they were based in Britain or in Canada, the societies had recruitment agents in place overseas. Continental Europe was eventually represented by interested parties. Genealogists are encouraged to explore such groups and sponsors if they are applicable.

Some classic or useful books about immigrant groups are listed in the Reading and Reference section. Numerous articles have appeared in periodicals like *Families, Ontario History, Canadian Historical Review, The Ontario Register,* back issues of the defunct *Canadian Genealogist* and local publications. The following list of articles is representative only. They may or may not have lists of emigrants.

"Baldoon: Success or Failure" by A.E.D. MacKenzie in *Families* Vol. 12, No. 3 (1973).

"Hessian Migration to the Canada Company's Huron Tract" by Stafford Johnston in *Families* Vol. 15, No. 4 (1976).

"The Irish Emigrant Settler in the Pioneer Kawarthas" by Howard Pammett in *Families* Vol. 17, No. 4 (1978).

"The Settlement of Manitoulin Island" by Shelley J. Pearson in *Families* Vol. 21, No. 1 (1982).

"Tracing Emigrant Networks: North East Scots in Canada, 1830-1900" by Marjory Harper in *Families* Vol. 30, No. 1 (1991).

"The Markham Berczy Settlers" by Robert J. Shank in *Families* Vol. 33, No. 1 (1994).

"Niagara Mennonite Settlers along the River and Lake Erie" by Harold Nigh in *OGS Seminar Annual, 1987.*

"Red River Colonists and Lake Erie Pioneers" by Robert A. Jones in *Canadian Genealogist* Vol. 4, No. 2 (1982).

"The Migration of Voyageurs from Drummond Island to Penetanguishene in 1828" by A.C. Osborne in *Ontario History* Vol. 3 (1901).

"First Settlements of Pennsylvania Mennonites in Upper Canada" by W.H. Breithaupt in *Ontario History* Vol. 23 (1923).

"Assisted Emigration from Ireland to Upper Canada under Peter Robinson in 1825" by Howard Pammett in *Ontario History* Vol. 31 (1936).

"Colonel Talbot's Principality" by Fred Coyne Hamil in *Ontario History* Vol. 44 (1952).

"The First Four Years of the Settlement on the Canadian Side of the Detroit River" by Rev. E. J. Lajeunesse in *Ontario History* Vol. 47 (1955).

"The Petworth Emigration Committee: Lord Egremont's Assisted Emigrations from Sussex to Upper Canada, 1832-37" by Wendy Cameron in *Ontario History* Vol. 65 (1973).

Ships' Lists and Border Crossings

Before 1865

Almost everyone wants to find their emigrating family on a ship's list—clear evidence that they did indeed endure the long and often cruel voyage—but most will be disappointed in the pre-1865 era. The critical element here for genealogists is that ships' manifests, also known as passenger lists, were not officially maintained before 1865 in Canada. Quebec City, the port most commonly associated with emigrants to Upper Canada and Canada West, was the first official port of entry for Canada. Its ships' arrival lists date from 1865.

By 1803 the British government required a ship's master, or captain, to list all passengers at his point of departure. By 1817 the same was required at his disembarkation port. These lists were never officially preserved by government although a few have been located, apparently kept for shipping company purposes. In the pre-1865 period, almost every passenger ship arriving in Canada was from the British Isles. There are some records of births, marriages and deaths at sea in the Board of Trade series at The National Archives in England. Some emigrants from other overseas countries did come to Canada in this period, but the majority would have first travelled to Britain to obtain the necessary passage.

A popularly consulted publication is Filby and Meyer's *Passenger and Immigration Lists Index*, a huge index to names arriving in North America from overseas, up to the end of the nineteenth century. Originally published in three volumes, several supplements have been added. Please be aware that the sources for these names are lists that have been *published*; they do not include original or manuscript sources that have never been published. In some cases, a published list is the only surviving source of the information. Ships arriving at Canadian ports, as well as American ones, are included. The compilers located some lists of passengers to Canada in obscure or out-of-print sources. Filby's article "Passenger Lists and Naturalizations" appeared in the OGS *Seminar Annual, 1985*. Many libraries with genealogy collections have the published series. The entire *Index* is now searchable at *Ancestry.com* or on CD-ROM.

Emigrants destined for this province sometimes took a perhaps less expensive passage to an American port. When attempting to track your ancestor's route into Ontario in this period, it is essential to understand the importance of available travel modes. For Americans coming into Canada from the east, and overseas emigrants who sailed to American ports, the opening of the Champlain, Erie and Oswego Canals by 1828 certainly facilitated migration from New York, New England and other points. Some emigrants from the British Isles taking passage to New York intended to remain in the United States. Not wishing to miss an opportunity to acquire reliable settlers, the British consul in New York in 1817 was instructed to give financial assistance to those who would agree to travel on to the Canadas or Nova Scotia. Those headed for Upper Canada received passage money for the trip between Oswego and York, or were charged only half fees for free land grants. Evidence can sometimes be found in Upper Canada land petitions, when the petitioner included a certificate or type of early passport signed by Consul James Buchanan. Doris Bourrie abstracted relevant names from another series, the Upper Canada Sundries, in "British Emigrants from New York to York, Upper Canada, 1817" in *Families* Vol. 29, No. 4 (1990).

Two notable websites for early ships' lists are *Olive Tree Genealogy* and *Immigrants to Canada*. Both feature some ships' passenger lists gleaned from the pre-1865 period, as well other sources and links that provide immigration information. Marjorie Kohli's site *Immigrants to Canada* is dedicated to all aspects of immigration in the nineteenth century. Besides the names of hundreds of ships, the website includes items from parliamentary and sessional papers, voyage accounts, immigration reports, handbooks for emigrants, steamship lines and port information. Whenever available, the names of individuals are listed.

Thomas Russell "passport" (1819), Upper Canada Land Petitions, RG 1, L 3, vol. 429, R bundle 12, petition 219; Library and Archives Canada microfilm C-2743

Quarantine

During the long ocean voyages to Canada early in the nineteenth century, contagious diseases carried by ship passengers made it necessary to establish quarantine stations. Grosse Ile in the St. Lawrence River northeast of and downstream from the city of Quebec was chosen as the control site in 1832, its function lasting for over 100 years. Thousands were detained in rudimentary facilities, and thousands died there from the ravages of such diseases as cholera and typhoid. The great majority were from Ireland. Upper Canada was the intended destination for many, and surviving family members eventually did arrive here. Comparatively few records of names or personal memorials of burials exist from the period of epidemics.

Parks Canada commemorates Grosse Ile with its Irish Memorial National Historic Site. When known, the names of those who died were inscribed on the Memorial. They can also be viewed online where a virtual tour of the island is also given. Highly recommended reading is *Grosse Ile, Gateway to Canada, 1832-1937,* which has appendices of orphaned children and some reported deaths from 1847, at the height of the typhus epidemic. Author Marianna O'Gallagher was an early advocate for the recognition of the island's role in immigration history. Thomas Dukes also wrote about "La Grosse Ile and Its Memorials" in *Families* Vol. 26, No. 4 (1987). Ireland Park now stands on the waterfront in Toronto, near the former immigration sheds, as another tribute to the famine immigrants. The Park is twinned with sculptures on Dublin's Custom House Quay.

In the 1820s, the *Quebec Mercury* newspaper was in the habit of publishing deaths that occurred in the Marine and Emigrant Hospital in that city. Lists of names from July 1829 to November 1830 were published in the Ottawa Branch OGS *News* Vol. 15, No. 4 (1982), the great majority of whom were Irish immigrants. "Some Scottish Emigrants of 1832" by George A. MacKenzie in *Families* Vol. 28, No. 4 (1989) gives an 1832 passenger list as published in the *Quebec Gazette.* The periodical *Lost in Canada?* also occasionally published passenger lists that appeared in the same newspaper, in the following issues:

Vol. 12, No. 2 (May 1986) for 1815

Vol. 12, No. 3 (August 1986) for 1805 and 1814

Vol. 15, No. 2 (May 1989) for 1815

Vol. 15, No. 4 (Fall 1990) for 1838

Vol. 14, No. 2 (May 1988) for 1824

Provincial Agents

Besides the controls that were developed at the entry port of Quebec, further bureaucratic measures were taken along the St. Lawrence River and Great Lakes routes into Upper Canada. The position of provincial emigration agent was created in 1833 to oversee the transit and placement of immigrants, and assist the sick or indigent. This action relieved the office of the Lieutenant Governor and Crown land agents from such duties. A few sources of such early assistance survive. The Society for the Relief of Strangers in Distress was formed in 1817 to aid immigrants arriving in the town of York. Its name was later changed to Society for the Relief of the Sick and Destitute, and a book of the same title by Harrison and Martin contains names and family information from its records. The patient register of admissions and discharges from Toronto's temporary Convalescent and Fever Hospital 1847-1848 is available at AO on microfilm MS 6916. Leone Hinds published "Destitute and Sick Emigrants at Prescott, 1835" in *Families* Vol. 33, No. 3 (1994) as another example.

Contained in the AO collection of Emigrant Office records are 22 volumes of material and names for emigrant arrivals at Toronto, Kingston, Hamilton and Quebec, ranging from 1835 to 1874. Among them are ledgers created by the chief emigrant agent for Upper Canada and Canada West, Anthony B. Hawke. See the Post-1865 section for further information, and the AO Inventory 11, Ontario Immigration Records.

After 1865

After the turning point of 1865, ships' passenger arrival lists to Canada are available and have been microfilmed. The two official ports of entry in the nineteenth century were Quebec, beginning in 1865, and Halifax from 1881. More official ports were later delegated on the east and west coasts, even though passenger ships had arrived there earlier: Saint John, New Brunswick, in 1900, and Sydney, Nova Scotia, in 1906. Pacific ports at Vancouver and Victoria (both 1905) are likely of less relevance for ancestors who came to Ontario. All these series extend to 1935 on microfilm at LAC (copies at FHL). Ships' manifests after 1935 are still in the custody of Citizenship and Immigration Canada.

While Ontario itself does not have ocean ports, thousands of emigrants each year landing in Quebec and Halifax were destined for Ontario. The microfilms have been arranged by the name of the port, with the Quebec lists also available at AO. Thereafter, the arrangement is chronological by year of arrival. From 1865 to 1900 there will be a list of the names of ships at the beginning of each year. Lists also exist 1905-1931 at LAC for passengers entering New York and other eastern U.S. ports, only for those who stated Canada as a final destination.

Passenger manifest, S.S. Virginian, Quebec, 1 June 1906, p. 1, RG 76, C1a; Library and Archives Canada microfilm T-487

Passenger lists vary a great deal in content depending on times and regulations, but the best for genealogical information will include the names of all family members or single travellers, their ages, country of origin (occasionally a county in England), occupation, class of travel and eventual destination if beyond the port of arrival. The passenger lists 1865-1922 are available digitally through the Canadian Genealogy Centre *without nominal indexes* at this time. For interlibrary loan, the CGC provides microfilm reel numbers correlated to a ship's year of arrival. The search time can be considerably shortened if you can estimate the port and year of arrival.

Nominal indexes to the lists were non-existent for years, making them tedious and very time-consuming to search on generally unsatisfactory-quality microfilm. However, *Ancestry.ca* and LAC have partnered to index names for the port of Quebec arrivals 1865–1935, to make them available online at both websites. Further work is planned to encompass the digitization and indexing for other major Canadian ports of entry. Meanwhile, progress has been made on selected projects:

- A searchable database for the years 1925-1935, for arrivals from overseas and the United States to all ports, is available at CGC. The indexing is not linked to images and is considered incomplete, in that Canadians returning to the country, passengers in transit, and visitors are not included.

- The goal of the Nanaimo Family History Society is to index names from the ports of Quebec and Halifax from 1900 until 1919 when a new individual format (Form 30A) was adopted for passengers from overseas.

- The *ShipsList* website has a good selection of passenger lists for early ship arrivals in Canada.

- The *Ingeneas* website continues to add ships' lists to its database, among many other sources, including 1901 census extractions for "year of arrival."

Immigrants heading for Ontario may have arrived at the ports of Halifax or Saint John, then proceeded by railway to their westerly destinations. East coast arrivals should not be overlooked if Quebec searches are negative. Canada's Immigration Museum in Halifax is at Pier 21, the last surviving ocean immigration shed. It's also possible that ancestors destined for Canada and Ontario may have landed at an American port. Therefore, some cases may warrant a search of arrivals at likely sites such as New York's Castle Garden 1820-1892 or its successor Ellis Island 1892-1954 (the database of the latter currently goes to 1924). The sites are searchable online for names, as are a growing list of other U.S. ports.

Passengers on ships outbound from all ports in the U.K. for Canada (among other world destinations) have been organized into a database at the *FindMyPast* website. Taken from The National Archives' BT 27 collection, "Passenger Lists Leaving the U.K." spans the years 1890 to 1960.

A photograph of the vessel on which your ancestor arrived adds special interest to your family history. Suggestions for finding photos are the LAC website, or the Steamship Historical Society of America which has collected thousands of photographs of ships.

Provincial Agents

To return to the provincial level, the combined Emigrant Office (also called the Emigration Office) for Canada West and Canada East became more official in 1841. Individual agents were in place at points along the incoming routes, under the supervision in Toronto of Anthony B. Hawke, the first chief agent in Upper Canada and Canada West. As time went on and political jurisdictions evolved, the province of Ontario's erstwhile immigration powers overlapped and shared authority with colonial and then federal governments. The sources of interest are the letterbooks, reports and other registers prepared by the chief agent and field offices. Many, but not all, have been microfilmed. Researchers should first consult the AO inventory/finding aid *Ontario Immigration Records*. Fawne Stratford-Devai's *Province of Ontario Immigration Records* is the best explanatory guide.

In the AO collection of the Toronto Emigrant Office, later the Department of Immigration, we find correspondence (series A) which has names or lists of immigrants scattered within them. AO has a searchable online database to four volumes of the Hawke letterbooks 1865-1883 called *Toronto Emigrant Office Assisted Emigration Registers*. Some arrival and destination registers (series M) exist from the field agencies at Kingston, Montreal and Quebec with nominal lists. Another responsibility of the Emigration Office was to keep details of bonus plans and other special assistance to immigrants. Bonuses were offered as advance payment for ship passage or as post-settlement entitlement (series G, I, J, K, T, U). Files of applications for a refund bonus 1872-1876 and refund bonus certificates 1873-1874 are arranged alphabetically. A different series relates to railway passes issued for immigrants (series N) heading onward to an Ontario destination.

A great variety of records held by LAC are from the central registry files of the federal department of agriculture's immigration branch and its predecessors 1842-1893 (some diffusion microfilm also at AO). Lists of immigrants are among the correspondence, reports, references to sponsoring organizations and the sub-series of miscellaneous arrival records 1861-1893. The finding aid is presently limited to paper, but further description may be forthcoming on the LAC website.

A database at *Ancestry.ca* called "Canadian Immigrant Records" is an amalgam of extractions from several sources. By far the largest source utilized is the answers to the year of immigration question in the 1901 census, but the complete Ontario census is not represented.

Border Crossings

Up until 1908, there was free movement across the land border from the United States into Canada. Beginning in 1908 border ports of entry were established across Canada for the inspection and recording of *incoming* immigrants. Sources for railway arrivals from the U.S. do not exist—train passenger lists were not preserved in Canada. Although the entry points are called ports, they include inland crossing points as well as ferry ports and ship landings on lake and coastal areas. The Library and Archives Canada arrangement of the records by port, the large number of entry points and the lack of nominal indexing could mean another long search. Where the ancestor lived before and after his entry might help to determine the crossing point, and using directories may pinpoint the year of arrival.

When a family arrived together at a Canadian crossing point, the names of children as well as adults were recorded. The collected information includes ages, nationality, occupations, mode of travel, amount of cash in hand, former residence and intended destination. Of the border ports that were created, the following were in the province of Ontario from west to east between 1908 and 1918. The records of some ports begin later than others, and some lists are not in precise chronological order. Canadian offices were also located in Lewiston and Charlotte (Rochester's port), New York, very active ports for ferries to Canadian points on Lake Ontario. The Canadian Genealogy Centre lists the dates of the records and microfilm numbers.

Rainy River	Blind River
Fort Frances	Cutler
Pigeon River	Gore Bay
Fort William	Little Current
Port Arthur	Depot Harbour
Sault Ste. Marie	Parry Sound
Bruce Mines	Collingwood
Thessalon	Goderich

Point Edward	Port Dalhousie
Sarnia	Toronto
Courtright	Port Hope
Sombra	Cobourg
Port Lambton	Brighton
Walpole Island	Trenton
Wallaceburg	Belleville
Walkerville	Picton
Windsor	Deseronto
Ojibwa	Bath
Amherstburg	Kingston
Port Stanley	Wolfe Island
Port Burwell	Gananoque
Port Dover	Rockport
Port Colborne	Brockville
Windmill Point	Prescott
Crystal Beach	Iroquois
Fort Erie and Erie Beach	Morrisburg
Bridgeburg	Aultsville
Niagara Falls	Cornwall

From 1919 to 1924, Form 30 (similar to Form 30A for ship arrivals) was used at border crossings, with one page filled out for each individual. The procedure then reverted in 1925 to lists again, with many entries on one page. The records as a group are available up to 1935 at LAC. Thereafter records of entry into Canada remain with Citizenship and Immigration Canada, under restrictions of the federal privacy act (see Appendix II). An Access to Information request form is necessary for copies of documents. Additional reading can be followed up in "Canadian Immigration Records of Entry in Genealogical Research" by Bennett McCardle in OGS *Seminar Annual, 1985*.

The United States also began to keep border crossing records of entry from Canada into the United States, from 1895. A large historic group of these records are known somewhat misleadingly as "St. Albans Border Crossings," but the record group contains country-wide ports of entry for U.S. immigration. The town of St. Albans in Vermont had both American and Canadian immigration offices. The original American crossing records are held by the National Archives and Records Administration (NARA) in Washington DC, with microfilm copies at LAC and FHL. The information gathered was very similar to the Canadian forms. The source material may be an individual card or a manifest of several entries for one period. *Ancestry.ca* has a searchable database for these *outgoing* records, "Canadian Border Crossings 1895-1956," with links to the digitized entry forms. In addition, LAC has microfilmed indexes to smaller sections of those records.

Passports

Questions about passports as a potential genealogical source arise at times. Few Canadian records other than statistical numbers are known to exist until about the First World War period, and those numbers were very low. A passport was originally a letter of request from a sovereign power for safe passage and protection in another country. During the American Civil War, the United States required such a letter from travelling Canadians, but application letters have not survived and the requirement was temporary. Nineteenth century Canadians planning to travel overseas needed a passport from the British Foreign Office. Again during the Second World War, demands by the United States led to special wartime passports for Canadians crossing the border. Canadian passports *per se* gradually evolved from letters issued by the Governor General to official certificates in the early twentieth century. The booklet-type of passport developed after 1920.

The former Department of External Affairs routinely destroyed records of "non-operational value" before passing documents for posterity to Library and Archives Canada. Nevertheless, you can find references at LAC for such items as the file for individual passport applications from British sources in colonial times, and the "1939 Central Registry" (items ranging from 1909 to 1939) for which LAC finding aid 25-4 should be consulted to determine access restrictions.

Home Children

It is estimated that at least 100,000 immigrant children arrived in Canada from Britain in the late nineteenth and early twentieth centuries through the auspices of charitable and parish organizations. The migration is generally considered to cover the period 1869-1939. Not always orphaned, some of the children had been abandoned or neglected by parents too poor or helpless to care for them. Workhouses already existed to accommodate the desperate underclass, but the establishment of various institutional homes for children was seen as a more humane solution. There, the youngsters received some education and practical training. However, in the late Victorian era, the homes grew more and more crowded. The resources of poor law unions and their boards of guardians were being unbearably stretched. At the same time, Canada had a high demand for workers in its agricultural economy. Thus the "push-pull" migration factor took effect.

The groups of children sent to Canada were accompanied by chaperones. Some of the sponsors for the groups were organizations like Dr. Barnardo's Homes, Church of England Waifs and Strays Society, Catholic Emigration Society, Father Berry's Homes, Liverpool Sheltering Home, National Children's Home and Orphanage, Mr. Fegan's Distribution Home, Maria Rye, Salvation Army, William Quarrier Orphan Homes of Scotland, Middlemore Homes and Macpherson Homes. Receiving homes, or distributing homes, were set up in Canada for placement of boys as farm workers and girls as domestic servants. Contracts for service varied but usually lasted until the child turned 18 years of age. Many books have been written about this phenomenon either from a historical or personal perspective. A home child's life in Canada was often a lonely experience.

The locations of the main receiving homes in Ontario were:

(Barnardo's) Toronto, Peterborough

(Macpherson) Toronto, Hamilton, Belleville, Galt, Stratford

(Quarrier) Brockville

(Rye) Niagara-on-the-Lake

(Catholic Emigration Society) St. George's Home, Ottawa

(Middlemore) London

(National Children's Homes) Hamilton

(Fegan) Toronto

(Church of England Waifs and Strays Society) Toronto, Niagara-on-the-Lake

Besides tracing such an ancestor in the traditional genealogical sources, including ships' passenger lists, a descendant will want to consult two useful databases being created by the British Isles Family History Society of Greater Ottawa (BIFHSGO) covering the period 1869-1930. The databases, available at the Canadian Genealogy Centre, include government-held immigration records and boards of guardians information for most of this period. The specifically related LAC sources and finding aids are:

- Information from no longer surviving inspection registers

showing names between 1878 and 1920—children organized by the boards of guardians of English poor law unions. You may find only the child's name and a page reference to a missing register. After 1897 you may find the child's age, year of arrival, the name of the poor law union and sponsoring agency, along with dates of inspection by Immigration Branch officials. "Remarks" were made by inspectors in somewhat less than half the cases. They may refer to the child's health, and activities, marriage, disappearance, deportation, mistaken identity, or First World War service.

- A Soundex card index for names of children who appeared in the files of the Immigration Branch's first central registry 1892-1932. Besides the child's name, the cards give a file number, and usually the name of the ship he or she arrived on with date and port of entry, and the sponsoring organization. This index appears to be most successful for finding the Barnardo children, but is not as complete for some other sponsored groups.

- In 1920 inspections of children at their placement locations became mandatory. An inspection card for each child is the result, with entries made at various times during his or her service. The alphabetically arranged cards also include a few children's groups emigrating from Europe.

LAC also holds the extensive Barnardo's Homes fonds, microfilm copies from the British parent office, which include several of the above-named sponsoring agencies as well. This material has restrictions, so family historians are advised to contact directly the Barnardo After Care Centre in England (Appendix III). LAC does give access to some unrestricted content in the fonds of the Church of England Children's Society (incorporating the former Waifs and Strays) and the Liverpool Sheltering Home.

The British Isles Family History Society of Greater Ottawa website has a database to search for Middlemore children. See also the articles there about the background and organization of the Middlemore emigration plan. The society's quarterly publication *Anglo-Celtic Roots* has featured several articles over the years on this particular group and their receiving homes.

The Archives of Ontario has its share of information about arriving children in the registers of the provincial Emigration Office. Indexed in the Hawke records (*Toronto Emigration Office*) database, the source registers have the child's name, age, place of

DR. THOS. BARNARDO IS DEAD
HIS LIFE SPENT FOR OTHERS

Career of World's Famous Friend of Children—Over 18,000 of His ''Family'' in Canada Alone.

Dr. Thomas John Barnardo, the friend and benefactor of thousands of poor urchins, died in England on Tuesday. Many and many a lad, rescued from squalid, perhaps criminal surroundings, will mourn the death of this famous philanthropist.

"Ee was werry good to me—'ee wos." These were the words of poor, ignorant, chivied Jo, one of the most pathetic creations of the immortal Dickens. Jo was befriended by a man who was as down in the depths as himself.

"He was very good to us" could well be said by over 55,000 whom he had rescued, trained and placed out in life. To them he has been as a father.

The sad intelligence caused profound sorrow at the distributing home in Farley-avenue yesterday. The reports were not believed, but a cable from Alfred B. Owen, who landed in England on Monday, showed that the sad news was only too true. Mr Owen left Toronto with the object of bringing out a party of boys and girls. They were to have sailed on the 28th. Whe-

THE LATE DR. BARNARDO.

ther that arrangement will hold good is at present unknown.

birth, workhouse location if applicable, year arriving in Canada and with which group, the name and address of employer or placement home, and so on.

Descendants of home children are numerous today, and many have had good results in tracing their ancestor with additional help from the original overseas sponsoring agency. Some of these organizations still exist and hold records from that period. Admission information, photographs, reports, inspections from Canada and other information may be available in a child's file. Barnardo's After Care Section in England has been encouragingly cooperative with family historians, within their own guidelines of confidentiality. Descendants recommend that you ask for a "complete file" and for known siblings of the emigrant.

A number of books on this subject are available. Marjorie Kohli's *The Golden Bridge* is a shining example. Look for authors such as Kenneth Bagnall, Gail Corbett, Phyllis Harrison, Anne Magnusson, Joy Parr, John D. Reid, Gillian Wagner and others. A shorter article by Bagnall, "Britain's Children Who Came to Stay," appeared in *Canadian Genealogist* Vol. 3, No. 2 (1981). Ann Rowe's "Tracing British Emigrant Children" in *Families* Vol. 30, No. 4 (1991) and "Miss Rye's Children and the Ontario Press, 1875" by Wesley B. Turner in *Ontario History* Vol. 68 (1976) are also useful and interesting for descendants. The National Archives UK has just published *New Lives for Old: The Story of Britian's Child Migrants* documenting the story from the UK to Australia, Canada, New Zealand, South Africa and Rhodesia between 1869 and, surprisingly, after the Second World War.

Obituary Thomas John Barnardo, Toronto World, *21 September 1905, p. 8, col. 4*

Naturalization, Ethnic Cultures

Anyone born in British North America, or anywhere within the British Empire, was a British subject. This is why emigrants from the British Isles were never required to become naturalized in Canada. All emigrants born outside the British Empire were considered aliens. The Canadian Citizenship Act was not passed until 1947.

Oaths of Allegiance

To obtain a land grant in Upper Canada before 1828, one requirement was an oath of allegiance, sworn before a magistrate (justice of the peace). All prospective recipients of the free land grants had to swear loyalty to the Crown, whether they were already British subjects or not. No other formal requirement for citizenship or naturalization of aliens existed until the late 1820s. Oaths of allegiance have not been purposely isolated as a separate collection of documents, although AO has an oaths of allegiance book 1837-1842 with names and dates. A small series 1800-1812 is in the Baldwin Room of the Toronto Reference Library, sworn before magistrates William Willcocks and Robert Baldwin in the town of York. They were published in *York Pioneer* (1961 and 1963) and in the old OGS *Bulletin* Vol. 8, No. 2 (1969).

Since oaths were a part of the documentation for acquiring Crown land, many are still found within the Upper Canada land petitions. Others may turn up in such divers places as Township Papers or Heir and Devisee Commission records. Most of them

John McEvers oath of allegiance (1823), Upper Canada Land Petitions, RG 1, L3, vol. 555, Renewal of Leases and Miscellaneous, petition 6; Library and Archives Canada microfilm C-2983

simply name the person, his residence and the date of the oath. A second person usually provided a character affidavit to support the person.

Political sensitivity over the loyalty of alien residents reached a height after the War of 1812, when great numbers of American-born arrivals were seeking land or employment in this province. For a time after the War of 1812, aliens were forbidden to own land, but this measure was almost impossible to enforce when there was so little discernible difference between English-speaking Canadians and Americans. Since the Americans had experienced a generation of republicanism, the government here felt their sympathies would be questionable, should hostilities break out again between the two countries.

Naturalization Registers

The passing of legislation in 1828 and the establishment of naturalization registers for each county was intended to alleviate this political tension. Again, aliens were required to swear or affirm the oath of allegiance "to the Sovereign of the United Kingdom of Great Britain and Ireland and of this Province" within a certain time period of being resident, thus conferring on them "the Civil and Political Rights of Natural Born British Subjects," as per the Act, 9 George IV. The information recorded was basic: name, county of residence, date of registration and signature. The registration was required after seven years and before ten years of residence. A second act in 1841 requested slightly expanded information: the person's residence on 10 February 1841, residence at the time of registration, expiry date of the seven-year residence term and a column for age if the person had been under sixteen upon his arrival here. Genealogically, the researcher can deduce from later registers when an ancestor arrived in Canada and possibly the year of birth of an emigrating child. County registrars forwarded the registers to the provincial secretary.

The series of naturalization registers extends from 1828 to 1850 at LAC. They are not always complete for each county. Donald A. McKenzie created a nominal index to the series, first published serially in OGS *Families*. OGS reprinted it as *Upper Canada Naturalization Records, 1828-1850*. Names can also be searched on a CGC database. Photocopies from the county registers can be ordered from LAC by citing the name, year, county, and entry numbers. An anomaly called "Waterloo County Allegiance Books" 1853-1872 can be seen at AO. The "books" are actually certificates, indicating this particular county clerk continued to compile records well after 1850.

Later Records

Naturalization records created and kept by the Department of the Secretary of State from 1854 to 1917 have been destroyed, but an index remains. The index is held only by Citizenship and Immigration Canada (Appendix II) and provides minimal but important information such as date and place of birth, date of entry into Canada, and names of spouse and children. A database created by the Jewish Genealogical Societies of Montreal and Ottawa is available at the CGC for naturalizations from 1915 to 1932. The pages of names were extracted from *Sessional Papers* and *Canada Gazette* of the period.

We have been told the files from 1917 on have been retained and contain more data. A search request to Citizenship and Immigration Canada is the first step and is only allowed for Canadian citizens or residents. If successful, the second step is applying on an Access to Information Request form for photocopies of documents. Proof of death is necessary unless the age of the immigrant exceeds 110 years. Access is barred to records created within the past twenty years.

Name	Country	Date of Certificate	Date of Oath of Allegiance	Occupation	Residence	Number and Series
Frankl, Edward	Germany		April 11, 1924	Farmer	St. Walburg, Sask.	29096 A.
Franklin, Michael Harry	Russia		April 28, 1924	Student	Montreal, Que.	29931 A.
Frasee, Thomas	Finland	Oct. 7, 1924		Merchant	Copper Cliff, Ont.	9302 E.
Frasen (Frasain), Swen Alfred Leonard	Sweden	Dec. 23, 1924		Farmer	Rolla, B.C.	34240 A.
Frases, Batista	Italy	Sept. 4, 1924		Plumber	Montreal, Que.	9113 E.
Frechtel, Ruben	Poland		Sept. 18, 1924	Tailor	Toronto, Ont.	11281 B.
Frechtel, Sara	Minor child					
Frederick, George	Roumania					
Frederickson, Howard William	U.S.A.		Feb. 9, 1925	Section foreman	Dugald, Man.	34896 A.
Frederickson, Roy	Sweden		July 9, 1924	Farmer	Spalding, Sask.	25126 A.
Fredrikson, Gus	Sweden		Aug. 17, 1924	Logger	Hanall, B.C.	22177 A.
Fredrikson, Viola Elvira	Minor child		Jan. 16, 1925	Farmer	Morson, Ont.	11645 B.
Freedman, Harry	Russia					
Freedman, Dora	Russia		Aug. 6, 1924	Truck driver	Toronto, Ont.	11185 B.
Freedman, Joseph	Poland		April 28, 1924	Peddler	Toronto, Ont.	10784 B.
Freedman, Izy	Minor child					
Freedman, Morris	Minor child					
Freedman, Joseph	Russia		Jan. 26, 1925	Grocer	Medicine Hat, Alta.	34685 A.
Freeman, Abraham	Poland		May 30, 1924	Merchant	Toronto, Ont.	30572 A.
Freeman, Ben	Poland		May 30, 1924	Tailor	Toronto, Ont.	30844 A.
Freestone, Annie	U.S.A.		Mar. 18, 1925	Housekeeper	Cousins, Alta.	35511 A.
Freire, Jose Fernandes	Spain	Oct. 31, 1924		Cigarmaker	Montreal, Que.	9267 E.
French, Hubert Charles	U.S.A.		Sept. 5, 1924	Sales manager	Windsor, Ont.	32409 A.
French, Ray Chester	U.S.A.		Feb. 18, 1925	Salesman	Vernon, B.C.	35045 A.
Frey, Carl	Austria		May 9, 1924	Paper mill employee	Woodfibre, B.C.	10845 B.
Frey, Barbara	Minor child					
Frey, Carl	Minor child					
Frey, Frederick	Germany					
Frey, Frederick William Charles	Germany		Jan. 15, 1925	Fireman	Cranbrook, B.C.	34540 A.
Frey, Jacob	U.S.A.		Mar. 3, 1925	Farmer	Edmonton, Alta.	35256 A.
Frick, Julius	Russia		Dec. 3, 1924	Farmer	Caldwell, Sask.	33937 A.
Frick, Thomas	Germany	Jan. 10, 1925		Labourer	Mossend, Sask.	9407 E.
Fridberg, Frederick	Germany		July 23, 1924	Hotel keeper	Edmonton, Alta.	31899 A.
Fridel, Waclaw	Poland		Nov. 19, 1924	Asst. manager	Toronto, Ont.	34183 A.
Friebel, Paul Oscar	Germany		May 19, 1924	Miner	Edmonton, Alta.	30442 A.
Fried, Jacob	Roumania		Aug. 27, 1924	Farmer	Consort, Alta.	32264 A.
Fried, Moses	Roumania		July 18, 1924	Jeweller	Montreal, Que.	31919 A.
Fried, Celia	Minor child		July 28, 1924	Rabbi	Montreal, Que.	11154 B.
Fried, Leah	Minor child					
Friedman, Aron	Minor child					
Friel, Rosalind	Russia	June 10, 1924		Carpenter	Winnipeg, Man.	9920 E.
Friesen, Jacob J.	U.S.A.		Mar. 3, 1925	Farmer	Vancouver, B.C.	35251 A.
Frimerman, Isaac	Poland		July 15, 1924	Retired	Hepburn, Sask.	31855 A.
Frimerman, Hershel	Minor child		Nov. 27, 1924	Harness maker	Toronto, Ont.	11808 B.
Frimerman, Leon	Minor child					
Frimerman, Phtzakel	Minor child					
Friscolanti, Giuseppe	Italy					
Friske, William	Russia		Nov. 27, 1924	Millwright	Hamilton, Ont.	32711 A.
Frisco, Joe	Russia	May 5, 1924		Farmer	Sutherland, Sask.	8810 E.
Frolak (Frolick), John	Hungary		May 1, 1924	Varnish maker	Brantford, Ont.	30067 A.
Fromas, Simon	Poland		Dec. 1, 1924	Cook	Welland, Ont.	32834 A.
Fromas, Sarah	Russia		Dec. 5, 1924	Fruiterer	Ottawa, Ont.	11544 B.
	Minor child					

LIST of Aliens to whom Certificates of Naturalisation under the Naturalisation Acts, 1914-20, etc.—*Continued*

DEPARTMENT OF THE SECRETARY OF STATE

List of naturalization certificates (1920-1921), Frankl to Froman, Jewish Genealogical Societies of Montreal and Ottawa, "1915-1932 Canadian Naturalizations," digital image, Canadian Genealogy Centre (www.collectionscanada.gc.ca/genealogy/022-908.011-e.html : accessed 23 February 2008)

LI-RA-MA

The odd name of this collection at LAC is derived from the surnames of Russian consuls in Canada from about 1898 to 1918: Likacheff (Montreal), Ragosine (Vancouver) and Mathers (Halifax). The three men represented Russian subjects living in this country, emigrants from the Czarist empire, which then encompassed a vast territory of eastern Europe. Family historians with East European roots may find a goldmine here. It is highly significant to note that files exist not only for the Russian-born, but for peoples from the Baltic states, Ukraine, Finland, Byelorussia, Georgia, Poland and Armenia. Some ethnic or religious groups included German Mennonites, Jews and Doukhobors. The collection is also referred to as Russian Consular Records like the similar collection in the United States in the same period.

While these are not official records of Canadian entry, and no consul was based in Ontario, the Montreal consul dealt with many emigrants who chose to live in this province. This collection

Victor Freiberg affidavit, LI-RA-MA Collection, MG 30, E 406, Series 4, vol. 102, file 6246; National Archives of Canada, Ottawa

provides an example of overlap between immigration information and what might be considered "ethnic" records.

LAC has a nominal index to over 11,000 nominal files of the series known as Passport/Identity Papers. The index can be searched online through a CGC database with links to digital images in the files. Care must be taken to imagine the spelling variations that might have been used in English. The files deal with Russian subjects who requested passports or visas, or were preparing for naturalization. Obtaining proper Russian identity papers enabled a man to avoid Canadian conscription in World War I. The prescribed forms in these files ask for name, residence in Canada, place of birth, with variations on age, date of birth, religion, marital status, nearest kin or dependents in Russian territory, date of departure or arrival, etc. Finding a personal photograph is not unusual. While the basic forms were created in the Russian language, it is not usually difficult to find a translator. Some forms and questionnaires were prepared in both Russian and English.

In the same collection, the records of the Montreal Consulate-General, Series I, especially volumes 3-15, may contain such material as requests for birth or death documents, assistance to Russians in difficulty in Canada, intervention in criminal cases, help with family problems, assistance for the emigration of relatives and/or accounts of Russians summoned for military service with the Czar or those who enlisted in the Canadian Expeditionary Force of World War I.

Ethnic Origins

Everyone who becomes a genealogist has some kind of "ethnic potential" because nearly all of us had ancestors who came from overseas at some point in time. The phrase "Canadian mosaic" was coined to counterpoint our American neighbour's "melting pot" concept of immigrant integration. Canada's espousal of multiculturalism encourages the collection and preservation of the immigrant experience. In Ontario, almost every group of non-traditional (meaning non-anglophone or non-francophone) newcomers has a historical society, social association or cultural centre.

The Multicultural History Society of Ontario (MHSO) is an educational and heritage centre, part of whose mission is to preserve material and memories that reveal the role of immigration and ethnicity in the history of Ontario and Canada. Since its founding in 1976, the society has aimed to collect "oral testimony," photographs and papers. Oral testimony—audio and visual materials—is the largest part of their vast collection and can only be consulted at the Oral History Museum in the MHSO centre (Appendix III). The collection of photographs and textual material up to 1986, comprising almost 1500 reels of microfilm, was transferred to the MSHO fonds at Archives of Ontario. These microfilms are not available on interlibrary loan. That transfer included a comprehensive accumulation of ethnic newspapers (mentioned in Chapter 2). A complete list of the newspapers is online at the MHSO website. You can also browse "Newspaper Lists" at the CGC website for cultural newspapers in the LAC collection, sorted by province. The main MHSO collection at AO can be consulted by the inventories arranged alphabetically for the name of the groups, for example, Americans, Armenians, Austrians, Belgians, Blacks and so on. Certain restrictions apply to the photographs.

Publications are another part of the MHSO mission, including the journal *Polyphony* and conference proceedings. Of most interest to genealogists would likely be their various series called *Ethnic and Immigration History, Ethnocultural Voices* and *Encyclopedia of Canada's Peoples.* The latter can be viewed and searched online. You can purchase *A Guide to the Collections of the Multicultural History Society of Ontario* through their website or by visiting the centre's library and museum.

Library and Archives Canada has a web portal to multicultural resources and services (see Reading and Reference), reflecting the cultural diversity from the private papers of individuals in ethnic communities to religious or benevolent associations. Many ethnic groups set up their own organizations in the past to assist immigration from their home countries or after arrival, depositing their records with LAC. A few examples are the Canadian Baltic and Immigration Aid Society, Ukrainian Canadian Committee and the Czechoslovak National Association in Canada. LAC has also published some ethnocultural guides to archival sources for Canadians of Finnish, German language, Jewish and Polish origins.

Numerous articles have appeared in *Families* and OGS *Seminar Annual* editions over the years with advice or personal experience in tracing ethnic ancestors. The book reviews in *Families* and other periodicals, as well as news about the formation of genealogy study groups for specific ethnic, cultural or religious backgrounds, are always sources for ongoing help. *Families* Vol. 29, No. 1 (1990) was dedicated to many cultures and included among other articles: "Family Origins in Ukraine" by Jeff Picknicki, "Hungarian Ancestry Research" by Peter B. Mérey, "The Armenian Boys at Georgetown" by Evelyn Berthrong and "Researching Welsh Genealogy" by Howard Rokeby-Thomas.

Mention of two groups is made here because of their relatively recent surge in exploring family history.

Jews

Jewish awareness of collective roots and researching family history has expanded with the activities of the Jewish Genealogy Society of Canada (Toronto) and the associated Ottawa and Montreal groups in researching personal family roots. From the website of the Toronto group of the JGS, you can link to their library catalogue and publications, and to fellow societies in Ottawa and Hamilton (addresses in Appendix IV). One society project is to record every Jewish burial in Toronto and all of Ontario in a database. Other efforts involve indexing and contributions to ongoing international projects, such as Yad Vashem for identifying and reconstructing holocaust families. Glen Eker's extractions of Jewish families from census returns 1851–1901, published by the Ontario Genealogical Society, are a major finding aid for researchers.

The Ontario Jewish Archives in Toronto also plays an important role for the preservation of archival materials. The archives has some synagogue records, family histories, cemetery recordings, and some marriage, naturalization and circumcision records. Additional material includes some files from Jewish immigration aid organizations and shipping agents. Jewish newspapers and some fraternal society records are available to consult. See also the archives' online 1925 and 1931 Jewish city directories.

One of the first publications from LAC's ethnocultural series was *Archival Sources for the Study of Canadian Jewry*, describing the LAC holdings in alphabetical order by subject and personal names. Author-archivist Lawrence Tapper also compiled *A Biographical Dictionary of Canadian Jewry, 1909-1914*. The Baron de Hirsch Institute fonds at LAC includes the Jewish Family Services section regarding social work, education, professions and other aspects of Jewish life in Canada. The Li-Ra-Ma collection and the Multicultural History Society of Ontario are other resources of interest.

Blacks

Interest in the history, heritage, and genealogy of Black settlement in Ontario also blossomed in the last decade or so. Much of the public awareness is due to the work of the Ontario Black History Society (OBHS). Blacks have been in the province since some of the Loyalists arrived with slaves. In 1793, an act was passed in Upper Canada forbidding the further introduction of slaves to this province. The law also guaranteed freedom for children of slaves by the age of 25, if they were born after 1793. This was the impetus for a long line of runaway fugitives and free Blacks coming into Ontario via the Underground Railroad. Many, but not all, remained. By 1834, British anti-slavery legislation was mandatory throughout the British Empire. After President Lincoln's emancipation proclamation of 1863, many former slaves or their descendants returned to seek family in the United States.

Black settlements in Ontario have been commemorated in publishing, film documentaries and museums. Places of historical interest are North Buxton in Raleigh township, Oro township and Sheffield Park on Georgian Bay. Josiah Henson's replica Uncle Tom's Cabin is at the Dawn settlement near Dresden. The Chatham/Kent Black Historical Society maintains a heritage room for information about the communities and genealogical research. The North American Black History Museum in Amherstburg is another major site for cultural information about African Canadians. Toronto was also a destination for Blacks. With a number of contributing partners, the OBHS is planning a museum and cultural centre in the city to celebrate the Underground Railroad, the African Methodist Episcopal faith and the later diversity of Black origins.

The OGS *Seminar Annual* for 1995 includes summaries of several presentations on researching Black ancestry. See also the special online exhibit at AO called "The Black Experience in Ontario, 1834-1914." All Black Ontarians do not share the same roots in slavery. The future will undoubtedly see the development of special interest groups for origins in the West Indies, Africa and elsewhere. As with other cultural groups, the same recommendation applies here: familiarize yourself with the existing literature, like authors Hill, Winks, Sadlier, Tulloch, Riendeau and others. Jerome Teelucksingh gives helpful advice on library/archival material and university theses in two articles in *Families* Vol. 42, No. 1 (2003).

Historical articles that can help with Afro-Canadian ancestry:

"The Black Image in Nineteenth-Century Ontario" by Allen P. Stouffer in *Ontario History* Vol. 76 (1984).

"Upper Canada's Black Defenders" by Ernest Green in *Ontario History* Vol. 27 (1931).

"Social Conditions Among the Negroes in Upper Canada before 1865" by Fred Landon in *Ontario History* Vol. 12 (1925).

"British Officials and Their Attitude To the Negro Community in Canada, 1833-1861" by Ged Martin in *Ontario History* Vol. 66 (1974).

"Blacks and the Rebellion of 1837" by Melody Brown in *1837 Rebellion Remembered.*

Reading and Reference

Acton, John A., compiler. *Index of Some Passengers Who Emigrated to Canada Between 1817 and 1849.* Toronto, ON: Ontario Genealogical Society, 2003.

Akwesasne to Wunnumin Lake, Profiles of Aboriginal Communities in Ontario. Toronto, ON: Ontario Native Affairs Secretariat & Ministry of Citizenship and Culture, 1992.

Antone, Bob. *The Longhouse of One Family: A Kinship Model of the Iroquoian Clan System.* Brantford, ON: Woodland Indian Cultural Centre, 1987.

Belkin, Simon. *Through Narrow Gates: A Review of Jewish Immigration, Colonization and Immigrant Aid Work in Canada, 1840-1940.* Montreal, QC: Eagle Publishing, 1966.

Bennett, Carol. *Peter Robinson's Settlers.* Renfrew, ON: Juniper Books, 1999.

Cameron, Wendy and Mary McDougall Maude. *Assisting Emigration to Upper Canada: The Petworth Project 1832-1837.* Montreal QC/Kingston ON: McGill-Queen's Press, 2000. See also www.petworthemigrations.com.

Cameron, Wendy, Sheila Haines and Mary McDougall Maude. *English Immigrant Voices: Labourers' Letters from Upper Canada in the 1830s.* Montreal QC/Kingston ON: McGill-Queen's Press, 2000.

Carpenter, Cecilia S. *How to Research American Indian Blood Lines: A Manual on Indian Genealogical Research.* Orting, WA: Heritage Quest, 1987.

Eker, Glen. *Jews Resident in Canada According to the 1851 to 1901 Censuses of Canada.* Toronto, ON: Ontario Genealogical Society, 2002.

Elliott, Bruce S. *Irish Migrants to the Canadas: A New Approach.* Montreal QC/Kingston ON: McGill-Queens Press, 2001.

_____, editor. "*The McCabe List*", *Early Irish in the Ottawa Valley.* Toronto, ON: Ontario Genealogical Society, 2002.

Ermatinger, Edward. *Life of Colonel Talbot and the Talbot Settlement.* 1859. Reprint. Belleville, ON: Mika Publishing, 1972.

Faux, David. *Understanding Ontario First Nations Genealogical Records: Sources and Case Studies.* Toronto, ON: Ontario Genealogical Society, 2002.

Fenton, William N. *The Roll Call of the Iroquois Chiefs: A Study of a Mnemonic Cane from the Six Nations Reserve.* 1950. Reprint. Oshweken, ON: Iroqrafts, 1983.

Filby, P. William and Mary K. Meyer. *Passenger and Immigration Lists Index: A Guide to Published Arrival Records of About 500,000 Passengers Who Came to the United States and Canada in the Seventeenth, Eighteenth and Nineteenth Centuries.* Detroit, MI: Gale Research, 1981 with supplements. See also Family Archive CD-ROM.

Forte, Nick G., compiler. *A Guide to the Collection of the Multicultural History Society of Ontario.* Toronto, ON: MHSO, 1992.

Graham, Elizabeth. *Medicine Man to Missionary: Missionaries as Agents of Change Among the Indians of Southern Ontario, 1784-1867.* Toronto, ON: Peter Martin Associates, 1975.

Harrison, Michael and Dorothy Martin, transcribers. *The Records of the Society for the Relief of the Sick and Destitute, 1817-1847.* Toronto, ON: Toronto Branch, Ontario Genealogical Society, 2002.

Heald, Carolyn. *The Irish Palatines in Ontario: Religion, Ethnicity, and Rural Migration.* Gananoque, ON: Langdale Press, 1994.

Hill, Daniel G. *The Freedom Seekers: Blacks in Early Canada.* Toronto, ON: Stoddart, 1995.

Kershaw, Roger and Janet Sacks. *New Lives for Old: The Story of Britain's Child Migrants.* London, UK: The National Archives, 2008.

Kohli, Marjorie. *The Golden Bridge: Young Immigrants to Canada, 1833-1939.* Toronto, ON: Natural Heritage Books, 2003.

Magocsi, Paul Robert, editor. *Encyclopedia of Canada's Peoples.* Toronto, ON: University of Toronto Press, 1999.

McCardle, Bennett. *Indian History and Claims: A Research Handbook.* Ottawa, ON: Indian and Northern Affairs Canada, 1982.

McKenzie, Donald A., compiler. *Upper Canada Naturalization Records, 1828-1850.* Toronto, ON: Ontario Genealogical Society, 1991.

McLean, Marianne. *The People of Glengarry: Highlanders in Transition, 1745-1820.* Montreal QC/Kingston ON: McGill-Queen's University Press, 1991.

Morrison, James. *Aboriginal Peoples in the Archives, a Guide to Sources in the Archives of Ontario.* Toronto, ON: Ministry of Culture and Communications/Archives of Ontario, 1992.

Mutrie, R. Robert. *The Long Point Settlers.* Ridgeway, ON: Log Cabin Publishing, 1992.

Neville, Gerald J., compiler. *Lanark Society Settlers: Ships' Lists of the Glasgow Emigration Society, 1821*. Ottawa, ON: British Isles Family History Society of Greater Ottawa, 1995.

Nin.Da.Waab.Jig. *Minishenhying Anishnaabe-aki or Walpole Island: The Soul of Indian Territory*. Wallaceburg, ON: Commercial Associates/Ross Roy Ltd., 1987.

Obee, Dave. *Destination Canada: A Guide to 20ᵗʰ Century Immigration Records*. Second edition. Victoria, BC: Interlink Genealogy, 2004.

O'Gallagher, Marianna. *Grosse Ile: Gateway to Canada, 1832-1937*. Quebec, QC: Carraig Books, 1984.

Ontario Native Affairs Secretariat and Ministry of Citizenship. *Akwesasne to Wunnumin Lake, Profiles of Aboriginal Communities in Ontario*. Toronto, ON: Ministry of Citizenship and Culture, 1992.

Parr, Joy. *Labouring Children: British Immigrant Apprentices to Canada, 1869-1924*. Revised edition. Montreal QC/Kingston ON: McGill-Queen's University Press, 1994.

Reaman, G. Elmore. *The Trail of the Black Walnut*. 1965. Reprint. Baltimore, MD: Genealogical Publishing Company, 1993.

Reid, John D. *Researching Canada's Home Children*. Toronto, ON: Heritage Productions, 2005.

Russell, Bill. *Records of the Department of Indian Affairs at Library and Archives Canada: A Source for Genealogical Research*. Second edition. Toronto, ON: Ontario Genealogical Society, 2004.

Sack, B.G. *History of the Jews in Canada*. 1945. Reprint. Montreal, QC: Harvest House, 1965.

Stratford-Devai, Fawne. *Province of Ontario Immigration Records: An Overview*. Campbellville, ON: Global Heritage Press, 2001.

Stuart, Donna Valley, editor. *Genealogy of the French Families of the Detroit River Region 1701-1936*. 2 volumes. Revised edition. Detroit, MI: Detroit Society for Genealogical Research, 1976. See also www. rootsweb.com/~mistcla2/Denissen.htm.

—————————, compiler. *Michigan Censuses 1710-1830, Under the French, British and Americans*. Detroit, MI: Detroit Society for Genealogical Research, 1982.

Tanner, Helen and Miklos Pinther. *Atlas of Great Lakes Indian History*. Norman, OK: University of Oklahoma Press, 1987.

Tapper, Lawrence. *A Biographical Dictionary of Canadian Jewry, 1909-1914*. Teaneck, NJ: Avotaynu, 1992.

Wallace, W. Stewart. *A Biographical Dictionary of the Nor'westers*. Toronto, ON: The Champlain Society, 1934.

Whyte, Donald. *Dictionary of Scottish Emigrants to Canada Before Confederation*. 4 volumes. Toronto, ON: Ontario Genealogical Society, 1986-2005.

Winks, Robin. *The Blacks in Canada: A History*. Revised edition. Montreal QC/Kingston ON: McGill-Queen's University Press, 2000.

Ancestry.ca. www.ancestry.ca

British Isles Family History Society of Greater Ottawa (BIFHSGO).
www.bifhsgo.ca

Castle Garden. www.castlegarden.org/

Citizenship and Immigration Canada.
www.cic.gc.ca/english/index.asp

Ellis Island. ellisisland.org

Encyclopedia of Canada's People. www.multiculturalcanada.ca/ecp

FindMyPast. www.findmypast.com

Grosse Ile. www.pc.gc.ca/ihn-nhs/qc/grosseile/index_e.asp

Hudson's Bay Company Archives.
www.gov.mb.ca/chc/archives/hbca/index.html

Immigrants to Canada.
ist.uwaterloo.ca/~marj/genealogy/thevoyage.html

Immigrant Ships Transcribers Guild. immigrantships.net

Ingeneas. www.ingeneas.com

Jewish Genealogical Society of Canada (Toronto). www.jgstoronto.ca

Jewish GenWeb. www.jewishgen.org

Library and Archives Canada. Multicultural Resources and Services.
www.collectionscanada.gc.ca/multicultural/index-e.html

Markham Berczy Settlers Association. markhamberczysettlers.ca

Montgomery County Archives, New York.
www.amsterdam-ny.com/mcha

Moravian Church Archives. www.moravianchurcharchives.org

Multicultural History Society of Ontario. www.mhso.ca

Nanaimo Family History Society. members.shaw.ca/nanaimo.fhs

Olive Tree Genealogy. www.olivetreegenealogy.com

Ontario Jewish Archives. www.ontariojewisharchives.org

Penetanguishene Centennial Museum & Archives.
pencenmuseum.com

The Ships List. www.theshipslist.com

Sneakers. www3.sympatico.ca/sneakers/genealogy.htm

State Historical Society of Wisconsin. wisconsinhistory.org

Steamship Historical Society of America. www.sshsa.org

Toronto Emigrant Office Assisted Emigration Records.
www.archives.gov.on.ca/english/db/hawke.htm

Trent University, First Nations Periodical Index.
www.lights.ca/sifc/journals.htm

Woodland Cultural Centre. www.woodland-centre.on.ca/index.php

9

Community and Family Development

This chapter looks at some of the context of life for ancestors after their settlement: the framework they lived in, education and training prospects and employment opportunities. Social life, barely touched on here, was liberally reported in local newspapers. Barn raisings, fairs, religious revival meetings, card parties, visitors from distant places, travelling performers, and veiled (or not so veiled) references to residents who absconded, spent the night in the drunk tank or courted popular young women all add community flavour to a family history. Also, the newspapers often took political stances, publishing detailed debates, provocative editorial comments and rousing letters to the editor. As you seek to add context to your ancestors, keep newspapers in mind as the expression of their times.

Municipal Records

Reference Dates

1788	Four districts created to establish local government in western Quebec
1792	First parliament of Upper Canada held at Newark (Niagara-on-the-Lake)
1842	District councils became overseers of local administration
1849	Districts were dissolved and counties assumed upper tier local government

1850	Municipal Act; according to population density, towns and townships became eligible for incorporation and management of local government
1867	Federal voters' lists were created each election year
1917	Canadian women gained full national voting rights
1968	Formation of some regional governments in Ontario

Settlement in pioneer and frontier societies demanded organized structure for the order and protection of the common good. Government originated with the lieutenant governor of Upper Canada who was -appointed by the Crown to represent colonial authority. The governor was served by an appointed executive council, akin to a cabinet, and a legislative council. Neither of the two bodies was accountable to the elected assembly. Councillors were entitled to very large grants of land, ensuring their personal prosperity and, in practice, they held their positions for life. Those were only two of the many grievances that grew up about the entrenched status quo of "the family compact." Dissatisfaction led to eventual rebellion in the 1830s and reform in the 1840s on the principle of responsible government. The governor-in-council appointed justices of the peace, also called magistrates, and other preliminary officials to establish order in the emerging settlements of what would become Upper Canada.

Justices and Clerks of the Peace

Justices of the peace were commissioned in each district of Upper Canada. In addition to their judicial roles (see Chapter 7), the justices governed local needs and community services. Thus they had impressive power and responsibility. They were usually influential and prominent residents of a district town, although each township needed representation. Collectively or selectively, in earliest times, they appointed the local sheriffs, clerks of the peace, registrars of deeds, coroners and other important functionaries. Justices of the peace met four times a year at Courts of Quarter Sessions of the Peace to authorize expenditures for public works, among other district duties and their judicial roles.

Part of the responsibility of early-appointed clerks of the peace, at the direction of the justices, was to ensure annual tax assessment and collection, population lists, statute labour for local roads and other necessities. As the population grew rapidly, administration had to evolve with it. The first district councils were created in 1841 with elected representatives from the surrounding organized towns or townships. County councils began to oversee local administration after 1850 and continued their role, even until today, in rural areas. Tax assessment rolls are probably the most useful records of municipal origin for the family historian. Minutes of council meetings will also be of interest for certain ancestors who were elected to, or participated in, local affairs.

The records were stored in the offices of various clerks, if they were indeed saved. Inevitably, the older records often became damaged, lost or destroyed for lack of space. Sometimes old registers or papers found their way into private homes or a local historical repository. Some years ago the Archives of Ontario made a concerted effort to collect old records from municipal offices, and most cooperated due to lack of storage room or preservation resources. The end result is that AO has the most *central* collection of nineteenth century municipal records for southern Ontario. However, LAC and many other institutions also have some, in addition to municipal town offices that may have retained their records.

Of special assistance is *Directory of Municipal Archives* produced by the Municipal Archives Interest Group of the Archives Association of Ontario. The *Directory* lists locations of municipal materials wherever they may be held and is entirely online in PDF format. The AO online and paper finding aid 209 "Municipal Records at the Archives of Ontario" shows their holdings in detail from early times till about 1900. Also highly recommended is the AO online exhibit *The Changing Shape of Ontario: A Guide to Boundaries, Names and Regional Governments*.

Tax Rolls

Tax assessment rolls record information about a resident's property in order to determine the amount of taxes payable on real property. In early days, assessment information was often combined with simple census recording. Collector rolls are similar in that they also record names and property locations, but have extra information regarding payments and possible tax arrears. The documents survive for intermittent periods or locations.

Assessment rolls note the concession and lot for the owner or occupant in a rural area. As the rolls became more detailed, information could include the amount of cultivated or uncultivated acreage, type of construction of house or buildings, numbers and types of livestock, orchard, garden and crop production and so on—all to determine the rate of

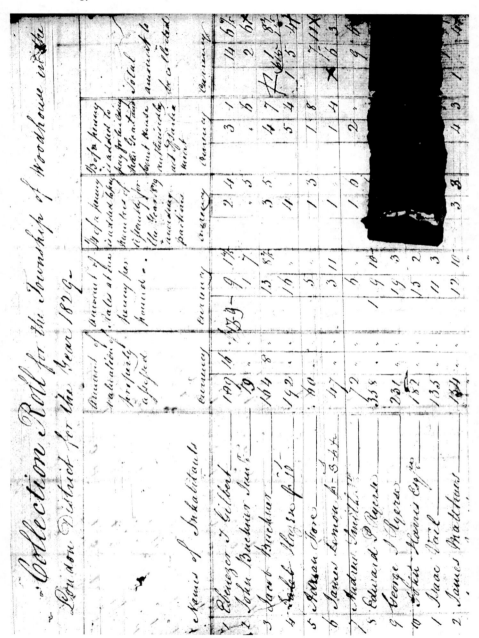

Collection Roll Woodhouse Township (1829), M 9, D8-35; Library and Archives Canada microfilm H-1100

taxation. Only the head of family or occupant of the property is customarily named in the early censuses, although when the tax roll is combined with a census there is usually some breakdown of household ages, sex, occupations, and perhaps nativity, religion or length of residence. Some of the early combined assessment rolls and census returns are listed in the finding aid *Catalogue to Census Returns on Microfilm, 1666-1891,* but only if they are available on LAC microfilm.

Surviving pre-1850 census and assessments for towns and townships in the following districts can be consulted at AO under the name of a district, county or town/township. These districts have the earliest material, which can include much more than assessment rolls:

Eastern District 1814-1850

Gore District 1816-1856

Huron District 1842-1848

Johnstown District 1796-1850

Niagara District, 1828-1849

Newcastle District 1802-1850

Ottawa District 1810-1850

Western District 1813-1850

Another notable resource centre for early material is the Regional History Collection, D.B. Weldon Library, at the University of Western Ontario. It has scattered records for some townships in the former districts of London, Brock, Talbot, Huron and Western. A few early records have been published by OGS branches, interested societies, and *The Ontario Register.* For example, Halton-Peel Branch OGS has indexed district census and assessment records for the districts of Gore, Newcastle and Ottawa. Niagara Branch OGS printed surviving parts of the 1828 census for the Niagara area.

Statute labour rolls for roadwork are sometimes appended to assessment rolls. Road building and maintenance were critical in pioneer society. The rolls include some or all of the men from community families whose properties abutted a road allowance. They were expected to work a certain number of days per year. Names, ages and residence are given. Quite often they are fit young men representing the family obligation. When such rolls are available, they could be a genealogical gem for sons and young husbands—who may not appear on the actual assessment roll if they had not yet acquired their own property and were still living in an older man's household.

Assessment rolls became much more common after 1850 or dating from the incorporation of a particular municipality. Because many more have survived in sequence from the second half of the nineteenth century, they can pinpoint a family's arrival or removal between census years. Many places began to compile their lists from this point in alphabetical order by the first initial of the surname. Information eventually became more or less standardized: land and building value, status as residence or business, religion (for school taxation purposes), age and occupation of head of household and number of people living on the property.

Family historians can watch for a noticeable increase in the value of an ancestor's property from one tax roll to the next. Such a leap in assessment often indicates that a new building has been added, perhaps a home or outbuilding, or perhaps a significant addition was made to an existing structure. Cross-checking with the Abstract Index to Deeds may also show a loan or mortgage at that time, indicating preparation for construction.

As towns and cities increased in size, it becomes more complex to use these records in the 1900s. Depending on their size and the years in question, town and city rolls are arranged by subdivision survey plans or by electoral ward boundaries. Knowing a street address will be of some help, but you may require assistance from land registry office staff for accessing latter-day records in their care. For our largest city, see the very useful Toronto Street Finder online at *OntarioRoots*. In order to interpret the figures relating to lot size on later assessment rolls, especially for the smaller sized lots of a village or town, it is helpful to read Janet Fayle's "Understanding Lot Sizes in Early Assessment Rolls" in *Families* Vol. 34, No. 2 (1995).

Councils

The Municipal Act of 1850 provided for the incorporation of local governments at the grassroots level of town or township when population size warranted it. Hillman's *A Statutory Chronology of Ontario Counties and Municipalities* provides the background framework. But even as these lower units developed, districts and then counties were still governed by councils overseeing wider concerns at a higher level tier. A county council of elected representatives from the towns and townships within county boundaries was headed by a warden. In addition to financial business and administrative documentation, county council records produce such records as cash books for municipal employees or for contracted labour projects, and lists of tax defaulters and non-resident landowners. Tax arrears were handled by the county sheriff who seized delinquent properties and sold them at auction on the county's behalf.

At the township level, rural responsibilities were foremost. An elected reeve with a relatively small council were the figureheads. One of the earliest appointed positions of rural responsibility was the pathmaster, under an overseer of highways and roads. See the article "Pathmasters of Glanford Township, Wentworth County" by Beryl Simpson in *Families* Vol. 23, No. 3 (1984) as an example. Although the article is specific to one township with lists of names, it outlines the responsibilities of the appointment. Additional rural appointments were positions like fence viewers, livestock valuers and pound keepers. Then, as now, typical problems for agricultural communities included livestock killed by wild animals, inappropriately constructed fencelines, straying livestock or disputes over water courses and rights. Meeting minutes of larger municipalities, with a mayor and larger number of councillors, clearly reflect urban concerns and the provision of services to householders.

The comprehensive AO research guide 209 has an alphabetical listing and description of its holdings, as well as introductory information and links. The collection includes county, town/township and village material. However, the previously mentioned *Directory of Municipal Archives* will locate records held by other repositories.

Genealogists are reminded that very early records of local appointments such as justices of the peace, sheriffs, bailiffs, constables, customs officers, harbour masters and other municipal or county officials can be found among records of district Quarter Sessions. Application requests for such positions can also be found at LAC in records of the Civil Secretary for Upper Canada and Canada West (Sundries) 1801-1867.

Voter Lists

Voter lists for election purposes were compiled by municipal officials within each electoral district, which in Ontario generally corresponded to county outlines. Beginning with the election of 1935, separate federal voters lists were created. As with assessment rolls, voters lists provide evidence of a an ancestral name with a date and place. In the British tradition, eligible voters were originally males of at least 21 years of age—although the age qualification was not spelled out in legislation until 1853—and freeholders (owners of real property). That means a large portion of the adult male population in Upper Canada was enfranchised because land tenure was commonly available to all. Women as owners of real property in Ontario had the right to vote for municipal school trustees from 1850 and gained full municipal voting privileges by 1900. It took until 1917 before *all* women in Ontario had the legal right to vote in provincial and federal elections.

Some town/township voter lists, occasionally pre-1867, are included in the portion of AO finding aid 209 alphabetically by place name. Other lists for election years 1874-1978 are in the AO library. Federal voters' lists 1935-1983 are available at LAC.

As of 2007, there have been 39 provincial elections since Confederation in 1867. Elections in the first half of the nineteenth century were well-covered by reports and political commentary in local newspapers. The *Journals of the Legislative Assembly* is another potential source of candidates and election results. The names of petitioners opposing or endorsing an elected candidate in the 1840s, originally published in the *Journals* were reprinted as "Contested Elections" in *Lost in Canada?* for:

Halton County, in Vol. 11, Nos. 3 & 4 (1985)

Middlesex County, in Vol. 12, Nos. 1-3 (1986)

Oxford County, in Vol. 13, No. 1 (1987)

Education Records

Reference Dates

1785	First school opened, at Kingston
1807	Legislation established a grammar school in each district
1816	Legislation establishing common schools
1827	King's College founded (later the University of Toronto)
1830	Upper Canada College founded at York
1847	Toronto Normal School opened
1850	County boards of education established; the School Act expanded Roman Catholic rights to separate school funding
1876	Royal Military College founded at Kingston
1896	Legislation required children aged from 8 to 14 to attend school for the entire academic year
1960	Consolidation of rural schools

Ontario has a free system of public elementary and secondary schools. Education is a provincial, rather than a federal jurisdiction. A major portion of any municipal budget these days is the portion spent for education, and it goes to an elected county or regional board of education. The first settlers made do with a local teacher who could gather a few students for lessons. The first grammar schools in the province operated with tuition fees, and thus were not accessible to most of the populace. Elementary schools were initially called common schools.

The school year now runs from September to June. This was not always the case in the early days, when the agricultural season dominated the work schedule of so many families. Children were expected to do farm and home work because the typically large family needed many hands. Before 1896, children were required to attend school only for a minimum of four months during the annual session. Eighteenth and nineteenth century children were often sent to work for a neighbour to provide financial assistance to the family or to learn a trade. Many such arrangements were informal. Documents of indenture or apprenticeship are seldom seen because there was no government requirement to register or record them.

Students and Schools

Detailed records for an individual student's academic progress, created at the school, became known as Ontario Student Records (OSR) folders. Originally the OSRs contained student progress reports and teachers' comments, and were highly confidential, although students could obtain a transcript of their academic marks for application to another institution. While such records are kept for over 75 years, most "extraneous" material is expunged within a year of the student's graduation or removal. What remains is the name of the student, date of birth, year(s) of attendance, course marks and names of teachers. There may or may not be an address for the student. The Ontario Freedom of Information and Protection of Privacy Act will govern access to any surviving personal student records less than 100 years old.

A school might have retained its older records or passed them to the county board of education office. Some family historians have experienced success with a local school board. Contact the Ontario Ministry of Education (Appendix II) for the address of a school or a school board, or use the simple search feature on its website.

Examination results for elementary or high schools, or provincial level post-secondary institutions, were often published in newspapers. Such news reports were usually printed at the end of a school term (before or after Christmas) or a school year (June).

A good source for student information would be school yearbooks, most common in the twentieth century among high schools. Prevalent features in the books are school activities, clubs, awards, photographs and mini-commentaries on the graduating classes.

When seeking an ancestor, remember to explore the Archives of Ontario's education records, RG 2. The collection is very large, requiring study of its on-site finding aid and the numerous appendices. Not every item is described online. You might find school attendance registers and/or other registers with names and ages of students, names of parents or guardians and, possibly, further information on graduation or movement from one school to another. Many such registers will fall within the 100-year privacy restriction, so AO recommends consulting with the appropriate archivist.

Among the AO holdings, the following may have items of genealogical interest:

- local school histories and teaching experiences, predominantly 1896 (RG 2-87), listed online with names and places.
- reports from district superintendents to the chief superintendent of education, 1842-1849 (RG 2-16) and 1850-1870 (RG 2-17), often detailing individual school conditions.
- miscellaneous school records 1829-1976, with a paper inventory list (fonds 1201).
- grammar school trustees' half-yearly reports 1854-1871, arranged by place name (RG 2-21).
- annual reports by local superintendents and boards of trustees, 1850-1870 (RG 2-17).
- *Schools and Teachers in the Province of Ontario* 1911-1966, annually published lists from the department of education.
- a few collections from various school boards (RG 2-142).

The relative scarcity of historical school and student records is a case for exploring local history books, museums and OGS branch publications. Nipissing District branch published students' names at some schools in their area in 1906 and 1914, in their newsletter *Public Relations*. Brant County branch has a list of rural school registers; Niagara Peninsula Branch has a 1921 reunion list of St. Catharines' Old Boys. The first few articles below also have names of students.

"The Strachan Lists" by Donald H. Lennox in *Families* Vol. 33, No. 3 (1994). Shown here are students living in 1827 who had been educated at grammar schools in Cornwall or York under the aegis of (later) Bishop John Strachan. Also included are students who matriculated from Trinity College, including theologues, from its inception and names of men admitted to holy orders by Bishop Strachan from 1840 to 1867.

"The Cornwall Grammar School under John Strachan, 1803-1812" by George W. Spragge in *Ontario History* Vol. 34 (1942).

"An Early Red School House and its Century-old Record Book" by John Barnett in *Ontario History* Vol. 48 (1956).

"Report of a Common School in Elizabeth(town) Township, Leeds County: 1842" by Lee Booth in *Families* Vol. 15, No. 3 (1976).

"Pioneer Schools of Upper Canada" by Frank Eames in *Ontario History* Vol. 18 (1920).

"Arguments Over the Education of Girls: Their Admission to Grammar Schools in this Province" by Marion V. Royce in *Ontario History* Vol. 67 (1975).

"Elementary Education in Upper Canada: The Enoch Turner Schoolhouse" by Duncan Urquhart in *1837 Rebellion Remembered*. This article gives a vivid "examination of the schools and the nature of the education they provided."

Private and independent schools for primary and secondary education have always operated separately, and should be contacted directly for possible information. Representative groups, like the Ontario Federation of Independent Schools (Appendix III) should be able to supply an individual school address. A collection of records from Bishop Strachan School for girls, with a variety of information from the nineteenth century to 1942, have been deposited with AO.

Post-Secondary

Universities and other learning centres beyond the high school level tend to retain their own older records, unless space is a problem or a faculty has closed down. First you need to determine which university or college an ancestor might have attended. The institution's own archives would be your primary contact. A nineteenth century search is not so difficult because there were relatively few universities: Queen's in Kingston; McMaster in Toronto, then later Hamilton; Ottawa; Western in London; and Toronto. McGill University in Montreal has historically been another popular choice for Ontario residents. Most of these started as "colleges" and may have had other names. Initially, most had religious affiliations. Nowadays, these early (and now largest) universities have their own professional colleges or faculties. In 2008, there are 18 publicly funded universities in Ontario. Another 17 institutions, mostly theology-based, are authorized to grant specific degrees. Colleges of applied arts and technology have existed for many years, adding 24 current institutions to the post-secondary education level. Addresses can be obtained from the Ministry of Education website or the annual *Directory of Canadian Universities.*

When you have selected the relevant institution, you will likely find cooperation in obtaining the ancestor's name on enrollment or graduation lists. However, the academic records are again subject to the expected privacy restrictions. University libraries are natural reference centres for their student programs, but they also have material about or from their graduates such as unpublished theses. The usual class yearbooks, student newspapers and alumni associations can be sources of lively information. "University Yearbooks as a Source of Migration" was published by Donald E. Read in *Families* Vol. 24, No. 4 (1985).

A few universities or their alumni have published retrospective rolls of registered students from the institutional beginnings. Others have long-term projects to collect biographical information. For instance, Trinity (Anglican) College in Toronto has unpublished files on all people who studied theology at the Diocesan College in Cobourg (1841-1851) and its successor, Trinity's Faculty of Divinity (1852 to the present), which are open to descendants and researchers. AO has the collection of University of Toronto and Upper Canada College correspondence, 1880-1905, nominally indexed.

See also "The Graduates of Kings College, Toronto" by W. Stewart Wallace in *Ontario History* Vol. 42 (1950) and "John Strachan and the Diocesan Theological Institute at Cobourg, 1842-1852" by J.D. Purdy in *Ontario History* Vol. 65 (1973).

Mechanics' Institutes were the forerunner of modern libraries. The concept originated in England to provide the adult working class with educational opportunities. After 1882 the province of Ontario was transferring Institute material, along with funding, to municipalities for building public libraries. The Mechanics' Institutes collection at AO 1848-1895 has papers and records from Belleville to Woodstock, with an online alphabetical place name finding aid.

Professions and Occupations

Reference Dates

1792	First agricultural society organized
1797	Law Society of Upper Canada formed
1839	College of Physicians and Surgeons of Upper Canada was formed
1841	Medical school established at Kingston
1843	Upper Canada medical school established in Toronto
1850	Upper Canada School of Medicine was affiliated with the University of Toronto
1872	First Trade Unions Act
1883	Women's Medical College established at Kingston
1897	Victorian Order of Nurses organized

Professional training faculties were few and far between in the early nineteenth century. Early students from Upper Canada in law, medicine, divinity and the sciences were often likely to become qualified in the British Isles or the United States. An example of the latter is our neighbouring state of New York where some training institutions were then more developed or advanced. It is not possible here to explore *all* professions and occupations in depth, but a few can be mentioned where additional sources are likely. See Chapter 10 for military personnel.

Associations and regulatory bodies exist for many established professions and trades. Some of these organizations have kept membership lists or applications. The names and addresses of many organizations can be found in *Directory of Canadian Associations*. If professions like medicine, the law, the ministry, engineering, science, architecture and others have produced more prominent citizens than "ordinary" jobs, past editions of *Canadian Who's Who* and *Dictionary of Canadian Biography* may prove to be rewarding sources. The latter documents the lives of significant citizens from Canada's beginnings.

Teachers   The first training schools for teachers were called Normal Schools. Model Schools were opened later in various counties for a different class of teaching certificate. The AO collection includes Normal and Model School admission applications 1847-1849 and 1869-1872, third class certificates 1877-1901, examination papers 1859-1879 and Toronto Normal School registers 1847-1859 and 1863-1873. There is also a collection from the Ontario Educational Association, a

professional teachers' organization, for the years 1861-1986.
Teachers' superannuation applications 1820-1919 in the

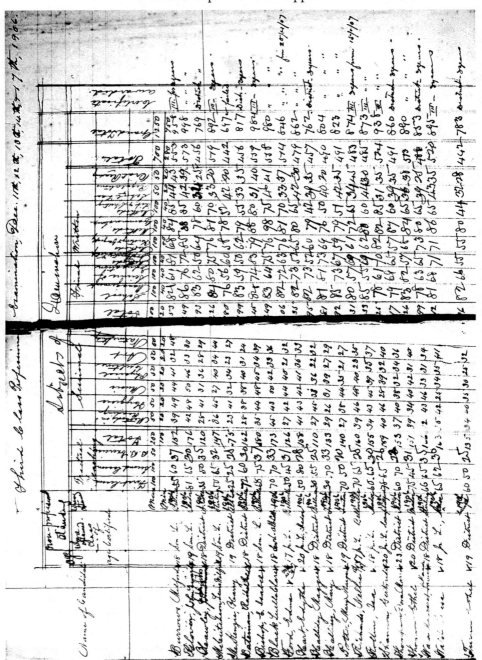

Teachers' third class professional examination, December 1906, County Boards of Education records, RG 2-142-0-13, Hastings County Board of Education Minutes 1882-1907; AO microfilm MS 5468

AO collection are an important source for historical information on a teacher ancestor. Types of training and locations of teaching experience for retired individual teachers are documented on the superannuation form. Other information given is birthplace, residence, religious affiliation, age and number of teaching years. Brant County Branch OGS published similar material in *First Superannuated Teachers in Ontario*, extracted from department of education reports on 170 retiring teachers from 1853 to 1856 and 1858.

Some material in the AO collection with regard to teachers has not yet been processed. In order to find other useful genealogical material, you should spend considerable time examining the finding aid or browsing archival descriptions on the website to relate accessible material to your ancestor's location and dates. If you can consult a library or archives in your target area, there may be some original school or education records in its holdings.

More information is available in the 28-volume set called *Documentary History of Education in Upper Canada* by John G. Hodgins. Articles of interest:

"Elementary School Education in Upper Canada: A Reassessment" by R.D. Gidney in *Ontario History* Vol. 65 (1973).

"Who Ran the Schools? Local Influence on Education Policy in Nineteenth Century Ontario" by D.A. Lawr and R.D. Gidney in *Ontario History* Vol. 72 (1980).

"Teachers' Institutes: Instituting Proper Training" by Harry Smaller in *Ontario History* Vol. 80, No. 4 (1988).

Lawyers   The legal profession represents the law, which permeates so many facets of our lives—the drafting of wills, assigning property title and deeds, the wording of contracts, justice in the courtroom and so on. The Law Society of Upper Canada (LSUC) is the body responsible for educational standards and regulating admission to legal practice. All lawyers in the province must be members of the society (bar admission) and are accountable to it for ethical and professional behaviour. Training in the law was originally akin to an apprenticeship. Students worked and clerked in law offices to obtain professional standing. Prior university attendance was not required, but completion of an academic course of study was not enough in itself to qualify someone. The first law school was formalized at Osgoode Hall in 1889. Student records from 1891 are now at the LSUC archives.

The archives has nominal rolls of the barristers and solicitors from the law society's inception in 1797. The rolls provide the name of the person and the date of his admission to the society or his call to the bar. Roy C. Schaeffer published them in *Families* Vol. 28, No. 4 (1989) with the title "Genealogy and the Legal Profession." Now the list also is available on the society's archives website as an alphabetical, biographical database 1797-1929. Minutes of the convocation of the society in the nineteenth century may also have additional information about admissions, such as the name of the applicant's father or sponsor. The archives has a research service but requires an appointment for a personal visit.

Genealogists can also consult the annually published lists such as *Ontario Legal Directory* or *Canada Law List*. They recorded practising lawyers and legal firms with addresses. In this way, a lawyer's career and locations can be traced through the years. The lists also include information on contemporary courts and their various officials. The records of some now-defunct law firms have been deposited with AO.

Doctors, Nurses Medical schools were established at the universities of McGill in Montreal in 1823 and Queen's in Kingston in 1841 and others followed. But, many doctors-to-be still went to London and Edinburgh to train. The early records of the medical school at Trinity College have gone to AO, which also has Kingston Women's Medical College school reports 1850-1894. See "Jenny Kidd Trout and the Founding of the Women's Medical Colleges at Kingston and Toronto" by Peter Dembski in *Ontario History* Vol. 77, No. 3 (1985).

At the Canadian Genealogy Centre under Medical Personnel, you can find a guide to microfilm numbers for medical board reports and certificates 1819-1854. Licences for medical practice, coroners, surgeons and midwives are available for varying nineteenth century dates. The CGC guide also gives more source suggestions for medical-type ancestors.

Early nursing training developed along with hospitals. Kingston and St. Catharines hospitals were among the first to have programs. Up until the beginning of the twentieth century and even later, it was common for women to take their training in New York state, for instance Rochester, where regulatory requirements had been in place for some time. The archives of the College of Nurses of Ontario (Appendix III) advises that they have no personnel records before 1923, which is when this province required nurses to be registered. If you have a photograph of a nurse ancestor, the archives may be able to identify where she trained by her uniform. Some of the few hospital records at AO include material from their affiliated schools of nursing.

Records for the Victorian Order of Nurses for Canada 1873-1972 are at LAC. Historically, the role of the VON was outreach, to serve patients some distance from medical facilities, developing Cottage Hospitals in rural areas. As well, the Order served the Canadian military during the two world wars. The LAC fonds includes correspondence and archival material for hospitals at North Bay, New Liskeard, Chapleau and other places. Reports, minutes, scrapbooks, clippings and more are described in the online finding aid.

An allied occupation is described in "The Case of the Missing Midwives: a History of Midwifery in Ontario, 1795-1900" by C. Lesley Biggs in *Ontario History* Vol. 75, No. 1 (1983). Midwives appear fairly frequently as *accoucheurs* on many birth registrations.

Farmers Many of us had ancestors who were farmers, and it is possible to find additional information on their modest but important occupation. A view of early rural life was given in *Families* Vol. 41 No. 3 ((2002) by Ryan Taylor in "Difficulties of Pioneer Life: Was It Really That Miserable?" The article "House-Building in Rural Canada West 1850" by Donald Read in *Families* Vol. 43 No. 4 (2004) gives a vivid eyewitness account of how the pioneer community often worked cooperatively.

Farmers can be found in county directories that show the owners or occupants of rural township properties. The best reference work for available directories is Mary Bond's *Canadian Directories, 1790-1987*. Both Library and Archives Canada and the Archives of Ontario have large collections of historical directories. The nineteenth century series of historical atlases often have some biographical sketches, photographs of local dignitaries and drawings of farms or buildings. Community histories are another source for family reminiscences. See Barbara Aitken's *Local Histories of Ontario Municipalities 1951-1977* and the later supplements.

The records of township or county agricultural societies, which often date back to the first half of the last century, are a little-used source. Local newspapers devoted extensive space to prize lists at the township or county fall fair. The rural Womens' Institutes were formed in 1897 and within two decades one of their ongoing projects was to collect historical details of their communities and first settlers. Thus the Tweedsmuir Histories,

Oct. 11, 1889.

East Huron Fall Show.

A Most Successful Ex-hibition..

Big Crowd on Friday.

The opening of the annual Fair under the auspices of the East Huron Agricultural Society took place on Thursday of last week. The day did not open auspiciously, for heavy rain set in and continued a good part of the forenoon. This did not discourage the exhibitors from taking their exhibits to the Fair grounds, however, and by 1 p. m. the "Crystal Palace" was well filled, about the only lack, compared with other years, being the dearth of fruit. This was the more noticeable from the fact that East Huron is not surpassed by any other locality for apple growing.

Among noticeable exhibits was a splendid show of light and heavy harness, buffalo robes, horse blankets, trunks and valises by our two harness-makers, H. Dennis and I. C. Richards. It was a creditable display. Brussels Woolen Mill also showed a large range of woolen goods, knitted goods, &c. It proved that they are able to put on the market good substantial lines that shou'd satisfy the public. The farmers of this section would do well to patronise this institution.

Messrs. Smith & Malcolm made a tip-top display of furniture, manufactured in their factory. They also exhibited sashes, doors, &c.

W. H. McCracken, E. Garvin, J. Stafford and others had a lot of garden produce in the building, the most of which was of excellent quality.

W. J. Fairfield was to the front with an unusually fine display of work from his photograph gallery. It was much admired. Mrs. Graham's paintings and the exhibit of Mrs. Whitley were also worthy of special comment.

In the ladies department the honors were divided. The largest prize-winners were Mrs. T. and Mrs. W. Ballantyne and Miss Nellie Ross, of Brussels ; Miss McClelland, of Belgrave, and Misses Watson & Gibb, of Listowel. Besides these there were dozens of others, who closely followed the prize winners. The judges had a big time in awarding the prizes in this department.

No section of the county can beat this for good bread makers and butter makers. To add to the interest this year a special prize was given by G. A. Deadman for the best cake baked with his baking powder, and about half the exhibit was devoured before the Show was over, thus proving that the good ladies are living up to the baking of the lighter order as well as the "staff of life."

R. Leatherdale had on exhibition two cases of stuffed birds and animals and a valuable collection of coins, the latter embracing almost everything known in the money market as far as gold, silver and copper are concerned.

On Thursday evening upwards of 400 people visited the 'Palace' and inspected all that was to be seen. The Hall was better lighted than usual, and the presence of the Band enlivened the proceedings. A number of girls gave an exhibition of club swinging on the platform. At 10 o'clock the Hall and its contents were left to the care of the watch...

...Friday, the second day of the ... was a big improvement over ... ing day as far as weather ... concerned, although the ... on the cool side. From ... morning until afternoon people

Portion of "East Huron Fall Show," The Brussels Post, 11 October 1889, p. 3

another under-used source, were instigated. A great many have been microfilmed and available at AO as well as local resource centres. Wellington County Museum and Archives was the first to digitize their county collection and create a searchable database.

Surveyors   Surveyors left diaries and field notebooks of arduous and often lonely journeys through the wilderness. Some of them noted the names of men they hired as axemen, labourers and cooks. At times their books mention someone's house or camp as a landmark or overnight stop. Those stops were often made with the earliest inhabitants, the ones who preceded official settlement records. At AO the surveyor records are found within the Crown lands finding aid. Additional information about surveyors can be found in Ladell's *They Left Their Mark.*

Marine Workers   Ancestors employed in maritime activities can be found among LAC's Central Registry of Seamen, for example, registers of marine certificates for masters (captains), mates and engineers of steam vessels 1872-1952. LAC also has such items as microfilm copies of Lloyd's Captains Registers 1851-1947 that include Canadian merchant marine captains with their place and year of birth, along with dates of service on named vessels and the destination of each voyage. More information on merchant seamen and their ships can be found in *History of the Great Lakes* and in the quarterly *Inland Seas*, published by the Great Lakes Historical Society. Edward Warner wrote about "Crew Members Aboard Great Lakes Sailing Vessels Project" in *Families* Vol. 30, No. 2 (1991). The Marine Museum of the Great Lakes at Kingston has extensive marine records including a database of over 13,000 ships from 1786, part of it accessible online.

Government Employees   LAC has some historical files for federal government employees, with explanations on the CGC website. Annual reports published by various government departments in *Sessional Papers of the Dominion of Canada* may contain lists of employees. The usual caution applies to some of the later records at LAC: they will be restricted by right to privacy legislation.

Postmasters LAC has an online database to post office locations across Canada with the names of known postmasters in chronological order by dates of their appointments. Donald E. Read's "Canadian Post Office Records for the Genealogist" in *Families* Vol. 25, No. 3 (1986) is a helpful article.

Police Police ancestors may have served with the Royal Canadian Mounted Police (RCMP), with the Ontario Provincial Police or with a town or city force. The first detachment of the North West Mounted Police—forerunner of the RCMP—was formed in 1873 and consisted of 150 men recruited mainly in Ontario. LAC has the surviving historical personnel files 1873-1904 and they are searchable online for that period. The RCMP archives in Regina has a nominal index to records from 1904 to 1920, which they will search, although the actual files were destroyed. Files after 1920 are not public unless the policeman has been deceased for 20 years or more. "The RCMP Honour Roll" by Norman G. Wilson in the RCMP *Quarterly* and reprinted in the Saskatchewan Genealogical Society's *Bulletin* Vol. 25, No. 2 (1994) listed members who were killed on duty from 1873 to 1993. "Ancestors on the Frontier" by Sandy Garland in *Ottawa Branch News* Vol. 27, No. 1 (1994) investigates an ancestor in RCMP records at LAC. A small Dominion Police Force existed from 1869 to 1919. The few surviving records have been incorporated into the early RCMP records.

Records for the Ontario Provincial Police (OPP) exist from 1909, the year they were formed. Some of the records in the AO collection include force members 1917-1921, applications 1909-1925, awards 1946-1976 and investigation files. The most genealogically rewarding would be Series E of the finding aid: personnel and training, and criminal investigation reports. Restrictions on the OPP records in AO custody vary between 25 and 50 years. Service records of policemen in the city of Toronto begin in 1834. Metropolitan Toronto police headquarters maintains a historian and a museum.

Photographers Photographers are of special interest to genealogists, not only as ancestors, but also because their names and locations on family photographs help to situate forgotten or missing family members. Scrutiny of wearing apparel also assists with date estimates. See the two very useful publications by Glen Phillips.

Railway Workers Railway employee ancestors are well-served by the Douglas book *Canadian Railway Records* and an article in *Families* Vol. 34, No. 3 (1995).

Architects   Both LAC and AO have collections donated by individual architects. In particular, the Canadian Centre for Architecture collects business records, drawings, and models from architectural firms.

Politicians   Politicians, by their very nature as elected representatives, receive great attention from their contemporaries and from historians. Their characters and contributions are reflected in newspapers, community histories, biographies and private papers, of which both LAC and AO have wide collections.

Inventors   Might your ancestor have invented a machine, a piece of equipment, a new tool or a scientific process? It's surprising how many instances of your surname might show up in the Canadian Intellectual Property Office's *Canadian Patents Database*. The database dates from 1867 to the current day, with dates, descriptions and drawings available for most inventions. Inventors from countries outside Canada are included if the patent was registered here. The same site has sections for registered trademarks, copyrights, and industrial design.

Other Occupations   Researchers are advised to consult library and archival catalogues by subject or key word for various occupations. Any number of books have been published on occupations ranging from blacksmiths and clockmakers to innkeepers and jewellers.

Business Records

AO has certain collections for business firms in the province. To ascertain whether employees are named, it's necessary to examine the description or finding aid of individual fonds. The papers and records may be more revealing of owners and management. In general, many of the collections could have such documentation as charters and letters patent, registrations, regulatory files and some commercial records. Expired partnerships and sole proprietorship records from about 1850 to 1973 (RG 55-17 at AO) include declaration forms to state when a partnership or company was formed, who the principals were, the type of business and its location, and when it dissolved. The list of records is arranged by county on the AO website. Indexes can be searched by the name of the firm or an individual's name for microfilm numbers.

Dun and Bradstreet reports in the twentieth century and *Dun's Review* 1893-1933 can be consulted at LAC and other reference libraries. They contain credit ratings and other information on commercial, business and manufacturing companies throughout Canada, as well as some information on banks and trust companies. Business directories are another source for tracing an ancestor's business or company. One of the earliest with coverage across the province is Wilson's reprint of *Directory of the Province of Ontario, 1857.* However, it does not necessarily include every single business or professional person at that time. "Tracing a Family Business" by David Bellhouse appeared in OGS *Seminar Annual, 1984,* advising universally applicable research techniques.

Obtaining information from insurance companies needs direct contact with a company's head office to explore whether it has old records and allows access to them. City directories have the names of such companies from early days. Both *Directory of Archives in Ontario* and *Directory of Canadian Archives* list some banks and life insurance companies that have archives: Bank of Nova Scotia, Toronto-Dominion Bank, Crown Life Insurance and London Life Insurance among them. Their business records have limited genealogical application, again depending on the existence of or accessibility to employment or personnel files. Appointments to see their material must be made in advance.

The historical records of the T. Eaton Company, the nation's largest retail employer, have been donated to AO. In this huge collection is a full series of in-house employee magazines from the 1920s to the 1980s. The Maclean-Hunter collection at AO has a separate finding aid for records of this publishing conglomerate. Another large employer, Steel Company of Canada (Stelco), has an archives in Hamilton with minutes, correspondence, annual reports and the like. The LAC collection relating to steam navigation on the Great Lakes 1809-1965 gives access to the development of merchant shipping companies. Shipping company records can also be found at the Marine Museum of the Great Lakes at Kingston.

Some of the major business collections at LAC are those for the historic Bank of British North America, Toronto Board of Trade, Toronto Stock Exchange, Henry Birks & Sons, Ltd., and others representing a national level of industry or employment. These are but a few representative samples of what you can find when you know your family's business or employment and are tenacious enough to follow through. Not only LAC and AO have large and small collections along this line, but regional or local repositories are alternate resources to pursue. "Business, Corporate, University and Municipal Archives: Summary of Panel Presentation" in *Readings in Ontario Genealogical Resources* can give you more ideas.

Labour Unions

Trade unions or associations had origins in the nineteenth century, but it was not until the Trade Unions Act of 1872 that industrial workers were given some recognition for their efforts to improve working conditions. Most labour unions in Canada have been of a national rather than provincial nature, hence the tendency to deposit historical material at LAC. Existing records date mainly from the twentieth century. The Canadian Labour Congress, an umbrella group of unions, placed its historical material with LAC in 1970. The Congress held its first convention in Toronto in 1873, with 31 unions attending. The largest collections for specific unions at LAC involve railway and transportation unions, and date from the 1940s. Examples of more at LAC are the past records of Clothing Workers, Association of Canadian Television and Radio Artists, Canadian Airline Employees, Knights of Labour, Steelworkers, Textile Workers, Automobile Workers and many others. Investigation of individual collections will show how much is administrative material, and whether membership names are included. Forsey's *Trade Unions in Canada, 1812-1902* is informative background reading.

Health and Welfare

Reference Dates

1812	Toronto General Hospital traces its roots to the War of 1812
1831	First Mechanics' Institute established, in York
1841	First lunatic asylum opened, in Toronto
1873	Ontario's first Public Health Act
1875	Forerunner of Hospital for Sick Children opened, Toronto
1880	Ontario Medical Association established
1882	Public Health Units were formed
1883	St. John Ambulance established in Canada
1912	Public health units re-formed on a county basis

Medical Records

Genealogists have more than a passing interest in a family's medical history. Information about cause of death and contributing causes are a valid part of family history and can increase understanding of family health and life cycles. Certain sources are available to us for this information, such as death certificates and perhaps newspaper notices or family hearsay. Nevertheless, our sources and information for health history are usually limited to two or three preceding generations. As medical professionals now recommend, it behooves us to gather information for the benefit of our own health and that of future generations. Instructions for compiling a family health tree are available from genealogical and medical sources, such as books by Bell and Arvanitis; McNabb, Curtis and Barclay Bowley; or the Mayo Clinic website.

A much more serious issue arises in this connection. Inherited disease and disorders have only come under study relatively recently by geneticists, especially with the advancement of human genome knowledge. The consequences of being able to trace a recurring disease through lineal and collateral generations of a family are obvious for early detection and treatment among living members. With a great deal of effort and cooperation, the methodology of genealogical research can work in tandem with medical specialists to help determine descendants at risk.

The reality is that personal health-related records are traditionally confidential. We can only mention some general avenues that might be of assistance. Doctors are not required to keep patients' case files longer than six years after the last reference in it, or their retirement from practice. Likewise, medical or clinical records for hospital patients are customarily destroyed after a set time. However, the medical profession has become aware of the archival and historical value of retaining some material. As an example, if older hospital admission registers were saved, they may be open to researchers. The specialized *Directory of Medical Archives in Ontario* lists medical and medicine-related locations.

On the other hand, many records of provincial psychiatric hospitals are saved at the Archives of Ontario in various forms. Psychiatric facilities were known as lunatic asylums in the nineteenth century. For a long time the asylums were largely of a custodial nature rather than being treatment centres. The records contain asylum correspondence, patient information and estate and maintenance files. The earliest patient casebooks and registers date from 1851 for Toronto, 1855 for Kingston, 1867 for London and 1876 for Hamilton. They are microfilmed and accessible up to the 100-year restriction. A nominal "Lunatic Index" at AO refers to patient committals and discharges 1889-1913, with some earlier entries, compiled from general correspondence of the provincial secretary. Records of the privately run Homewood Psychiatric Hospital in Guelph 1883-1944 are also subject to certain privacy restrictions.

Background reading could be "'In Charge of the Loons': A Portrait of the London, Ontario, Asylum for the Insane in the Nineteenth Century" by Cheryl L. Krasnick in *Ontario History* Vol. 74, No. 3 (1982). For more information on health types of records, see "Genealogical Research into Medical and Social Welfare Records" by Carolyn Gray and Tom Belton in *Families* Vol. 30, No. 4 (1991). The online exhibit "Medical Records at the Archives of Ontario" relates the heritage of health care and some of AO's specific holdings. In addition, AO holds historic records for special institutions like the Deaf and Dumb Institute at Belleville and the Ontario School for the Blind at Brantford with some information on inmates, but are mostly of an administrative nature. A series of licenses for private hospitals and rest homes dating from 1925 is also at AO.

Social Assistance

It was already mentioned that some of the helpless and destitute in the early days of this province were kept in local jails for want of separate, more appropriate shelter. Upper Canada did not initially provide for an authority like the poor law unions in England. Concern was soon evident about society's accommodation of the needy. See Chapter 8 regarding assistance for poor and ailing immigrants.

Upper Canada Courts of Quarter Sessions records sometimes refer to indigent widows with children in need of food or shelter. Orphanages frequently began as religion-affiliated organizations, and thus one city or county may well have had both a Protestant and a Catholic home. Boards of health have existed since the mid-1800s to provide a measure of disease control and public care. Hospitals became necessary for the isolation or treatment of contagious disease and the chronically ill, and other community medical services developed with professional personnel. In many cases, records have not survived for the early facilities, but related records may be found in municipal or county council minutes or committee reports.

It was not until 1866 that each county was required to have

"Bruce County House of Refuge, Walkerton," photograph, accession 9258 S14381; Special Collections, AO

a House of Refuge or House of Industry, although numerous establishments had been created before that date. Home for the Aged, Home for Men and Home for Women were other names or uses for these public buildings. It is worth noting that these homes often had their own cemeteries on the grounds for the burial of people unclaimed by relatives. Inspectors and other agencies made reports on conditions in these homes, some of which can be found at AO.

Houses of Industry were set up for the unemployed poor. Those who were able to work would contribute to the upkeep of the institution. Two articles give some description: "The Industrial Home, Newmarket, Ontario" by Norman Jolly in *Families* Vol. 26, No. 4 (1987) and a follow-up by Corlene Taylor, "Some Notes on Norman Jolly's 'The Industrial Home,'" in *Families* Vol. 27, No. 4 (1988). The pamphlet *County Paupers and County Houses of Industry* of 1894 explains the role of these charitable institutions and their services. After 1874, delinquent children may have been sent to one of the industrial schools or reformatories. The pamphlet and more material on a number of industrial schools can be found at AO.

Benevolent/Fraternal Societies

As families grew and prospered, more time became available beyond the necessities for survival. Some of us may question just what a genealogist can learn from charitable, fraternal or social organizations, but membership alone can add some depth of character to an ancestor. If records are available, they might show the ancestor's position on issues within the group or his participation in projects. Benevolent societies usually began with the purpose of addressing local needs of the less fortunate. For example, in Chapter 8 some reference was made to immigrant aid from government, but locally raised volunteer societies also sprang up. Many of them had only a brief existence. One of the first was the Loyal and Patriotic Society of Upper Canada, which Doris Bourrie wrote about in *Families* Vol. 26 No. 4 (1987). The society, existing from 1813 to 1817, was formed to financially assist the hardships incurred by the militia and their families during the War of 1812. Other societies developed wider commitments and had affiliations beyond their own communities. Some groups are directly related to a cultural heritage, like those described in Harney and Hamilton's *Benevolent and Mutual Aid Societies in Ontario*. Some organizations were based on religious, occupational or pastime interests, while others have a national or international base in which fathers, sons and grandsons have been members.

Fraternal and benevolent societies began to provide important membership benefits such as life insurance or funds for widows. Masonic lodges existed as early as 1787 in Newark and 1794 in Kingston. Helen Schmid wrote about the Ancient Order of United Workmen assessment notices which were for death benefits to the kin of deceased members, giving name, age, date and cause of death, and name and location of the lodge. Her articles appear in *Families* Vol. 21, No. 2 (1982), Vol. 22, No. 1 (1983), and Vol. 26, No. 4 (1987).

AO has some historical records for the Canadian Order of Foresters, Independent Order of Odd Fellows, Rotary Club, the Loyal Orange Association, Order Sons of Italy of Canada, and so on. Others are scattered among papers donated by private individuals or families. You may have to contact a current organization to learn its policy on retention or disclosure of older records. The Knights of Columbus (Appendix III) headquarters has been helpful for some family historians. The Orange Order is accustomed to requests from genealogists. OGS has indexed a database of names from the Independent Order of Odd Fellows' life insurance program 1875–1929. To decipher cryptic initials on cemetery stones—usually referring to the deceased's membership in a fraternal organization—see "grave symbols" on the Olive Tree Genealogy website.

Some records deposited at LAC are from Sons of England, Sons of Scotland, the Irish Benevolent Society, Young Men's Christian Association (YMCA), Imperial Order of the Daughters of the Empire (IODE), and the list goes on. Knowing the name of a society or association will speed up a search for online textual material. The LAC library search returns hundreds of published reports and histories of benevolent associations. *Directory of Associations in Canada* may be the most useful guide for finding current addresses. Older province, county, or city directories usually had lists of the various organizations in their areas, with names of officers or executive members. Histories have been published for numerous such organizations. *The St. George's Society of Toronto* is a particularly good example because it includes burial transcriptions from the society's special plot in St. James Cemetery.

Reading and Reference

Municipal Records

Armstrong, Fred. *Handbook of Upper Canadian Chronology.* Revised edition. Toronto, ON: Dundurn Press, 1985.

————————. *Upper Canada Justices of the Peace and Association, 1788-1841.* Toronto, ON: Ontario Genealogical Society, 2007.

Cote, J.O. and N. Omer. *Political Appointments and Elections in the Province of Canada from 1841 to 1867.* 2 volumes. Second edition. Ottawa, ON: Lowe-Martin, 1918.

Directory of Archives in Ontario. Toronto, ON: Archives Association of Ontario, 2001.

Directory of Canadian Archives. Ottawa, ON: Canadian Council of Archives, 1990.

Dunford, Fraser. *Municipal Records in Ontario: History and Guide.* Toronto, ON: Ontario Genealogical Society, 2005.

Forman, Debra, compiler and editor. *Legislators and Legislatures of Ontario, 1792-1984.* 3 volumes. Toronto, ON: Ontario Legislative Library, 1984.

Hillman, Thomas A. *A Chronology of Ontario Counties and Municipalities.* Gananoque, ON: Langdale Press, 1988.

McGrath, Paul, editor. *The Great Contest for Responsible Government: The City of Toronto Poll Book of 1841.* Toronto, ON: Toronto Branch OGS, 2004.

Millar, Ellen, editor. *Directory of Municipal Archives.* Revised third edition. Toronto, ON: Archives Association of Ontario, 2007.

Mosser, Christine, editor. *York, Upper Canada, Minutes of Town Meetings and Lists of Inhabitants, 1793-1823.* Toronto, ON: Metropolitan Toronto Library Board, 1984.

Obee, Dave. *Federal Voters Lists in Ontario, 1935 to 1979: A Finding Aid.* Victoria, BC: D. Obee, 2004.

Association of Municipalities of Ontario.
www.amo.on.ca/AM/Template.cfm?Section=Home
OntarioRoots. www.ontarioroots.com

Education

1837 Rebellion Remembered. Toronto, ON: Ontario Historical Society, 1988.

Directory of Canadian Universities. Ottawa, ON: Association of Universities and Colleges of Canada, annual.

Hodgins, John G. *Documentary History of Education in Upper Canada.* 28 volumes. Toronto, ON: Warwick Bros. & Rutter, 1894-1910.

Houston, Susan E. and Alison Prentice. *Schooling and Scholars in Nineteenth Century Ontario.* Toronto, ON: University of Toronto Press, 1988.

Stamp, Robert M. *The Schools of Ontario, 1876-1976.* Toronto, ON: University of Toronto Press, 1982.

_____. *The Historical Background to Separate Schools in Ontario.* Toronto, ON: Ontario Ministry of Education, 1985.

Ontario Ministry of Education. www.edu.gov.on.ca/eng

Occupations

Baldwin, Mary and Margaret Dunn, compiler and editor. *A Directory of Medical Archives in Ontario.* Toronto, ON: Hannah Institute for the History of Medicine, 1983.

Beers, J.H. *History of the Great Lakes.* 1899. Reprint. Cleveland, OH: Freshwater Press, 1972.

Bond, Mary E. *Canadian Directories, 1790-1987: A Bibliography and Place Name Index.* 3 volumes. Ottawa, ON: National Library of Canada, 1989.

Bourgeault, Ivy Lee. *Push! The Struggle for Midwifery in Ontario.* Montreal QC/Kingston ON: McGill-Queen's University Press, 2006.

Canniff, William. *Medical Profession in Upper Canada, 1783-1850.* Toronto, ON: Briggs, 1894.

Directory of Associations in Canada. Toronto, ON: University of Toronto Press, 1973-1997.

Douglas, Althea and J. Creighton Douglas. *Canadian Railway Records: A Guide for Genealogists.* Revised edition. Toronto, ON: Ontario Genealogical Society, 2004.

Forsey, Eugene. *Trade Unions in Canada, 1812-1902.* Toronto, ON: University of Toronto Press, 1982.

Godfrey, Charles M. *Medicine for Ontario: A History*. Belleville, ON: Mika Publishing, 1979.

Ladell, John L. *They Left Their Mark: Surveyors and Their Role in the Settlement of Ontario*. Toronto, ON: Dundurn Press, 1993.

Langdon, John Ernest. *Clock and Watchmakers in Canada, 1700 to 1900*. Toronto, ON: Anson-Cartwright Editions, 1976.

Ontario Legal Directory. Toronto, ON: University of Toronto Press, published annually since 1925.

The Ontario Medical Register. Toronto, ON: The College of Physicians and Surgeons of Ontario, published intermittently from 1867.

Phillips, Glen C. *Ontario Dairy and Creamery List, 1900-1950*. Sarnia, ON: Iron Gate Publishing, 1989.

_____. *Ontario Drug Store and Druggist List, 1851-1930*. Sarnia, ON: Iron Gate Publishing, 1989.

_____. *Ontario Photographers List, 1851-1900*. Milton, ON: Global Heritage Press, 2002.

_____. *Ontario Photographers List, 1901-1925*. Milton, ON: Global Heritage Press, 2002.

Travill, A.A. *Medicine at Queen's, 1854-1920: A Peculiarly Happy Relationship*. Montreal QC/Kingston ON: McGill-Queen's University Press, 1988.

Wilson, Don, editor. *Readings in Ontario Genealogical Sources*. Toronto, ON: D. Wilson, 1978.

Wilson, Thomas B., editor. *Directory of the Province of Ontario, 1857*. 1857. Lambertville, NJ: Hunterdon House, 1987.

Archives Association of Ontario. aao.fis.utoronto.ca/aa/maig.html

Canadian Centre for Architecture. www.cca.qc.ca

Canadian Intellectual Property Office. Canadian Patents Database. www.canadalegal.com/gosite.asp?s=626

Law Society of Upper Canada Archives. library.lsuc.on.ca/GL/arch_general.htm

Marine Museum of the Great Lakes. www.marmuseum.ca

Royal Canadian Mounted Police Archives. www.rcmp-grc.gc.ca

Health and Welfare

Bell, Sherilyn and Constandina Arvanitis. *The Genes in Your Genealogy*. Toronto, ON: Heritage Books, 2001.

Briggs, Elizabeth and Colin Briggs. *Before Modern Medicine: Diseases and Yesterday's Remedies*. Winnipeg, MB: Westgarth Publishing, 1998.

Godfrey, Charles M. *The Cholera Epidemics in Upper Canada 1832-1866*. Toronto, ON: Seccombe House, c1968.

Harney, Robert F. and Jean Hamilton, editors. *Benevolent and Mutual Aid Societies in Ontario*. Toronto, ON: Multicultural History Society of Ontario, 1979.

Harrison, Michael and Dorothy Martin. *Records of the Society for the Relief of the Sick and Indigent.* Toronto, ON: Toronto Branch OGS, c2003.

Houston, Cecil J. and William J. Smyth. *The Sash Canada Wore: A Historical Geography of the Orange Order in Canada.* Second edition. Campbellville, ON: Global Heritage Press, 2000.

McNabb, Luanne, Elizabeth Curtis and Kathleen Barclay Bowley. *Family Health Trees: Genetics and Genealogy.* Second edition. Toronto, ON: The Ontario Genealogical Society, 2005.

National Genealogical Society Quarterly: Your Family Health History. Special issue. Vol. 82, No. 2. Arlington, VA: National Genealogical Society, 1994.

Robertson, John Ross. *History of Freemasonry in Canada.* Toronto, ON: Hunter, Rose, 1899.

Storey, Anne, compiler and editor. *The St. George's Society of Toronto: A History and List of Members, 1834-1967.* Toronto, ON: Generation Press, 1987. See also www.ourroots.ca

Grand Orange Lodge of Canada. www.grandorangelodge.ca

Knights of Columbus, Ontario State Council. www.osc-koc.com

MayoClinic.com. How to Compile Your Medical Family Tree. www.mayoclinic.com/health/medical-history/HQ01707

Olive Tree Genealogy. www.olivetreegenealogy.com

United States Department of Human & Health Services. U.S. Surgeon General's Family Health Initiative. www.hhs.gov/familyhistory

10

Military and Associated Records

Reference Dates

1783	Treaty of Separation; end of Revolutionary War
1796	Jay's Treaty took effect regarding boundary with U.S.; British withdrew from Detroit and Michilimackinac
1812	War of 1812 began
1814	Treaty of Ghent was signed to end the War
1828	Removal of British garrison on Drummond Island to Penetanguishene
1837–38	Rebellion in Upper and Lower Canada
1855	Militia Act; a paid peace-time active militia was organized
1861–65	Civil War in the United States
1866, 1870	Fenian raids into Canada
1870	Military expedition to the Red River
1871	British troops withdrew from Canada
1885	Militia participated in the North West Rebellion
1899	A Canadian contingent was organized for the South African (Boer) War
1910	Department of Naval Service was established
1914	First World War began
1924	Royal Canadian Air Force established
1937	Mackenzie-Papineau Battalion of Canadian volunteers fight in Spanish Civil War
1939	Second World War began
1940	National Resources Mobilization Act
1950	A Canadian contingent created to serve in the Korean War

| **1967** | Unification of Canadian Armed Forces was completed |

The main line of defence in the North American colonies was provided by British Army troops until the mid-nineteenth century. During that time, a soldier ancestor was generally someone born and enlisted in the British Isles. Native-born Canadians were seldom signed up in colonial posts, with a few exceptions. Many soldiers at the end of their service terms made the decision to stay or return here as settlers. Thus we look to British government and military records for much of the material relating to soldiers in early Canada. The withdrawal of British troops from Canada after 1870 overlapped with the formation of the Canadian armed forces, although the 1870 Red River expedition was a joint effort.

Since Confederation, defence and the military have been under federal authority, so Library and Archives Canada is the repository for most of the accessible records, including microfilm copies of many series from The National Archives in England (formerly the Public Record Office). A huge amount of information has been published, both in print form and on the Internet. Researchers would do well to initially consult "From Colony to Country," an online LAC overview of Canada's military history with annotated bibliographies for each period. *Canadian Military History Gateway* is an educational and interactive website developed by the Department of National Defence in partnership with a number of leading institutions. The Canadian Genealogy Centre and other websites mentioned throughout the chapter also provide reliable military information.

To distinguish somewhat between militiamen and professional soldiers, this chapter will deal first with the militia, then with historic British army records as they pertain to this province, followed by the Canadian armed forces. Books by Bercuson and Morton are recommended reference works for more historical background.

Pre-1870

Militia

The British concept of a universal militia system existed in Upper Canada from the eighteenth century. Able-bodied men between the ages of sixteen and fifty (later raised to sixty) were required to assemble for training once a year on the King's birthday in June.

The exercise was little more than a reminder of their obligation to serve and defend if the need arose. These militia regiments or battalions were usually organized on a county basis. The officers were frequently men with some experience from either the Revolutionary War or were ex-British military, but also men of community prominence were coopted as leaders. In 1829, first battalions consisted of men aged nineteen to thirty-nine; second battalions were formed for older men aged forty to sixty. Certain exemptions were allowed for members of pacifist faiths and public officials or occupations considered vital to civic life. Otherwise, men who did not appear for the annual muster were fined.

Militia rolls give a man's name, sometimes his age, the name of his regiment and normally the company or captain he served under. A great number of militia rolls and pay lists are found in the records of the Department of Militia and Defence (RG 9 at LAC), although others are scattered throughout different collections or resource centres. For example, the Lincoln Militia fonds at both LAC and AO includes nominal pay lists in 1795 and 1838. At LAC, see the paper or online finding aids for the various departments titled Upper Canada Adjutant General's Office 1794-1852, Department of Militia, Upper Canada 1846-1869 and Department of Militia and Defence 1846-1960. AO has some personnel lists in its Military Records collection, with material for about a dozen counties. An inventory is not available yet, so seeking advice from an archivist is appropriate. Some lists and records have also survived in papers of former county officers, and may be found in manuscript collections under their names.

By far the most definitive publication for the family historian in early days is *Men of Upper Canada: Militia Nominal Rolls 1828-1829* exhaustively compiled by Elliott, Walker and Stratford-Devai. Lists of names have been extracted from LAC material to cover nearly every county of the time period. Where a few townships or militia company lists are missing, contemporary tax assessment rolls have been substituted when available. Often the regimental rolls or the compilers indicate from which townships within the county they were drawn, a clue to a man's residence.

Militia lists for various periods are also found published in local historical society periodicals, or local or county histories. A few of the earliest lists in print are:

"The Lincoln Militia" by Albert Stray in *Canadian Genealogist* Vol. 7, No.
4 (1985), with an excellent introduction to the militia in general, and 1813 lists of Lincoln County names.

"Lincoln Militia Returns, 1818" by J.A.C. Kennedy in *Families* Vol. 10, No. 2 (1971).

"Militia Roll of Talbot Street, Kent County, 1818" in *The Ontario Register* Vol. 7, No. 1 (1983).

"2nd Regiment, Prince Edward Militia, 1822" in *The Ontario Register* Vol. 2, No. 3 (1969).

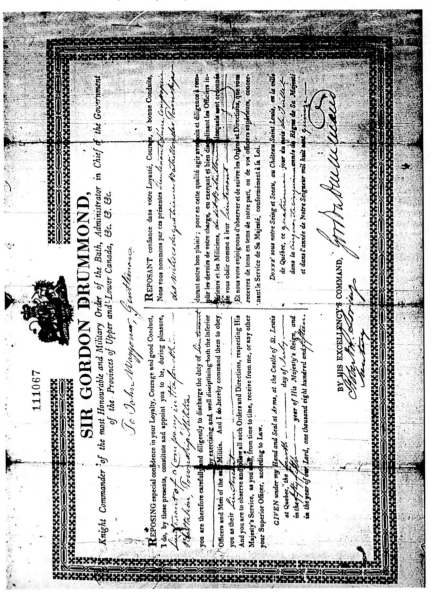

John Waggoner militia appointment (1838), Civil Secretary's Correspondence, Upper Canada Sundries, RG 5, A 1, vol. 201, p. 111067; Library and Archives Canada microfilm C-6901

"Militia Returns of Thurlow, Hastings County, 1830 and 1837" by Gordon Crouse in *The Ontario Register* Vol. 3, No. 2 (1970).

"Hastings Militia Return" [1834] by Gordon Crouse in *The Ontario Register* Vol. 1, No. 4 (1968).

"Muster Roll of the 1st Hastings Independent Rifle Company" [1836] by Roger Reid in *Families* Vol. 39, No. 1 (2000).

"Militia Roll of Rainham, Haldimand County, 1832" in *The Ontario Register* Vol. 3, No. 4 (1970).

1812–1814

Many militiamen saw local action in the War of 1812, for which LAC has some pay lists arranged by regimental units. Fewer than 1500 British army regulars, stationed at existing forts, were the main defenders with professional experience. Fencible units such as the Canadian Fencibles and the Glengarry Light Infantry— raised in the colonies, with more training and discipline than the county militia—augmented the sparse number of regulars. The support of native allies and the then under-trained militia was essential in many instances. Their actions during the war are regarded as the birth of pride in the Upper Canadian militia.

The AO has an online exhibit called "War of 1812" that features a timeline and descriptions of battles, leaders, the aftermath, sources, and links, with plentiful illustrations. An article of interest is "'Deeds Speak': Militiamen, Medals and the Invented Traditions of 1812" by George Sheppard in *Ontario History* Vol. 82, No. 3 (1990). Numerous books have been written to examine this historical period, including Pierre Berton's popular double set, *The Invasion of Canada* and *Flames Across the Border*. William Gray's *Soldiers of the King* and Johnston's *The Glengarry Light Infantry* both have lists of the rank and file in the War of 1812 period.

In related matters, Paul Pepper published "War of 1812, Lists of Orphans, Pensioners and Widows" in *Families* Vol. 31, No. 3 (1992). Transcribed from the *Kingston Gazette* in early January 1817, the list includes all who had been approved for militia pensions as of that date. The names of the applicants, their relationship to a deceased or disabled militiaman, and his regiment, battle action and size of pension are stated. One odd item located in the New York State Library is "Survivors of the War of 1812," transcribed by Barbara Nethercott in *Families*, Vol. 33, No. 3 (1994). The list shows pensioners or widows of Canadian veterans of the War of 1812 who were living in New York State in 1883. This may be a chance to locate a missing ancestor or collateral relative.

Legislation was enacted in 1819 to award land grants to those who had served, and many militiamen took advantage of the government bounty. Petitions from the men for land grants were mentioned in Chapter 6. LAC holds a great variety of additional material in its Department of Militia and Defence collection, RG 9. Wilfred Lauber's *An Index to Land Claim Certificates* deals with as-yet unmicrofilmed documents for these militiamen at LAC. The documents may include discharge papers and affidavits of service, with a fair amount of personal information. Some of the veterans were still alive in 1875, when the Dominion Parliament voted to pay an additional gratuity to survivors, who were asked to produce verifiable identification. *Dominion Sessional Papers* of 1875 and 1876 printed the lists of those who responded and the names were reprinted in *Canadian Veterans of the War of 1812* by Eric Jonasson, with an informative discussion about the course of the war.

1837 Rebellion

Some militia regiments were called out during the Rebellion of 1837. They served into 1838, mainly when American incursive attempts were halted at Windsor and Prescott. Again, some lists of names can be found, ranging from those in LAC to published county histories and militia histories in particular. The British Military and Naval "C Series" at LAC (copies at AO) has scattered records of some militia units, with an alphabetical listing of names and subjects within the series, all microfilmed. The First Battalion, Incorporated Militia, was formed in November 1838, mainly from the Gore District. Their records at AO include attestations, courts martial and certain other material with name references.

A list of militia names for 1839 was printed in *The Toronto Almanac and Royal Calendar of Upper Canada for the Year 1839*. The names of officers and men who died during this period were printed in the 1904 *Bureau of Archives Second Report*. A publication commemorating this event, with a number of expert articles, is *1837 Rebellion Remembered* while Fryer's *Volunteers and Redcoats, Rebels and Raiders* is excellent reading.

Dawn Broughton offered "Canada's Gallant Volunteers of 1837-38: Roll Call, Winter of 1890-91" in *Families*, Vol. 27, No. 1 (1988). This consolidated list was first published in the Kingston newspaper *British Whig* in 1891, compiled by a public-spirited Belleville man who feared that the names of the "ordinary" volunteers might be forgotten. The list shows hundreds of men still living over fifty years after their militia service.

Losses Claims

Other types of records associated with war and the military are the claims for losses submitted by residents of Upper Canada during the two above periods of warfare and unrest. Civilians whose property was destroyed by invading forces, or had goods and food seized by either side for provisioning soldiers and militiamen, could apply to the government for compensation. Military boards heard claims for the War of 1812, creating many volumes of registers 1813-1848 that document names, locations, decisions and details. The records are at LAC (copies at AO) with some nominal indexes in the microfilmed finding aid. See Larry Kulisek's "The War of 1812 Losses Claims, a Note on Sources for Genealogical Research" in OGS *Seminar Annual, 1986.* The article has in-depth information on sources with examples taken from the Western District. Doris Bourrie's "The Loyal and Patriotic Society of Upper Canada" in *Families,* Vol. 26, No. 4 (1987) describes successful civilian efforts to provide for needy families of militiamen and to honour certain War of 1812 veterans with medals.

Doris Bourrie also compiled names in *Rebellion Losses for Upper Canada* from surviving records for various districts. The claims were under consideration for compensation by a commission in 1849. The names of the petitioners come from returns of the provincial secretary in 1849, a source at LAC in RG 19. Also, other claims petitions may be found interspersed in British War Office (WO 9) records.

Active Militia

A major reorganization in the militia system occurred in 1855. A new active militia force with uniforms, arms, pay and more regular training was created. The active militia, also called the permanent force, was to become the foundation for the Canadian army later in the century. Early militia pay lists will provide the patient researcher with some personal information. One researcher ascertained from pay lists of 1868 that her ancestor was paid 50¢ per day for sixteen days of drill that year.

The annual *Militia List* (re-named the *Defence Forces List* in the twentieth century) became a standard publication during this period, although it recorded only officers and not noncommissioned officers and privates. Records from the 13th Battalion Volunteer Militia from its formation in 1862 (later known as Royal Hamilton Light Infantry, Wentworth

Regiment) in Hamilton, are available on microfilm at AO. They contain service rolls, medical registers, regimental scrapbooks and more. Researchers should also consult LAC on-site finding aids. Somewhat later registers of the Royal Canadian Artillery, properly described as the permanent force, can be borrowed

Militia pay list (1868), 22nd regiment Oxford Rifles, RG 9, II F 6, vol. 71, p. 115; Library and Archives Canada, Ottawa

through interlibrary loan from LAC: births 1871-1911, marriages 1870-1915, deaths 1895-1905; they are nominally indexed.

U.S. Civil War

The American Civil War was a major conflict from 1861 to 1865. While the government of the Canadas had no involvement with the war, thousands of men from this province headed south to enlist for adventure. See the AO online exhibit "Ontario During the American Civil War Era." Help is available for finding an ancestor rumoured to have taken part, especially if you don't know in which state he might have enlisted.

A good place to start is the website of the British Isles Family History Society of Greater Ottawa. It provides a "Table of Canadian Pensioners" from an 1883 list, with their certificate numbers. This will help you access further information in files at the U.S. National Archives and Records Administration (NARA). Another useful tool is the *Civil War Soldiers and Sailors System* online database. Based on the NARA index cards, the database was a cooperative effort by the National Parks Service with many volunteers and several partners, including data checking provided by the Genealogical Society of Utah and the Federation of Genealogical Societies.

The Old Military and Civil Records Branch of NARA in Washington, DC, has the compiled military service files and pension files. Their extensive Union and Confederate records are microfilmed, as are indexes to the material. You can use the card indexes yourself at NARA or one of its regional archives or through the FHL in Salt Lake City and its local Family History Centers. Online, NARA has plenty of guides and finding aids to describe the records. Copies of original material can be ordered from NARA on their specific forms. There is a great deal of additional material available for Civil War soldiers, not all at NARA, but this is a beginning to determine if your ancestor is on record as a participant. NARA has already partnered with the Genealogical Society of Utah for the digitization of images from Civil War pension files, to become freely available on the FHL's *FamilySearch* website.

Fenian Raids

Lesser known military actions were the 1866 Fenian raids into Upper Canada. The raids followed on the heels of the U.S. Civil War with the American counterpart of the Irish Fenian Brotherhood attacking England at its North American colonies.

The Canadian militia was expecting trouble. Relatively minor border fights took place, notably at Fort Erie and Ridgeway on the Niagara peninsula. Later incursions took place in Quebec in 1870 that put the Ontario active militia on alert again. Senior's *Last Invasion of Canada: The Fenian Raids 1866-70* is vital reading for anyone whose ancestors took part in the defensive actions.

Nominal records available from those actions are similar to surviving records discussed for earlier periods: bounty claims for land grants, disability pensions and compensation claims with corresponding documentation. The land grants were offered in the 1900s so the records relate only to those veterans who were alive at that time. As with land grants offered to earlier veterans, the series cannot be considered comprehensive for the overall complement of actual participants. AO has microfilmed nominal indexes to applications and files by Fenian volunteers 1901-1922—see Fenian and South African land grant records (RG 1-99) in the AO Archives Descriptive Database. The Ontario Land Records Index will also indicate an entry relating to a veteran's (V) land grant.

The AO online exhibit "Ontario During the Civil War Era" has a small section about Fenian times. Medals were awarded, upon application, for service. More information about medals can be seen on the Veterans Affairs Canada website under "Canada Remembers." "Nineteenth Century Military Records in the National Archives: An Introduction" by Glenn Wright is in *Families*, Vol. 33, No. 4 (1994). This is especially recommended for detailed treatment of sources and reference material.

The British Army

Many soldiers from the British army decided to settle in Canada after serving here in the eighteenth and nineteenth centuries. Upper Canada land petitions are often a rewarding source, since the men were entitled to a grant of land as military claimants. Petitions may include information about how and when he served, perhaps accompanied by a discharge document or officer's affidavit. Beyond that, descendants will want to trace an ancestor through army documentation. Some information for the revolutionary war period is found in material like the Haldimand Papers and the British Military and Naval "C Series." Microfilms of these records are available mainly at LAC (MG 21 and RG 8, respectively). AO also has much of the "C Series" with its name and subject inventory. Check the FHL catalogue for its microfilm holdings. In most cases you must consult the paper finding aids. *Only* the microfilm reel guides to the "C Series" and others are presently on the Canadian Genealogy Centre website. The CGC military section gives many external links to additional websites.

By far the most comprehensive records are those in the British War Office series held at The National Archives (TNA) of England and Wales. Microfilmed copies of some series are available at LAC and FHL. LAC finding aids are 1800 (inventory, calendar and card index to British Military Records) and 90 (a shelf list guide to the microfilm reels). However, we strongly recommend the excellent research guides and finding aids on the TNA website for the best descriptions. Explore the "British Army" pages under "Military History" and choose your category from there, between 1760 and 1920. Most importantly for family historians, a great number of discharged soldiers 1760-1854 are nominally indexed in "The Catalogue," TNA's online searchable database of millions of items from diverse record types. Documents can be ordered for a fee as paper copies or digital images. The TNA also features podcasts on its website for military information.

Apart from the records entered into the TNA database, the remainder of the enormous military collection can be accessed only by way of its chronological and regimental arrangement, which means knowing the name or number of the regiment your ancestor served in. Kitzmiller's *In Search of 'The Forlorn Hope'* assists genealogists to determine a specific regiment. Knowing which regiments served in British North America and Upper Canada, at which forts and when, can also be very helpful. To learn about regimental movements and postings, the first survey could be made in Stewart's *The Service of British Regiments in Canada and North America*. Regiments serving during the American Revolution are listed on the website *Orderly Books of the Crown Forces in North America*, while *Land Forces of Britain, the Empire and the Commonwealth* covers much broader scope. Searching the latter entails digging deeply through the site.

See also the link at CGC for a website called *British Regiments in Canada*. Once you can determine the name or unit number of the regiment, a wide variety of military and regimental histories for Canada is available. Perkins' *Regiments: Regiments and Corps of the British Empire and Commonwealth, 1758-1993* is one source. The Royal Canadian Military Institute in Toronto (Appendix III) has an extensive library on military subjects.

Again, consult TNA website pages for detailed information on which War Office series would be of most relevance for an ancestor, and how inclusive each series is. Some series or registers were created according to when and how a man was discharged or died. The series called Soldiers' Documents (WO 97) can be greatly rewarding for soldiers who served as ordinary privates or non-commissioned officers. Service records exist from 1760 and can contain enlistment papers with the parish of birth, physical appearance, his occupation or trade at the time, among other documentation. Within each regiment the muster rolls also have details of service and physical description.

Accessible at LAC, bearing in mind the regimental arrangement in most cases, are:

- WO 12, Muster Books and Pay Lists for selected regiments; service details and often physical description.
- WO 17, Monthly Returns for each overseas regiment (1758-1865 for what became Ontario and Quebec).
- WO 25, Various Registers, mainly Regimental Description and Succession Books 1756-1875 and Casualty Returns 1812-1815.
- WO 42, Certificates for miscellaneous births, marriages, and deaths with some wills and service papers 1776-1881, originally included in correspondence regarding members of the King's German Legion and British American regiments.
- WO 97, Royal Hospital Chelsea Soldiers' Documents 1760-1882 (6,383 volumes) for soldiers discharged to pension; this series gives the most detailed service records and descriptions for each man.
- WO 120, Royal Hospital Chelsea Regimental Registers 1713-1868 (70 volumes), similar to above.

Some of the British regiments with long service in Canada were the Royal Canadian Rifle Regiment, the 100th Prince of Wales Royal Canadian Regiment and the Corps of Sappers and Miners among others. "Military Register of Baptisms for the Station of Fort George, Upper Canada, 1821-1827" was published in *Ontario History* Vol. 15 (1917)—for that limited period, it may be useful for some ancestors. Marriages for soldiers and the baptisms of their children are also found in churches adjacent to forts. "Life and Times of a Professional Soldier" by David Owen in OGS *Seminar Annual, 1987* gives historical details of the common British soldier's experience in the late eighteenth and early nineteenth centuries. Timothy Dubé's "Tommy Atkins,

We Never Knew Ye: Documenting the British Soldier in Canada, 1759-1871, Military Organization and the Archival Record" was published in *Canadian Military History*, Vol. 4, No. 1 (1995). In fact, the journal *Canadian Military History*, from the Laurier

Thomas Thomas, British army discharge (1837), Upper Canada Land Petitions, RG 1, L 3, vol. 504, T bundle 21, petition 5; Library and Archives Canada microfilm C-2837

Centre for Military Strategic and Disarmament Studies, is geared to all aspects of Canadian military history with articles by professional historians.

Chelsea Pensioners

Royal Hospital Chelsea began as a home for elderly soldiers as well as those affected by injury or disease. By the time of the Napoleonic Wars, pensions were also being allowed for long and loyal service, as well as disability. Therefore the records are not solely related to disabled in-pensioners, but to discharged soldiers as out-pensioners. A soldier's entry is based on the last regiment he served with, in case he had transferred during his service. The Regimental Registers (WO 120) note discharge to pension or death, if applicable. LAC finding aid 1915 lists the regiments and their respective microfilm reels. Norman Crowder's book *British Army Pensioners Abroad* is also of great interest for anyone with an army ancestor.

During the 1830s, some Chelsea pensioners were given the option of commuting their pensions in exchange for land in Upper Canada. This was a British plan to relieve itself of a financial burden and strategically populate the province with experienced soldiers against any future threat of invasion. Many of these men did not successfully adapt to farming, and drifted to towns and cities, or eventually returned to England. Some of the commuted pensioners and their families came to Simcoe County and Penetanguishene in 1835. See Barbara Aitken's "Chelsea Pensioners in Upper Canada and Great Britain" in *Families* Vol. 23, Nos. 3 & 4 (1984) which lists sources for research and the names of 654 pensioners who were alive in 1839. Another article is "The Forgotten Veterans of 1812" by Albert M. Fortier Jr. in *Families* Vol. 5 No. 2 (1983), dealing with discharged soldiers of the Tenth Royal Veterans Battalion who chose to settle in Canada, listing 200 men.

Hessians/Germans

During the American Revolution, due to his Hanoverian origins, King George III called upon five battalions of Germanic mercenaries to form part of his regular forces. Although widely referred to as "Hessians," they came from several German principalities, including Brunswick, Waldeck and Anhalt-Zerbst. Hundreds of them became military claimants (OLRI in Chapter 6) for land grants when the revolutionary war ended. Besides tracing them through land petitions, a descendant researching a Germanic name would do well to consult DeMarce's *German Military Settlers in Canada, After the American Revolution* or *Register of German Military Men* by John (aka Johannes) Merz. These authors have done extensive research in Canadian, German and British archival records to produce some real treasures of compiled information. Clifford N. Smith has written a number of books on German mercenaries from Ansbach, Bayreuth, Hessen-Kassel and Hessen-Hanau.

Post-1870

Books of Remembrance

Canadians who died in wartime service, or as a result of it, are memorialized in Books of Remembrance in the Peace Tower on Parliament Hill, Ottawa. Each of seven books commemorates one war or aspect of service. They range from the Nile Expedition to the Korean War and the more recent "In the Service of Canada." To view the original books in their setting is a moving experience, but the pages can be seen online at the Veterans Affairs website under "Canada Remembers – Records and Collections." The website offers much more to explore in the way of personal letters and stories, medals, war artists and the "Canadian Virtual War Memorial." The latter is a searchable database with information from burial sites to additional material or a photograph, if available.

The Department of National Defence's *Directorate of History and Heritage* website also offers a variety of online collections about war memorials, military dates and operations and soon, "Official Lineages of the Canadian Armed Forces" from 1855.

Medal Registers

From the War of 1812 to the South African War, the medals awarded to men of Ontario and all of Canada have been registered by the military. Different kinds of medals were awarded at different times for specific actions or expeditions. Veterans Affairs website (see "Canada Remembers") has particulars about the individual honours with digital illustrations. An LAC on-site nominal card index, finding aid 9-20, provides a start for names. Further details can be requested with the online form at CGC or in person at LAC. War of 1812 medal registers are in a separate collection at LAC and microfilmed. Publications by Donald G. Mitchell and David K. Riddle describe First World War medals and awards to members of the Canadian Expeditionary Force. See the cited Veterans Affairs website or *Directorate of History and Heritage* for later twentieth century medals.

Red River Expedition

Federally organized forces were sent to western Canada during an uprising in 1870, in what became Manitoba. Colonel Garnet Wolseley commanded the expedition against Louis Riel's provisional government with a few army regulars, but predominantly militiamen. Young men from Ontario formed a large part of the contingent. LAC has records for this campaign, not extensive, but similar to those for earlier military engagements, in RG 9—for example, registers of muster rolls and pay lists 1870-1877, disability claims and a few records of courts martial and desertions 1870-1873. A list of participants' names, taken from the registers, is available under "Red River Expeditionary Force," Appendixes II and III, at the military section of *Olive Tree Genealogy* website. Military service bounty in the form of land grants was available, with some claims for land grants after the Red River expedition published in *Dominion Sessional Papers* Vol. 5, No. 6 (1872) and Vol. 8, No. 8 (1875). *Sessional Papers* can be searched via the Internet at *Early Canadiana Online*. See George Stanley's *Toil and Trouble: Military Expeditions to Red River*.

North West Rebellion

Historian Glenn Wright gives a highly recommended introduction to the next period of Canadian military history in "Short Guide

"Officers of the Governor General Body Guard, North West Rebellion," photograph, accession 2381, S5436; Special Collections, AO, Toronto

to Sources for Documenting Military Service in Canada and Abroad, 1885-1918" on the British Isles Family History Society of Greater Ottawa (BIFHSGO) website. In 1885 a North West Field Force was formed to combat still unsettled conditions on the prairies where the North West Mounted Police were not sufficient to control the disturbances. The Canadian active militia was mobilized again, at this time still under the leadership of an experienced British officer. Colonel Frederick Middleton commanded the combined field force of militia, the "Mounties" and volunteers. BIFHSGO has created a North West Rebellion database for all members of the North West Field Force, giving the man's rank and company or type of service.

Existing government records for the North West Field Force of 1885 at LAC are the usual nominal rolls and pay lists, grants of land and an index to pension claims for injury. The land grants for the Red River Expedition and the North West Field Force were given in western Canada, and may explain the disappearance of a male family member from Ontario after 1885. Pension files for individuals can be found in either the Department of National Defence (RG 24) or Department of Veterans Affairs (RG 38) in LAC custody. The on-site finding aid 24-1 lists the file names. One volunteer company taking part was the Ottawa Sharpshooters of the Governor General's Horse Guards. Their names and ages are listed on a roll call on the BIFHSGO website. BIFHSGO also published John Reid's *The Ottawa Sharpshooters* with biographies of all members of the unit.

South African War

The service records from the South African War are held by LAC in the Department of Veterans Affairs collection. The surviving files or registers (approximately one-quarter of the files are no longer extant) contain enlistment information such as age, physical attributes, occupation and name of next of kin. Medical reports, discharge papers and medal notations may also be included. The veterans' subsequent applications for the customary land grants, in Department of the Interior records (RG 15 at LAC), give the man's post-war residential address.

The search for a participant in this wartime event is greatly facilitated by the CGC searchable database "Soldiers of the South African War (1899-1902)." Database information is based on three of the most important document types created during and after the war: service files, medal registers and applications for bounty land grants. Digital images of documents or pages from a service file, and a medal register if applicable, are linked to names. Land grant applications are *not* digitally linked. Each person's name in the database usually has a regimental number or name, type of record, and an archival reference—most useful for pursuing the land grant applications. Due credit is given to BIFHSGO which partnered in the indexing for this fine project. CGC also features a thematic guide on this war.

At AO you will find the nominal indexes and files for land grants in a sub-series of Fenian and South African Land Records (RG 1-99). The article "Serving the Empire: Canadians in South Africa, 1899-1902" by Glenn Wright in *Families* Vol. 21, No. 1 (1982) discusses the variety of records available for these men.

First World War

There is also a database finding aid at the CGC website of First World War soldiers in the Canadian Expeditionary Force (CEF) called "Soldiers of the First World War – CEF." The database is an index that provides you not only with the critical regimental number and archival reference but also, in many cases, links you to a digital image of the attestation (enlistment) form. Since more than 600,000 names are in the database, you will likely find several men with the same or a similar name. When the date of birth is shown on the results page, it should assist with identifying the man you want. If it happens there is no digital link, you can still access/order his file by the archival reference description.

An actual service file contains much more than the attestation paper, with probably a minimum of 25 pages and possibly twice or three times that amount. With the name, regimental number and archival reference, you can order the complete file on-site at LAC or by using the online order form at the CGC database site. Service files contain all the details of a soldier's life from enlistment to demobilization. For example, attestation forms ask for the expected data of current address, date and place of birth, name and address of next of kin, marital status and trade or occupation. The reverse of the form adds more personal information such as colour of hair, eyes, and complexion, height, religion and distinctive marks or scars.

The CEF was a large and complex military organization and, in addition to the infantry, included artillery, service corps, medical personnel, engineers and so on. Women were involved in support services. Genealogists will want to understand the nature of the military system in which an ancestor found himself and

Unit 221st.Battalion   Rank Lieut.   Name Dougall,Hector Fraser

OFFICERS' DECLARATION PAPER

CANADIAN OVER-SEAS EXPEDITIONARY FORCE

QUESTIONS TO BE ANSWERED BY OFFICER

[ANSWERS]

1. (a) What is your Surname? .... Dougall

   (b) What are your Christian Names? .... Hector Fraser

2. (a) Where were you born? (State place and country) .... Winnipeg, Manitoba

   (b) What is your present address? .... 251,Bell Avenue,Winnipeg.

3. What is the date of your birth? .... August 23rd, 1896.

4. What is (a) the name of your next-of-kin? .... Isabel Dougall

       (b) the address of your next-of-kin? .... 251,Bell Avenue,Winnipeg.

       (c) the relationship of your next-of-kin? .... Mother

5. What is your profession or occupation? .... Clerk

6. What is your religion? .... Presbyterian

7. Are you willing to be vaccinated or re-vaccinated and inoculated? .... Yes

8. To what Unit of the Active Militia do you belong? .. 100th.Winnipeg Grenadiers.

9. State particulars of any former Military Service .... 79th. Cameron Highlanders

10. Are you willing to serve in the

     CANADIAN OVER-SEAS EXPEDITIONARY FORCE? .. Yes

The undersigned hereby declares that the above answers made by him to the above questions are true.

.... *HFDougall* .... (Signature of Officer)

Taken on strength (place) .... Winnipeg, Man.

        (date) .... May 8th. 1916.

(Signature of Commanding Officer.)

CERTIFICATE OF MEDICAL EXAMINATION

I have examined the above-named Officer in accordance with the Regulations for Army Medical Services.

I consider him* ..... Fit .... for the CANADIAN OVER-SEAS EXPEDITIONARY FORCE.

Date ...... May 8th 191.6

Place ...... Winnipeg, Man. .... Capt.

*Insert here "fit" or "unfit"   Medical Officer.

M. F. W. 51
100m.—4-16.
II. Q. 1772. 39-917

Hector Dougall, officers' declaration paper (1916), Canadian Over-Seas Expeditionary Force, RG 150, P-CE-706; Library and Archives Canada, Ottawa

the broader scope of dramatic events in which he played a small part. Books by military historians, such as Nicholson's *Canadian Expeditionary Force*, provide insight and context to make family history even more interesting.

Wartime "Sailing Lists" are available at large reference libraries in *Canadian Expeditionary Force Nominal Rolls*, or at LAC in RG 9. The lists were published as the battalions embarked for England and the European war theatre. On the lists are the serviceman's name, regimental rank and number, country of birth, date and place of enlistment, former service (if any), next of kin, name of ship and embarkation date. There are no published lists for the homebound ships, but at LAC in the Ministry of the Overseas Forces of Canada fonds (RG 150, finding aid 150-2) are records of all personnel shipping home to Canada, especially for the demobilization period 1918-1919. Besides the names and a detailed description of the voyage, regular ship reports may include medical examinations, onboard complaints and deaths at sea. The records are arranged by the name of the ship and date.

Many Canadians served with British forces such as the Royal Flying Corps (RFC) during the First World War. LAC has copies of thousands of Imperial War Service Gratuities files for Canadian personnel from Britain's land, sea and air units. See the notes on the CGC website which lead to a search of the Government of Canada database. LAC finding aid 9-56 lists the names, which are alphabetical by initial of the surname, but not strictly alphabetical within each grouping. Copies of a file can be requested using the relevant archival reference numbers. It's possible that the online files may be linked to digital images in the future.

War Diaries are logs kept by the various battalions and units describing their daily field actions. They exist for the CEF units fighting in France and Belgium. LAC has digital images of pages from the majority of the diaries in a database searchable by the name of a unit under the CEF command. The database is accessible from the CGC website. AO has microfilm copies of some of the War Diaries from LAC for 1915-1919. Other kinds of records at LAC in RG 9 include casualty lists and awards and honours. Published *Militia Lists* are an important source for information on commissioned officers and nursing sisters.

The OGS journal *Families* and branch newsletters often have articles about servicemen in wartime. Examples are:

Jane MacNamara wrote "Researching a CEF Ancestor" in *Toronto Tree* (Toronto Branch OGS) Vol. 26, No. 6 (1995) and "Soldier's Insurance in Trust" in *Toronto Tree* Vol. 25, No. 6 (1994), regarding City of Toronto life insurance provided for residents on active duty. "The Roll of Honour of the Ontario Teachers Who Served in the Great War 1914-1918" by Tordiff and Mulligan appeared in *Families* Vol. 43, No. 2 (2004).

Second World War

Service files for Second World War participants are also held at LAC. Access is open to anyone (a family relationship is no longer required) if the service person has been deceased more than twenty years. Instructions and an application form are given on the Canadian Genealogy Centre website under "Military" and then "Canadian Forces after 1918." Applicants should be prepared to wait a minimum of thirty days and perhaps many months, due to the volume of requests. The researcher will find even more documentation in these files than for First World War servicemen. Along with the basic enlistment form are service history, service assessment reports and discharge information. Additional Second World War records are much the same as described for the First World War: war diaries for every serving unit, casualty lists, awards and honours.

Unrestricted access is available to files for personnel of army, navy or air force who were killed in action or died during the war. OGS has published a two-volume series by compiler Bruce Thornley, arranged alphabetically, called *Index to Overseas Deaths of Ontario Servicemen and Servicewomen 1939–1947*.

"Standing on Guard for Us: Canadian Military Service in the Twentieth Century" by Glenn Wright in *Families* Vol. 33, No. 2 (1994) is an excellent overview from a specialist in the archival records. Again, the websites of Veterans Affairs and the Canadian Genealogy Centre offer a wide selection of subjects and links. Novices and military enthusiasts alike may enjoy a visit to *Maple Leaf Up* website and "The Canadian Army Overseas in WW2" with links to volunteer sites about battles, equipment, training, armour, organizations and a discussion forum. The Directorate of History and Heritage currently has much more material in its collections than can be seen online, so visiting their physical site would be equally productive.

Korean War

Documentation for armed forces individuals who participated during the Korean War 1950-1953 and subsequent United Nations peacekeeping duties is subject to right to privacy conditions. The Korea Veterans Association of Canada has a very complete website with a list of participating army forces, naval commands and air force squadrons. The site has an honour roll, battle maps, awards, photographs, a story archives, The Last Post for deceased members and much more. The association itself is organized into regional units. Veterans who died because of this conflict are in the Korean War Book of Remembrance in Ottawa, as well as on the national Korea Wall of Remembrance in Brampton, Ontario. More than 500 names are memorialized, along with each man's regimental number, rank, age, date of death, unit and location of remains.

Naval History

Not to ignore other branches of the Canadian forces, naval history had a similar pattern with the British Royal Navy providing protection in colonial times. The navy originally supplied ships on the lakes and rivers so important for travel, communication and defence long before the American Revolution occurred. Britain developed naval establishments in North America along with its military posts. Navy Island above Niagara Falls, Detroit, Carleton Island near present-day Kingston and Michilimackinac became some of the strategic naval yards. During the War of 1812, some civilians were called upon to provide expertise and labour in shipbuilding or naval engagements. Unlike the land grant provisions made for Loyalists who served in militia units during the Revolution, volunteers in the provincial naval service at this time were not specifically recognized. However, there are existing petitions for land grants made by some of these men after the Revolution and the War of 1812.

In the British Admiralty Office series at LAC are some muster rolls of Royal Marines and Navy seamen in the sub-series Admiralty Lake Service records 1814-1833 (RG 8), but the bulk of Royal Navy material for the nineteenth century remains at The National Archives in England. One article of interest is "The Navies on Lake Ontario in the War of 1812" by Barlow Cumberland in *Ontario History* Vol. 8 (1907). Books for this period include Forester's *The Age of Fighting Sail: The Story of the Naval War of 1812*.

Provincial Marine   The Provincial Marine grew out of the former naval establishments and from the provincial naval service after the American Revolution as a protective fleet on the Great

Lakes waterways. It also became the mode of transportation for government and commercial supplies. Some early documentation can be found among the Haldimand Papers at both LAC and AO. See also the British Military "C Series" at both LAC and AO for the period between the Revolution and the War of 1812. See W.A.B. Douglas' article "The Anatomy of Naval Incompetence: the Provincial Marine in Defence of Upper Canada Before 1813" in *Ontario History* Vol. 71 (1979). The Provincial Marine deteriorated after that war, especially with the growth of private shipping and navigation companies. You can also refer to the registers at LAC for marine certificates and the Lloyd's Captains Registers for commercial ships' officers; see Occupations in Chapter 9.

Penetanguishene   In 1817 construction of a Naval Establishment at Penetanguishene on Georgian Bay was completed to establish a strategic transport link to northwest areas and to strengthen Upper Canada's vital defence. The post was joined in 1828 by the "Drummond Islanders" who were a mixture of military and civilians from one of the last outposts to be turned over to the Americans. As a naval base, its usefulness declined until it was closed in 1834. However, the military section continued until 1856. The entire site is now the province's chief marine heritage attraction in season, called Discovery Harbour. Visitors can explore King's Wharf, the dockyard, replicas of supply ship *HMS Bee* and warship *HMS Tecumseh*, the restored officers' quarters, and workshops with staff in period costume.

What makes this particular Establishment unusual is the work that has been done to identify the original military and navy personnel who resided there during its 39-year history. The project of researching over 1,300 families was described in two detailed articles by Gwen Patterson in *Families* Vol. 27, Nos. 1 & 2 (1988), "Descendants of the Establishments in Penetanguishene." The family files are available at the nearby Penetanguishene Centennial Museum and Archives in their Genealogy Research Centre. Descendants of first families of the Establishment, and of fur trade and native ancestry, can study a great deal of historical material including many relevant church and mission registers of the era. A searchable database for at least a dozen local cemeteries is online. If a personal visit is not possible, archives staff will provide genealogical research at a reasonable fee.

Canadian Navy and Air Force

The Royal Canadian Navy and the Royal Canadian Air Force have less history than the army because they didn't come into full strength until the Second World War. In its RG 24, the LAC has an on-site "Guide to Sources Relating to Canadian Naval Vessels" for every ship commissioned since 1910, and other finding aids to Royal Canadian Navy records 1914-1965. Nominal indexes to such material are yet few and far between, so it is helpful if the ancestor can be associated with the name of a ship. The website *Canadian Navy of Today and Yesterday* has some archival photographs with a great deal of ship information. The Macpherson and Burgess book *The Ships of Canada's Naval Forces* has details of ships and commanding officers. War-related naval deaths are commemorated in the Books of Remembrance. See also the *Awards to the Royal Canadian Navy* website for service history of honoured individual seamen.

Service files are available for the Royal Canadian Naval Volunteer Reserve 1914-1919, including men who joined prior to the First World War. LAC finding aid 24-167 is an alphabetical list. Compiled in 1948, it gives home addresses at the time of enlistment. Informative background reading is "The Army Origin of the Royal Canadian Navy" by Lt.-Col. George Stanley in *Journal of the Society of Army Historical Research* Vol. 32 (1954). For seamen in the Merchant Navy see the guide "Royal Canadian Naval Third Central Registry" in RG 24 at LAC.

Air Force personnel service records, besides the usual papers, can include such items as an occupational history, pilot training reports and assessments, individual flying record, a pay book, Bomber Command hospital or sick list record, casualty notification form, dental charts and medical reports.

Personal information about individuals of the RAF Ferry Command, which flew aircraft from Montreal to the United Kingdom in World War II, is available and indexed at the Directorate of History and Heritage (not yet online). Microfilms can be borrowed from LAC for certain RCAF-related operations books, also called squadron diaries, during World War II (RG 24). The British Commonwealth Air Training Plan schooled more than 130,000 Commonwealth air crew in Canada during World War II. Training school diaries may include their newsletters, newspapers, activities and other information about social life on the bases (LAC finding aid 24-104). Fred Hatch's *Aerodrome of Democracy* is a testament to this venture, and among much other information, the book lists the base locations of the schools in Ontario.

1940 Mobilization Act

The National Resources Mobilization Act and the War Measures Act of 1940 gave the federal government extraordinary powers for the defence of the nation. The 1940 national registration was also mentioned in Chapter 5 as a census "alternative." What we have is a register of all people in Canada in August of 1940 age sixteen and up. British subjects and aliens were all expected to register. Questionnaires asked for full name and permanent address, age and date of birth, place of birth of registrant and both parents, health information, occupation and training and much more. Potentially the government could use this information to relocate skilled people for the war effort.

These records are now held by Statistics Canada in their Census Pension Searches Unit (Appendix II). Once again, access is restricted by right to privacy legislation unless proof of death at least twenty years ago can be provided by the enquirer. It is necessary to provide the name and the residence where the person was living in 1940; the latter could be a township, town, city or even a street address. You can view sample questionnaires at the Canadian Genealogy Centre website. Current fee information and an online order form is on the Statistics Canada website by searching for "1940 National Registration." See also "The National Resources Mobilization Act, 1940" by Wayne C. Renardson for more details and an example, in *Families* Vol. 28, No. 1 (1989).

War Graves

The Commonwealth War Graves Commission cares for military graves and cemeteries around the world, and can provide the burial location for most Canadians who died in the two world wars. The CWGC database "Debt of Honour Register" is searchable for cemetery names or casualties among army, air force, navy, merchant navy and civilian personnel. Precise details are given for the name of the cemetery, its physical location and directions and the individual's marker. If next of kin returned a verification form at or near the time of burial, a fair amount of additional information may be available. The website has a separate news page for people who plan to visit any location.

A list of local war memorials across Ontario can be found on the website *We Will Remember* and at the *Directorate of History and Heritage.* There are many, many other resources that have been mentioned, such as "Books of Remembrance" and "Virtual War Museum" on the Veterans Affairs website.

Dorothy Martin wrote about "The Ontario Military Hospital, Orpington, England" in *Families* Vol. 25, No. 3 (1985) and Ronald Illidge contributed "The Kinmel Park Military Cemetery, Bodelwyddan, Wales" to *Families* Vol. 33, No. 4 (1994). Both give names of Canadian servicemen buried there. Personnel records for the Ontario Military Hospital at Orpington are at

The Victoria Cross replaced the original British Victoria Cross awarded to Canadians during several conflicts between the creation of the award and the end of the Second World War. The new Victoria Cross, formally adopted into the Canadian Honours System in 1993, is identical to the original award, only the motto on the obverse having been changed from "For Valour" to "Pro Valore".

The original Victoria Cross was awarded to eighty-one members (81) of Canada's military forces (out of a total of 1,351 crosses and three bars awarded throughout the British Empire). Canada's last surviving recipient of the Victoria Cross, Sergeant Ernest Alvia "Smokey" Smith, V.C., C.M., O.B.C., C.D., (Retired), passed away on August 3, 2005.

His Royal Highness The Prince Albert, Prince Consort to Queen Victoria, designed the British Victoria Cross. Bruce Beatty designed the modifications incorporated into the new Victoria Cross. The details of the recipient will be engraved on the reverse of the suspension bar while the date of the action will be engraved on the reverse of the Cross itself.

The Victoria Cross Gallery of Canada's Military Forces

South African (Boer) War   First World War   Second World War

Full citations to these awards are recorded in *1000 Brave Canadians*, published by The Unitrade Press.

Opening page of the Victoria Cross listings on the VA website. www.forces.gc.ca/dhh/ collections/vc_gallery/engraph/home_home.asp?cat=7. Reproduced with the permission of the Minister of Public Works and Government Services, 2008.

AO in the William Hearst Papers. Some stray RCAF burials in the United Kingdom were transcribed in "Canadian Servicemen Buried on the Isle of Man" by Roger Christian in *Families* Vol. 29, No. 1 (1990), and "Some War Graves" by Dorothy Mahoney in *Families* Vol. 31, No. 1 (1992).

Royal Canadian Legion

The Legion is the largest veterans' organization in Canada and a familiar institution in towns across the country. It maintains a vital membership of veterans and their descendants, as well as associate members. Among their extensive activities is the sacred trust to keep Remembrance Day alive through services on the 11th hour of the 11th day of the 11th month. Their successful efforts have made the red poppy a proud national symbol every November. *Legion Magazine* has a searchable online feature for "Last Post" death entries. The Royal Canadian Legion fonds at LAC in MG 28 is a collection of about 100 years' worth of administrative papers, including a central registry in the microfilmed material, photographs, and moving image documentaries. Of special mention are the oral interviews with ex-servicemen in sound recordings. Other subject material includes battle sites and commemorations, along with scenes of Legion parades, buildings and veterans' groups. The 240-page LAC finding aid 1783 is online. Recommended reading is Morton and Wright's *Winning the Second Battle.*

The website *Canadian Military History Gateway* has a splendid three-volume military history from native and Viking times to modern information about the Regular Force and Reserve Force. Unification of Canada's armed forces was a lengthy process that culminated in 1967.

Reading and Reference

Bercuson, David J. and J.L. Granatstein. *Dictionary of Canadian Military History.* Toronto, ON: Oxford University Press, 1994.

Berton, Pierre. *The Invasion of Canada, 1812-1813* and *Flames Across the Border, 1813-1814.* Toronto, ON: Doubleday, 2001.

Bourrie, Doris. *Rebellion Losses for Upper Canada.* 10 volumes. Thornhill, ON: Doris Bourrie, 1989.

Canadian Expeditionary Force Nominal Rolls. 13 volumes. Ottawa, ON: King's Printer, 1915-1918.

Chambers, Ernest A. *The Canadian Militia: A History of the Origin and Development of the Force.* Montreal, QC: L.M. Fresco, 1907.

Crowder, Norman. *British Army Pensioners Abroad.* Baltimore, MD: Genealogical Publishing Company, 1995.

DeMarce, Virginia. *German Military Settlers in Canada, After the American Revolution.* Sparta, WI: Joy Reisinger, 1984.

Douglas, W.A.B. *The Creation of a National Air Force.* Toronto, ON: University of Toronto Press, 1986.

1837 Rebellion Remembered. Toronto, ON: Ontario Historical Society, 1988.

Elliott, Bruce, Dan Walker and Fawne Stratford-Devai, compilers. *Men of Upper Canada: Militia Nominal Lists, 1828-1829.* Toronto, ON: Ontario Genealogical Society, 1995.

Forester, Cecil S. *The Age of Fighting Sail: The Story of the Naval War of 1812.* New York, NY: Doubleday, 1956.

Fryer, Mary Beacock. *Volunteers and Redcoats, Rebels and Raiders: A Military History of the Rebellion in Upper Canada.* Toronto, ON: Dundurn Press, 1996.

Gray, William. *Soldiers of the King: The Upper Canadian Militia.* Toronto, ON: Boston Mills Press, 1995.

Hatch, Fred J. *The Aerodrome of Democracy: Canada and the British Commonwealth Air Training Plan, 1939-1945.* Ottawa, ON: Department of National Defence, 1983.

Johnston, Winston. *The Glengarry Light Infantry, 1812-1816: Who Were They and What Did They Do in the War?* Charlottetown, PE: Winston H. Johnston, 1998.

Jonasson, Eric. *Canadian Veterans of the War of 1812.* Winnipeg, MB: Wheatfield Press, 1978.

Kitzmiller, John. *In Search of 'The Forlorn Hope': A Comprehensive Guide to Locating British Army Regiments and their Records (1640-WWI).* 3 volumes. Salt Lake City, UT: Manuscript Publishing Foundation, 1988.

Lauber, Wilfred, compiler. *An Index of Land Claim Certificates of Upper Canada Militiamen Who Served in the War of 1812-1814.* Toronto, ON: Ontario Genealogical Society, 1995.

Livingston, Mildred R. *Dundas County Militia: 1814, 1831, 1832, 1835.* Prescott, ON: M.R. Livingston, 1988.

Macpherson, Ken and John Burgess. *The Ships of Canada's Naval Forces 1910-1985.* Toronto, ON: Collins Publishers, 1985.

Merz, Johannes. *Register of German Military Men.* Winnipeg, MB: Wolf Verlag Ltd., 1993.

Mitchell, Donald G. and David K. Riddle. See various titles regarding military medals.

Morton, Desmond. *A Military History of Canada: From Champlain to Kosovo.* 4th edition. Toronto, ON: McClelland & Stewart, 1999.

_____ and Glenn T. Wright. *Winning the Second Battle: Canadian Veterans and the Return to Civilian Life, 1915-1930.* Toronto, ON: University of Toronto Press, 1987.

Nicholson, G.W.L. *Canadian Expeditionary Force, 1914-1919.* Ottawa, ON: Queen's Printer, 1962.

Perkins, Roger, compiler. *Regiments: Regiments and Corps of the British Empire and Commonwealth, 1758-1993: A Critical Bibliography of their Published Histories.* Newton Abbot, Devon: R. Perkins, 1994.

Reid, John D. *The Ottawa Sharpshooters.* Ottawa, ON: British Isles Family History Society of Greater Ottawa, 2005.

Senior, Hereward. *Last Invasion of Canada: The Fenian Raids 1866-70.* Toronto, ON: Dundurn Press, 1996.

Sheppard, George. *Plunder, Profit and Paroles: A Social History of the War of 1812 in Upper Canada.* Montreal, QC: McGill-Queen's Press, 1994.

Smith, Clifford N. *British and German Deserters, Dischargees, and Prisoners of War Who May Have Remained in Canada and the United States, 1774-1783: Part 1 and Part 2.* Baltimore, MD: Genealogical Publishing Company, 2004.

Stanley, George F.G. *Toil and Trouble: Military Expeditions to Red River.* Toronto, ON: Dundurn Press, 1989.

Stewart, Charles H. *The Service of British Regiments in Canada and North America: a Resumé.* Ottawa, ON: Department of National Defence, 1962.

Thornley, Bruce, compiler. *Index to Overseas Deaths of Ontario Servicemen and Servicewomen, 1939-1947,* 2 volumes. Toronto, ON: Ontario Genealogical Society, 2006.

Turner, Wesley B. *The War of 1812: The War That Both Sides Won.* Toronto, ON: Dundurn Press, 1990.

Wilson, Barbara M. *Ontario and the First World War: A Collection of Documents.* Toronto, ON: The Champlain Society and University of Toronto Press, 1977.

Blatherwick, John. Awards to the Royal Canadian Navy. www.rcnvr.com/.

British Isles Family History Society of Greater Ottawa. www.bifhsgo.ca

Canadian Military Heritage Project. www.rootsweb.com/~canmil/.

Canadiana.org. Early Canadiana Online. www.canadiana.org/.

Commonwealth War Graves Commission. www.cwgc.org.

Cross, Wes. British Regiments in Canada. freepages.genealogy.rootsweb.com/~crossroads/regiments/.

"The Canadian Army Overseas in WW2." Mapleleaf Up. www.mapleleafup.org/.

Huronia Historical Parks. Discovery Harbour. www.discoveryharbour.on.ca/.

The Korea Veterans Association of Canada. www.kvacanada.com

Laurier Centre for Military and Strategic Disarmament Studies. www.wlu.ca/lcmsds/.

"Legion Magazine." Dominion Command, The Royal Canadian
    Legion. www.legionmagazine.com
McClearn, Sandy. Canadian Navy of Today and Yesterday.
    www.hazegray.org/navhist/canada/.
Mills, T.F. Land Forces of Britain, the Empire and the Commonwealth.
    regiments.org/milhist/index.htm.
National Archives and Records Administration (U.S.).
    www.archives.gov
The National Archives (UK). www.nationalarchives.gov
National Defence Canada. Canadian Military History Gateway.
    cmhg.gc.ca/html/browse/default-en.asp.
National Defence Canada. Directorate of History and Heritage.
    www.forces.ca/dhh
National Park Service. Civil War Soldiers and Sailors System.
    www.itd.nps.gov/cwss
Penetanguishene Centennial Museum and Archives. Museum of
    Penetanguishene, Ontario. www.pencenmuseum.com
Robertson, John K., Don Hagist, Todd Braistead and Don Londahl-
    Smidt. Orderly Books of the British Forces in North America,
    1775-1884. www.revwar75.com/crown/index.htm.
Schulze, Lorine McGinnis. Olive Tree Genealogy.
    olivetreegenealogy.com/mil/index.shtml.
Statistics Canada. "1940 National Registration." www.statcan.ca
STEM-Net, Memorial University of Newfoundland. We Will
    Remember. www.cdli.ca/monuments
Veterans Affairs Canada. "Books of Remembrance."
    www.vac-acc.gc.ca/remembers
Veterans Affairs Canada. "Canada Remembers."
    www.vac-acc.ca/general

11

Loyalist Ancestors

Reference Dates

1775–83	American Revolutionary War
1783	Treaty of Separation
1783–84	Major influx of Loyalists to old Quebec
1789	Lord Dorchester's resolution created a Mark of Honour for the Loyalists: the hereditary capitals UE to distinguish them from other settlers
1794	Detroit and Michilimackinac territory ceded to Americans
1796	Governor Simcoe's proclamation for creating District Loyalist Rolls
1798–1839	Additions and exclusions were made on the lists
1896	Loyalist societies were formed
1914	United Empire Loyalists' Association of Canada was chartered

The word "Loyalist" is used here to describe those who supported the royal cause in what Canadians call the American Revolution and Americans call the War of Independence. Among the Loyalists who left the American colonies for refuge during and after the war, were those who came to old Quebec and became the founding families of Upper Canada. The Loyalists themselves emerged from differing degrees of pre-war backgrounds, motivation and experiences, but they all shared the sacrifices of being dispossessed and displaced. Discovering a Loyalist ancestor may come from word of mouth as a family tradition, or from research references as you work backward in time on a family line. While much has been published about Loyalists, their times and troubles, there is no single, determining source that lists their names. It's up to you to uncover satisfactory documentation about the individual.

Lord Dorchester, Governor General and Commander in Chief of the Colonies of Quebec, Nova Scotia and New Brunswick, resolved in 1789 that a Mark of Honour was to be established upon the families who had adhered to the Unity of Empire during the American Revolutionary War. The mark of honour was to distinguish them (on the proposed militia rolls in the same resolution) "and all their Children and their Descendants by either sex" by the "following capitals affixed to their names: UE." In addition, the intent was to allot *privileged* land grants to the Loyalists and their sons and daughters. In the majority of cases, it is their children who provided the documentation we now use to identify a Loyalist who came to Upper Canada.

Upper Canada followed Dorchester's resolution more carefully than other British colonies. The UE designation became a convenient measure for the land committee and the land boards, which, for many preliminary years, had to handle great throngs of newcomers needing assistance and direction. Most of all, the Loyalists needed land to cultivate, plant and harvest food for their families. In the first stages of moving and settling them into the "uninhabited" western area of Quebec, government officials dispensed certificates to locate Loyalists on specific plots of hastily surveyed land. It seems the Loyalists themselves rarely practised the usage of UE after their names. Their priorities were to survive in new, and often isolating, circumstances. Some were initially unaware of the bureaucratic initiatives or directives on their behalf.

The UE postnominal initials represent Canada's sole hereditary honour (as in "all their children *and their descendants,*" above) [italics added]. The honour has guidelines for the unfamiliar who may want to add the initials to their names. Whether or not you choose to join the United Empire Loyalists' Association of Canada (UELAC), their studies have shown that contemporary authorities generally recognized Loyalist privilege for a person who:

- resided in the American colonies prior to the war against Britain;
- joined or served the British forces ("the Royal Standard") in some capacity before 1783; and
- experienced the loss of property, assets or livelihood in that period.

- Members of the Six Nations and other Indian allies who met the same conditions and came to the province were included. They received collective reserves rather than individual land grants.

The Loyalist privilege of receiving land grants free of all fees, and having each child benefit from the same bounty, was very attractive. In the early 1790s, Governor Simcoe made it widely known that Upper Canada welcomed new settlers to take up land and increase the population. Of the numerous American settlers who arrived, some would claim to be post-facto Loyalists.

Reality dictated the necessity of distinguishing Loyalists from "common" settlers who were expected to pay fees for survey and administrative costs. Records had to be created for keeping track of names and locations and the size of each grant. It suited the land boards and other officials to mark petitions and documents with UE or SUE (son of a Loyalist) or DUE (daughter of a Loyalist) as a bookkeeping method. While the original certificates were often issued for a regular 100-acre parcel, or family lands according to the number of dependents, a Loyalist could later petition for additional land commensurate with his militia rank.

True Loyalists were expected to have settled in Upper Canada by 1789. That date was later extended to 1796. Nevertheless, fine distinctions are not always clear in the surviving documentation. Anomalies can be confusing when privilege was allowed—or not allowed—for certain individuals. For example, some *Late Loyalists* persuaded the government they had legitimate reasons for not arriving earlier. *Maritime Loyalists* who re-located to Upper Canada were ostensibly not eligible for land grants here free of fees. *Treasury Loyalists* had originally spent time as pensioned refugees in England, coming to Canada in 1792. *Associated Loyalists* had served in a corps not attached to a regular Army regiment. *Military Claimants* were veterans of the professional army or could be officers of a provincial corps. Some Mennonites or Quakers, although conscientious objectors to the bearing of arms, had been more than sympathizers, providing support services. More in-depth discussion can be found in Merriman, *United Empire Loyalists: A Guide to Tracing Loyalist Ancestors in Upper Canada.*

Loyalist Lists

A list is frequently the first source sought by family historians, in the hope that it will supply the magic name without further ado. Furthermore, some CD-ROMs or databases package "Loyalists" into one neat unit from multi-source compilations. It's essential that you know the sources that were drawn from to create that package, especially a reference you want to follow up. Alas, there is no one definitive, accurate roll of Loyalists, although there are at least four contemporary lists. *Any* name that looks promising on a list is only a starting point, or one more piece of information, in your search to establish proof.

All lists contain some ordinary settlers or ex-soldiers who wanted to ensure their own property rights or perhaps claim similar bounties. The reason for differences and discrepancies in the lists lies in the evolving provincial administration and the various offices through which approval was to be sought. Over the years many names were suspended or expunged from Loyalist lists as the authorities wrestled with the eligibility of claimants. The ongoing petitions for privileged land grants, interpretation of qualifications, bureaucratic mistakes, confusion with fathers and sons who had each served in their own right, or numerous men with the same name, all caused additions to and removals from the lists.

By 1795 a system of land registration was in place. In effect, this meant that anyone with a proper claim to a piece of land could then petition for a Crown patent (title deed). In 1796 Governor Simcoe gave the district land boards the task of drawing up rolls of deserving Loyalists.

The District Rolls of Loyalists show the man's name, the district he was in at the time and sometimes his township of residence or a brief remark—the rolls vary from one district to another. Loyalists could turn in their original land certificates for proper deeds by filing affidavits or evidence to clarify their status and identities. The procedure, before a district magistrate, also required confirming an oath of allegiance. Unfortunately, not all Loyalists heard about this obligation in a timely way. Some had died in the meantime and some were unable to travel to the district towns to fulfil it. The rolls are at Library and Archives Canada (RG 1, L 7, vol. 52b). Published as *Ontario People 1796-1803* by Keith Fitzgerald, the book contains a good explanatory introduction by Norman Crowder. Fitzgerald's transcription, praised as "of facsimile quality" by a knowledgeable archivist, can also be seen on Archives of Ontario microfilm MS 803.

As a very small example of the problems the government had to contend with, one man serving in the Indian Department at the end of the War had managed to have himself placed on the Eastern District Loyalist roll. Subsequent enquiry revealed him to be an American soldier who had been taken prisoner by "our Indians" and talked himself into a turncoat job. He wanted to remain in Canada, but his loyalty was considered suspect and his name was suspended from the list.

The other available lists of Loyalists are apparently based on the same sources—the district rolls initiated in 1796. The Executive Council UE List at LAC (RG 1, L 7, Vol 52a) is often considered the most reliable, perhaps only in comparison with others. It was created and kept by the clerk of the executive council, and was being altered until about 1839. Again, all names on this list will not necessarily coincide with other lists. The Executive Council UE List is the second item (called "List of United Empire Loyalists") on microfilm C-2222 at LAC and AO.

The Crown Lands Department List is commonly called "the Old United Empire Loyalists List" and was published as a book in 1885 with numerous reprints since. The full title is *The Centennial of the Settlement of Upper Canada by the United Empire Loyalists, 1784-1884*. Because of its wide availability, it is too often seized upon as "the" authoritative source. The original register was created in the surveyor general's office for property location purposes, after a chain of acknowledgment from certain other offices, and was inherited by the provincial Crown lands office. However, the book derives from a *transcription* of the original list. Both the transcription and the book fail to note names that were crossed out in the original. The list is in two parts, with some initialled short-form references, many of which are not always elucidated or self-explanatory—they were abbreviations for inter-departmental usage. The original register is the first item on Archives of Ontario microfilm MS 4029. The transcription (PAC, MG 9, D 4, Vol 9) is the first item on microfilm C-2222 at LAC and AO.

A fourth contemporary list is the Register of the Inspector General, created after 1801 when the office came into being. From this time on, one job of the inspector general was to review the petitions for privileged Loyalist land grants. Thus this official too was amending his own register for years. It appears on AO microfilm MS 4029 as the second item.

Most of these lists have notes on what the recorder was told about how a person served the Crown during the war and which district he was in. Sometimes reference is made to an appearance on very early district provisioning lists, or possibly relationships to other people. A name on a Loyalist list is not considered adequate evidence of a Loyalist ancestor. Supporting evidence must come from additional sources. Illustrations of the above four lists are shown in *United Empire Loyalists: A Guide to Tracing Ancestors in Upper Canada.*

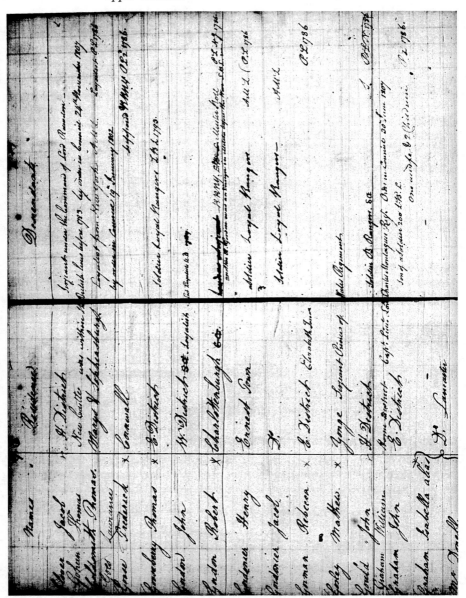

Crown Lands (Surveyor General) Loyalists list, RG 1-515-0-0-1; AO microfilm MS 4029

Other Lists

Another important and well-used list, compiled post facto, is the book by William D. Reid, *The Loyalists in Ontario, Sons and Daughters of the American Loyalists of Upper Canada*. If you look on *Ancestry.ca*, you will find it among the Canadian databases. Reid reconstructed Loyalist families based on orders-in-council (OC) issued to the children who claimed a Loyalist father. Reid clearly used a few additional sources such as fiat and warrant books, Township Papers, Heir and Devisee Commission files, and some published early church or ministers' registers, to provide extra family information. An index to all stray names is included. The OCs unquestionably provide the names of fathers who were considered Loyalists. The drawbacks with the compiled families are that some children may be missing—the ones who did not petition for their privileged land grant. Some Loyalists do not appear at all, and others are confused with men of the same name. Nevertheless, this book is a valuable guide leading to original sources.

Refugee lists or provisioning lists were created by army or government officials during the somewhat chaotic period during and immediately after the war when thousands of refugees were flooding into British territory. These desperate people had been ordered or threatened into exile, leaving behind their homes, their stock and crops and, often, their belongings and some family members. When men were away fighting, it was a wretched time for their dependents and wives, who often became widows. Potter-McKinnon's book *While the Women Only Wept* describes

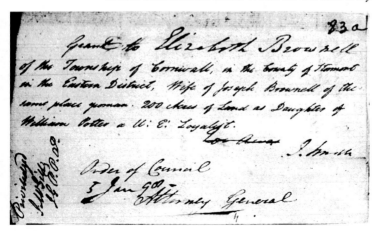

Elizabeth Brownell, order-in-council (1798), Upper Canada Land Petitions, RG1, L3, vol. 31, B bundle 4, petition 83; Library and Archives Canada microfilm C-1620

the trials of women and their families in eastern Ontario. See also "Loyalist Women" by Jennifer Taylor in *The Loyalist Gazette* Vol. XLII, No. 2 (Autumn 2004).

The British had limited means of assistance for the families of Loyalist men who were fighting. Wives, children and wounded men were taken into fortified areas where they helped to build refugee camps at safe points like St Jean, Chambly, Sorel (Fort William Henry), Machiche, Montreal, Carleton Island and Niagara. Babies were born, couples were married and people died in this interim while the war persisted. Quebec Governor Frederick Haldimand made plans to relocate most of them upriver. Boats, tents, blankets, cooking utensils and other necessities were supplied for the post-war journey on the Saint Lawrence to the upper part of the province. Elinor K. Senior wrote "Loyalist Regiments After the American Revolution" in *Canadian Genealogist* Vol. 2, No. 1 (1981) with accompanying maps showing refugee paths and subsequent settlement areas of the various Loyalist corps.

Some provisioning or refugee lists that relate directly to the British Northern Command area and Quebec during this resettlement time survive in the Haldimand Papers. LAC has copies of both the original papers (MG 21) and a transcription series, the latter microfilmed. LAC finding aid 599 contains a descriptive calendar, not yet online, of the entire fonds. Four volumes of Loyalist material are available with an index on microfilm C-1475. The books *Loyalist Lists* by Keith Fitzgerald and *Early Ontario Settlers* by Norman Crowder are compendiums of several of the available lists. In many instances, only the head of the family is named. By careful reading of the introductions and attention to detail, it is often possible to determine the number of people in one refugee family and approximate ages of children by the quantity of the rations they were issued. Occasionally a list will mention wives, children or ages, acting as a mini-census for a precise time and place. If "remarks" were made, they can be valuable information.

Other lists have been published in *Families* and local historical society periodicals, for example:

"Loyalist Stragglers in Montreal, September-October, 1784" by E. Keith Fitzgerald in *Families* Vol. 24, No. 1 (1985).

"Loyalist Victualling Lists of the Niagara Area, 1786" by Robert Halfyard in *Families* Vol. 24, Nos. 2 and 4 (1985).

"Returns of the Asylum at (Fort) William Henry for Loyalist Invalids" by George Neville in *Families* Vol. 16, No. 3 (1977).

"Loyalists of William Henry (Sorel)" by Walter S. White in *The Loyalist Gazette* Vol. XII (Autumn 1974) and Vol. XIII (Spring 1975).

Early Vital Records

Baptism, marriage, and burial information for ancestors who spent any time in the Montreal district settlements and refugee camps might exist in some Quebec sources, although few date back to Loyalist times. See Chapter 4 for more about early religious sources in Upper Canada.

- The Quebec Family History Society published *Marriages 1766-1850, Christ Church Cathedral, Montreal,* as well as the *Christ Church Sorel (Anglican) 1784-1899, Births, Marriages, Burials.* On its website, the society offers a free surname search and library catalogue, and a members-only database that includes Montreal-area Protestant marriages (most date from post-Loyalist times).

- The Anglican registers for Sorel (as well as many other Eastern Townships church records) have been extracted and indexed in a database by Marlene Simmons on her website *Quebec and Eastern Townships Genealogy Research Page;* free online searching and a modest fee for obtaining abstracts.

- Check LAC's *Checklist of Parish Registers (1986)* for the province of Quebec, for availability of Catholic and Protestant church registers through interlibrary loan.

- The register for St. Andrews Presbyterian Church, Williamstown, Glengarry County, began in Montreal in 1779 with Rev. John Bethune, chaplain for the Royal Highland Emigrants (microfilm C-3030 at LAC and AO).

- St. Gabriel Street Presbyterian Church registers, Montreal, are available at AO on MS 351, dating from 1796 and might contain some come-lately family members.

Military Service

Identifying a Loyalist ancestor means finding evidence that he participated in the fighting action, or otherwise provided support for the royal cause. The composition and activities of the provincial militia corps, known as Loyalist regiments, are a chief source for establishing that evidence. The corps were raised from volunteer civilians to support the regular British army troops. Lists of names in the form of musters and pay lists resulted, taken fairly regularly from their formation until their disbandment after the Treaty of Separation. Not as many survive as family historians would like—rolls or returns for some corps have never been located. Some of the original lists are found within the Haldimand Papers, British Military "C" Series and War Office records (see also Chapter 10). Many lists have been published in historical and genealogical periodicals by military historians and aficionados. If a list fails to state a man's previous residence in the colonies, researching his corps and where it was raised may get you closer to the truth.

The British had four major command, or department, areas during the confllict:

Northern Department, aka Canadian Command, based in Quebec City

Central Command, based at New York City

Eastern Command, based at Halifax

Southern Command, based in Florida

For most Ontario researchers, the greatest interest will be in the Loyalist corps of the Northern Command which were disbanded around Sorel (also known as Fort William Henry), Montreal, Niagara and Detroit. Militia and civilians were ultimately evacuated from the Central and Southern areas, notably to Nova Scotia or England, but certainly there were Loyalists in Upper Canada before 1800 from New Jersey, Pennsylvania, Maryland, Virginia and the Carolinas. Murtie Jean Clark's *Loyalists in the Southern Campaign of the Revolutionary War* is a classic for that region. Also, a considerable number of Loyalists who were first settled in what became New Brunswick made their way to Upper Canada after a few years.

The following Loyalist Corps were associated with the Northern Command, in addition to the Indian Department:

Royal Highland Emigrants (promoted post-war to regular British army establishment as the 84th Regiment)

King's Royal Regiment of New York (KRRNY)

Butler's Rangers

Loyal Rangers

King's Rangers

Older, smaller corps, before a reorganization in 1781, sent most of the men from these units into the Loyal Rangers or the Second Battalion of the KRRNY:

King's Loyal Americans

Queen's Loyal Rangers

Loyal Volunteers

Units led by Daniel McAlpin, Samuel McKay, Samuel Adams and Robert Leake

Unincorporated or associated corps not attached to a regular army regiment (several working with the Indian Department):

Joseph Brant's Volunteers

Loyal Foresters

Detroit Volunteers

Claus's Rangers

Major Van Alstyne's Company

Captain Grass' Company

(these last two originated in the Central Command)

Fryer's *King's Men, the Soldier Founders of Ontario* is recommended introductory reading for background on the Northern Command corps—their formation, officers and activities. The book provides not only richly detailed endnotes, but also the historical drama of the war and its key people. *Rolls of the Provincial (Loyalist) Corps, Canadian Command, American Revolutionary Period* by Fryer and Smy lists men in the major corps of the Northern Department of British operations. We must remember that human components in any company or regiment were fluid, as men came and went through injury, death or transfer. The compilers wanted to show the corps at their most complete size, between the years 1781 and 1784. Information for each man may simply be his name, while some have age, place of birth (the initials N.B. mean North Britain, which refers to Scotland), height, length of service or perhaps his residence when he enlisted. What is *not* included in this publication are members of the Indian Department, and men who died, were discharged or disappeared from the rolls before the end of the war.

Authors Cruikshank, Smy and Watt are of special interest as military historians. Gavin Watt's *The History and Master Roll of the King's Royal Regiment of New York* reproduces Cruikshank's original 1931 text on the subject, with new footnote annotations. Watt adds his own outstanding work in appendices, especially "The Revised Master Roll" which is alphabetical with as much service and settlement details as he could glean from many original sources. Another example is Watt and Morrison, *The British Campaign of 1777*, an in-depth study of the St. Leger expedition and each unit that took part in it, both attackers and defenders. Their research provides lists of men and their positions at the time.

Lieutenant Colonel Smy compiled *An Annotated Roll of Butler's Rangers, 1777-1784* from his studies devoted to the Loyalist era. Besides the preliminary information about Colonel John Butler, the recruiting of the Rangers and their lives at Niagara during the war, Smy includes an alphabetical biographical listing of known Rangers. Precautions apply, as always, to any derivative lists and the potential for mixing or combining men of the same name.

More published histories and articles can also be found about other individual regiments. They can be located through LAC's online library search engine or the catalogues of repositories you visit. As well, the personal papers of many officers of these corps have been deposited at public institutions.

Many men served out of Fort Niagara with the Indian Department, which played a key quasi-military role in Northern operations. Others worked for the Provincial Marine based at Carleton Island near Kingston. Some served the British cause in an effective spy network or on garrison duties, while some served unofficially as couriers, provisioners, drivers and boatmen or as guides for escaping Loyalist families. Again, the Haldimand fonds (MG 21) at LAC with finding aid 599, and British Military and Naval Records (RG 8) with finding aid 1800, are sources of primary information. Selections from these two series are available at AO.

Definitely worth mentioning are the numbers of French Canadians who were active on the Loyalist side during the course of the war. They not only acted as valuable agents, scouts or employees with the Indian Department at places ranging from Fort Niagara to Michilimackinac, but they also formed the bulk of the Detroit Volunteers militia. French farmers and traders had occupied both sides of the Detroit River and its vicinity for years before the British victory of 1763. To this day, French communities still ring the eastern and southern shores of the Detroit and St. Clair Rivers, and Lake Huron. Finding evidence to demonstrate a French ancestor's loyalty can be more of a challenge. Because they lived in a colony (Quebec) that was not rebelling and, in most cases, did not lose property, they did not exactly fit the criteria by which Loyalists were given privileged land grants. On the other hand, families who had to re-locate from Detroit across the river into Upper Canada after 1794 may be represented in the land petitions.

John P. Dulong's "French-Canadian and Acadian Loyalists" in the OGS *Seminar Annual, 1986* is one of the few articles to address this subject. "Canadian Participants in the American

Revolution, An Index" [meaning French Canadians] by Virginia DeMarce was published serially in *Lost in Canada?* from Vol. 6, No. 2 (May 1980) to Vol. 10, No. 4 (November 1984). Donna Stuart's *The Genealogy of the French Families of the Detroit River Region, 1701-1936* is also a potentially useful compiled resource. "The Partnership that created Canada" by Hereward Senior in *The Loyalist Gazette* Vol. XLIII, No. 2 (Fall 2005) dwells on the how the American Revolution influenced the merging of Canada's two great cultures.

American Sources

Momentum built up from the first year of the Revolution to penalize royalist sympathizers. Fines, imprisonment, the seizure of goods, dispossession and, gradually, eviction were the lot of the hapless families who tried to remain in their homes. Vigilante groups such as Committees of Safety and Commissioners for Detecting and Defeating Conspiracies were formed. As a type of finding aid for rebel/patriot documents, Butler's extensive *Index to Papers of the Continental Congress 1774-1789* covers personal names and many subjects, such as refugees, prisoners of war, confiscations and escheated estates. Penrose's *Mohawk Valley in the Revolution: Committee of Safety Papers and Genealogical Compendium* is a research aid specific to New York State.

State libraries, archival institutions, and historical societies in American states can offer much additional material to the genealogist who has identified his ancestor's colony of prior residence. Historic churches dating back to the eighteenth century in those states are of prime interest for baptismal and marriage information. There are also books written about the Loyalists of Connecticut, Delaware, Massachusetts, New Jersey, Pennsylvania and Vermont that will guide you to original sources.

Indian Loyalists

Indian participation in the Loyalist cause has been less well-known in the public mind, but scholarship is working to remedy it. At least four of the Six Nations of the Mohawk Valley, influenced by Joseph Brant and his sister Molly Johnson, declared loyalty to the King at the beginning of the Revolution. Native knowledge of the land and experience in the woods played a large supportive role for British troops. The New York tribes, too, lost their homes and traditional lands at the conclusion of the war. Like the other Loyalists, they were unsuccessful in petitioning the Americans for redress. However, Governor Haldimand made good on an earlier promise to recompense the loyal Indians. A very large grant of land in the new settlement area, six miles on either side of the Grand River, was assigned to the Six Nations. As well, another grant was given on the Bay of Quinte that became the Tyendenaga reserve. See Reaman's *The Trail of the Iroquois Indians: How the Iroquois Nation Saved Canada for the British Empire.*

The colonial Indian Department was a precursor to the federal Department of Indian Affairs. Some records of the successive administrations under Sir William Johnson, Guy Johnson and Sir John Johnson have been preserved in LAC's RG 10, but many other papers generated by these men have been scattered among different institutions and private collectors. This is also true for some papers of military and militia personnel who served in the Indian Department, although LAC has several important fonds under family names. Bill Russell advises, in his *Records of the Department of Indian Affairs,* that LAC's RG 8 (British Military and Naval Records) and MG 21 (Haldimand Papers) are also sources for native information. Therefore researchers interested in the pre-Upper Canada period should consult LAC finding aids and search its online inventories, as well as using Internet search engines for archival material.

Robert Allen's *The British Indian Department and the Frontier in North America, 1775-1830* includes an annotated list of Indian leaders. Penrose's *Indian Affairs Papers, American Revolution* contains almost 400 pages of information. See also *Loyalist Families of the Grand River Branch.* More information on general native ancestry research is in Chapter 8. Supplementary information for Indian Loyalists and Loyalists in general can be sought from the usual genealogical sources studied for any early Ontario settler.

The following articles may be of particular interest:
"The Loyalists and the Six Nations Indians in the Niagara Peninsula" by Wilbur H. Siebert in *Proceedings and Transactions of the Royal Society of Canada,* Vol. 9 (1916).
"The Indian Loyalists: Their Place in Canadian History" by Helen Caistor Robinson in the OGS *Seminar Annual, 1984.*
"Feathered UELs (Mohawks)" by Enos T. Montour in *The Loyalist Gazette* Vol. XI (Autumn 1973).
"Joseph Brant—Thayendanega" by Howard Thomas in *The Loyalist Gazette* Vol. XII (Autumn 1974).
Others can be found in past issues of *The Loyalist Gazette.*

Special mention should be made of the ambitious and growing Loyalist Collection at Brock University's James A. Gibson

Library. The Friends of the Loyalist Collection at Brock University is a registered charity that is raising funds for this centralized study facility, located in Special Collections and Archives of the library on the campus in St. Catharines. Plans are to duplicate material and microfilms of the most heavily used historical sources from LAC, TNA and other repositories. Available are selections of records from the British Treasury office, the Haldimand Papers, British Miliary and Naval Records "C Series," Upper Canada land books and petitions, Crown lands schedules, maps, Joseph Brant papers and those of allied families or other officials. See the PDF file at the website as the listing grows.

The Online Institute for Advanced Loyalists Studies website has a potpourri of selections from various sources for Loyalist material—lists of corps volunteers, samples of petitions or memorials, military instructions, letters to and from officers, lists of "traitors," contemporary accounts and so on. The site continues to develop for all aspects and geographic areas of Loyalist activities, not just those who came to Upper Canada.

Land Grants

Land records provide the greatest wealth of information on individual Loyalists because their status was inevitably linked to privilege in acquiring land. The first townships were allotted more or less to specific Loyalist corps, partly as a defensive measure, placing veterans in groups along the front townships. Tables for the amounts of land were devised and revised.

1783: Loyalist heads of families and privates from a Loyalist corps were designated for 100 acres each, and:
50 acres for each member of a Loyalist family and single men;
200 acres for non-commissioned officers;
500 acres for lieutenants and warrant officers;
700 acres for captains;
1000 acres for field officers (majors and colonels).

1787: The grant to Loyalist refugees and ordinary settlers increased to 200 acres each, and the provision for 200 acres for the daughters and sons of Loyalists came into effect when they reached the age of majority, or when a daughter married.

1788: The Royal Highland Emigrants had been allotted more favourable sizes of grants, but other Loyalists successfully

lobbied to have their grants increased to the same scale:
2000 acres for Loyalist corps lieutenants and warrant officers;
3000 acres for captains;
5000 acres for field officers.

Thus, both the soldiers of the regular British regiments who decided to stay in Canada and the Loyalists who had enrolled in a provincial corps were entitled to military claimant (MC) land grants. The difference between them lies in the *privilege* only for Loyalists—no bureaucratic fees to be paid, and recognition of sons and daughters. Inevitably, some confusion followed among administrative officials and the populace, because the regulations and calculations governing all land granting fluctuated for many years. Occasionally soldiers were mistakenly given Loyalist status, while some Loyalists leave evidence of only military grants.

John Canniff (1817), Upper Canada Land Petitions, RG 1, L 3, vol. 99 Part I, C bundle 11, petition 24; Library and Archives Canada microfilm C-1652

The date and the size of a man's grant can tell you something about your ancestor's status as an army veteran or privileged settler. Infrequently an American-born man might have joined a regiment of the regular army, which caused confusion in his status after the war. If a man received a grant only as an MC but his children received Loyalist sons' and daughters' grants, the context shows he was considered a Loyalist.

Land Petitions

Writing to the governor with a request was called a petition. Loyalists would ask to ensure their names were on a list or for additional lands for which they qualified or to clarify their land ownership. Generally speaking, a petition from a Loyalist himself rarely names any relationships. In fact, comparatively few petitions requesting a land grant exist for Loyalist heads of families. The call for district Loyalist rolls in 1796 had more or less created a foundation for sorting out Loyalists from other settlers. However, some Loyalists' names did not make it onto the district rolls, for various reasons. Some may have been unaware of the need to exchange their original certificates and to reaffirm their status and allegiance. Others may have considered the certificates to be adequate proof of land ownership. Unfortunately, many deserving Loyalists died in battle action, along the refugee routes, or after a few years of pioneer privation. Their families were left to deal with the situation as best they could.

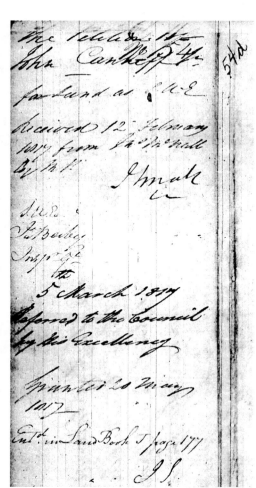

The Upper Canada Land Petitions series includes the bulk of Loyalist-related petitions, held at LAC (RG 1, L 3), but also available at AO, FHL and other institutions, with 26 reels of nominal indexes. Many widows or sons represent deceased Loyalists, as well as the still-living men who applied. The Loyalist or his next of kin would have had to provide evidence of his right to Loyalist privilege, such as proof of service in a Loyalist corps, where he lived before the advent of the Revolution and so on. The Canadian Genealogy Centre is working to have the indexes online in 2008.

By far the majority of Loyalist land petitions came from the grown children. Thus, the date of the petition can sometimes be a clue to their ages. They may mention that they have just turned 21, or where and when they were born. Daughters often applied shortly after marrying, identifying their husbands' name and residence. Both sons and daughters gave the name of their Loyalist father and his residence, indicating if he was deceased at the time. The relationship provides the link between generations.

George Bond (1808), Upper Canada Land Petitions, RG 1, L 3, vol. 35, B bundle 8, petition 129; Library and Archives Canada microfilm C-1622

The most important point to look for on a petition is whether it was granted. Some petitions from putative Loyalists were not approved because insufficient evidence was submitted about their service or loyalty, meaning a document of discharge or deposition from a former officer or comrade in arms. Some petitions were denied because a man had arrived after one of the cut-off arrival dates, or had already received his due allotment. Or the petitioner might have requested a location in a certain township or a specific property. He could have been refused because all lots in that township had already been granted, or the township was not yet officially surveyed or open for settlement.

Children's petitions were sometimes not recommended because the father's name was not found on the UE list. That event could have triggered additional petitions from the son or daughter, in the effort to provide acceptable evidence. The blended Loyalist families, created when a widow and widower married, caused some confusion if a child petitioned using the name of the Loyalist step-father. Many SUE or DUE grants were allowed on the predication of a step-relationship. Then in mid-1802 an executive council decision stated such a petition would only be considered if the child's biological father was a Loyalist.

Notations were made on the outside of petitions by various government officials as they investigated their records. Whatever the text of the petition says, no matter how persuasive the request, it is the back or outside of the petition that gives the government verdict. Approval shows the initials UE or SUE or DUE. The word "recommended" is commonly used, or "approved" or "confirmed." Unsuccessful petitions may have the note "not recommended" or "father not on UE list." Occasionally when a son or daughter was recommended for a grant, the petition was marked UE (rather than SUE or DUE). The same clerical mistake would be repeated on the Ontario Land Records Index (Chapter 6). Successful petitions are direct evidence of a Loyalist ancestor.

If you find a petition that did not succeed, it may not be the only one sent by the Loyalist or his family members. He may have tried again, perhaps with additional evidence, or his children may have been successful later. Be sure to search the index thoroughly for the surname, using spelling variants. In any event, it is wise to search for petitions from all his known children. In case of a petition possibly omitted during microfilming, a search of the published land book indexes (Chapter 6) would be of value.

Petitions were being made by the children of Loyalists into the 1850s. The later *pro forma* petitions required a great deal of family information. The petitioners, usually well advanced in age, had not made the customary application early in their lives. Forms with printed instructions were to be sworn before a Court of Quarter Sessions magistrate. If the Loyalist father was not then living, the year of his death, his age at the time and his wife's year of death were requested. Sometimes the father's age "if alive" is given in years. The petitioner's date and place of birth and relationship to the Loyalist are given. Provision is made for naming the petitioner's siblings and their ages, sometimes giving the names of husbands of the married sisters. One of the forms specifies to list only the siblings born since 1821 and to distinguish between different mothers (if the Loyalist had had issue from more than one marriage).

Researchers should not overlook the Crown lands series of petitions (Chapter 6) wherein a number of these late petitions appear. The Upper Canada series has some as well. Since free land grants to Loyalists had been officially discontinued in 1839, these petitioners could expect a "scrip" bounty equivalent to a 200-acre land grant. In 1850, the sum of £40 was the norm.

Claims for Losses

In addition to free grants of land in the new country and temporary provisioning relief, Loyalists were eligible for some compensation due to their loss of property and goods in the former colonies. A special government commission convened in Montreal, Halifax and London, England, to hear and adjudicate the claims for losses. Records in the British Audit Office group at The National Archives (TNA) in England (AO 12, 146 volumes & AO 13, 141 boxes and bundles. MG 14 at NA contains the proceedings of these hearings and the descriptive evidence that was submitted as valuations. Once again, you cannot expect every Loyalist ancestor to be found in these records. News travelled slowly from officialdom into the hinterlands and, even then, few in the area west of Montreal could afford the time or cost of travel. Relatively few Loyalists responded by the unrealistic deadline of March 1784. An extension until the spring of 1786 made it possible for two commissioners to take evidence in person at the settlements in Niagara, Cataraqui, New Oswegatchie and New Johnstown (see first map) and thus more Loyalists were accommodated. A few Loyalists submitted claims through agents John Porteous or Alexander Ellice (their papers at LAC in MG 23 and MG 24).

A researcher may find such information as the individual's

place of residence in the American colonies, description of acreage, crops or livestock, how long he had lived there, maybe his country or colony of birth, occupation, number of dependents, the date he joined the Royal Standard or otherwise justified his claim and his residence at the time of the claim. Supporting statements are often supplied by witnesses who knew him and his situation before or during the Revolution. Some claims include the names of relatives and relationships, particularly when inherited property had been lost. Compensation for a claim is primary evidence of a Loyalist ancestor, although the records are not always clear if he was successful or what amount he received.

British Audit Office

In discussing these records, AO is the designated archival reference for (British) Audit Office records, not to be confused with our general overall reference to Archives of Ontario. Historians seem to agree that the original chronological notes about evidence recorded by the two travelling commissioners are in the Library of Congress, Washington, DC (MSS 18,662). The transcribed version is in British Audit Office 12 (TNA, AO 12, first 56

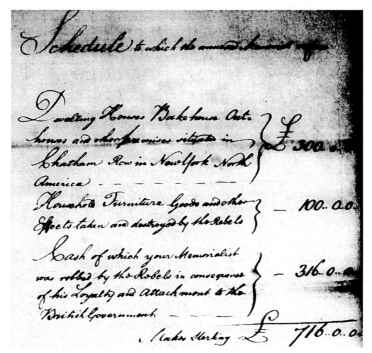

Frederick Brautigam, memorial claim for losses (1786), MG 14, Audit Office 13, vol. 63, p. 286; Library and Archives Canada microfilm B-2428

volumes), in books arranged according to the American state in which the claimant formerly resided. Ten volumes of notes are missing from the Washington manuscripts, and one book for New York State is missing from the AO 12 records.

A different transcription of the commissioners' books was published in the *Bureau of Archives Second Report* in 1904, but this version omits the claims that were rejected. This is another case where a publication, the "1904 Report," is widely available and highly visible, often without due observance of its omissions and limitations. More to the point, Bruce Antliff's *Loyalist Settlements, 1783-1789* has reconstructed the ten missing volumes and added the omissions from the *Second Report*. Antliff includes a name index to both the "new" material and the *Second Report*. Together, these two publications give the most complete transcripts of Audit Office 12 records and act as a finding aid. A government-published summary on microfilm C-9821 at LAC and AO contains a guide to each volume of AO 12 with microfilm numbers, a name index and, in Volume 109, "reports and statements" of claims paid out.

Audit Office 13 contains the original supporting documentation brought to the commissioners: handwritten memorials from the claimants, certificates or affidavits from witnesses or commanding officers, family papers of land ownership or transfer, evaluations of goods and property and/or business accounts. Here is where evidence can be found of harassment, intimidation and outright persecution. Loyalists who held official documents from an American state about the confiscation of their land or forfeiture of estates produced them for the claims commission. In *American Migrations 1765-1799*, Peter Coldham abstracted the files of AO 12 and 13 and arranged them in alphabetical surname order within each state of Loyalists' previous residences.

Coldham's masterful work virtually replaces his earlier *American Loyalist Claims* and is a treasure in itself. He has added six appendices to include abstracts for some East and West Florida claimants, and a list of ships known to have transported Loyalists with dates, sailing point of departure and destination.

LAC finding aid 250 has alphabetical indexes to claimants in Part II for AO 12 and Part III for AO 13. Part I of the finding aid is the shelf list for microfilm numbers. The finding aid is not currently available online. Both Archives of Ontario and the FHL also have microfilm copies of both Audit Office series. The FHL catalogue reference to AO 12 is clear, but AO 13 has been named "American Loyalist Claims, 1730-1835. Great Britain: Exchequer and Audit Dept."

Treasury Board

British Treasury records (T50 and T77 at TNA; MG 15 at LAC) are of additional interest. Treasury books in T50 recorded payments to successful claimants. T50 also includes "Miscellaneous Documents Relating to Refugees" and more. T77 has reports from special agents for some claims, unacceptable cases, confiscated property in Virginia and some duplications of, or adjuncts to, material in AO 12. The Treasury collection is best known by genealogists for its records of claimants and property losses in Florida, hence the term Treasury Loyalists. LAC has selected volumes from these records with a separate index to claimants.

United Empire Loyalists' Association

The United Empire Loyalists' Association of Canada (UELAC), organized in 1896 and incorporated in 1914, is a lineage society of UE descendants who submit documented pedigrees for approval and acceptance as regular members. Affiliate membership is available for those who submit the same approved research but are unable to swear the oath of allegiance to the Crown, an integral part of regular membership. Associate memberships are open to anyone who supports the aims of the association and for those in the process of proving their lineage.

Application for any type of membership goes to a branch of the UELAC. You can choose from more than a dozen branches in Ontario or others across the country, depending on where you live or your Loyalist ancestor lived. Each branch has its regular meetings, local activities, communications and resources. To apply for membership, you fill out a preliminary application that determines which type of membership is best. If you are seeking to document a Loyalist ancestor, a branch genealogist will give you instructions, explain the forms and, often, give you research advice. Relationships from one generation to the next must be documented by standard genealogical procedures and sources. Evidence of the Loyalist ancestor's status is also expected. When you complete and submit the final application, the branch genealogist sends it on to the Dominion genealogist for review.

Collectively, the UELAC is represented by a Dominion headquarters office in Toronto. The association publishes *The Loyalist Gazette* twice-yearly, holds an annual Dominion conference and steers a number of projects in which all branches participate. They have been proactive in public education about Loyalists, with the erection of monuments, provincial recognition of a yearly Loyalist Day, commemorative postage stamps and anniversary celebrations, often supported by re-enactment militia displays. Project 2014 preparations are underway to celebrate the centennial of the UELAC founding, with the dedication in Ottawa of a United Empire Loyalists' Memorial. Each branch also has plans for corresponding local activities.

The association does not have a central library but branches have their own resources. The UELAC website has many helpful and educational features, including a history and timeline of the Loyalist era, plus a directory of individual Loyalists to which members are contributing. Under References and Links is a thorough bibliography of Loyalist publications and a reading list for elementary schools. A chronological index of *Gazette* articles is online. See also individual branch websites. Volunteers manage the United-Empire-Loyalist listserve on *rootsweb.com* and the regular email newsletter *Loyalist Trails*. Both are open to all interested parties. You can subscribe to the latter from the UELAC website.

The bicentennial of the province of Ontario in 1983 and the associated arrival of the Loyalists sparked a flurry of new publications, so there is a good range of available literature. Several UELAC branches have produced memorable histories or genealogies for their areas. One to mention is Toronto Branch's *Loyalist Lineages of Canada, 1783-1983* in two volumes (volume 2 is divided into two books). They contain summaries of the pedigrees submitted by the membership between 1970 and 1983, arranged alphabetically by the surname of the Loyalist ancestor. The families are not only for Ontario, but for all Loyalist areas and branches.

Another special item of note is the Loyalist Cultural Centre (see Appendix III), a museum and genealogy library, operated by the Quinte branch. The Centre is located in Heritage Park in some of the original Loyalist country, where an annual re-enactment of the Loyalists' Landing takes place.

Reading and Reference

Allen, Robert S. *A History of the British Indian Department in North America, 1755-1830.* Ottawa, ON: National Historic Sites Service, Department of Indian Affairs and Northern Development, 1971.

_____. *His Majesty's Indian Allies: British Indian Policy in the Defence of Canada.* Toronto, ON: Dundurn Press, 1992.

Antliff, W. Bruce. *Loyalist Settlements 1783-1789: New Evidence of Canadian Claims.* Toronto, ON: Ministry of Citizenship and Culture, 1985.

Brown, Wallace. *The King's Friends: The Composition and Motives of the American Loyalist Claimants.* Providence, RI: Brown University Press, 1965.

Butler, J.P. *Index to Papers of the Continental Congress, 1774-1789.* 5 volumes. Washington, DC: National Archives and Records Administration, 1978.

The Centennial of the Settlement of Upper Canada by the United Empire Loyalists, 1784-1884. Toronto, ON: Rose Publishing, 1885 (reprints from Genealogical Publishing Company).

Clark, Murtie Jean. *Loyalists in the Southern Campaign of the Revolutionary War.* 3 volumes. 1981. Reprint. Baltimore, MD: Genealogical Publishing Company, vol. 1: 2003, vol. 2: 1999, vol. 3: 1999.

Coldham, Peter Wilson. *American Migrations 1765-1799: The Lives, Times and Families of Colonial Americans Who Remained Loyal to the British Crown Before, During and After the Revolutionary War, as Related in Their Own Words and Through Their Correspondence.* Baltimore, MD: Genealogical Publishing Company, 2000.

Crowder, Norman K. *Early Ontario Settlers: A Source Book.* Baltimore, MD: Genealogical Publishing Company, 1993.

Cruikshank, Ernest A. and Gavin K. Watt. *The History and Master Roll of the King's Royal Regiment of New York.* Revised edition. Campbellville, ON: Global Heritage Press, 2006.

Fitzgerald, E. Keith. *Ontario People, 1796-1803.* Baltimore, MD: Genealogical Publishing Company, 1993.

_____. *Loyalist Lists: Over 2000 Loyalist Names and Families from the Haldimand Papers.* Toronto, ON: Ontario Genealogical Society, 2000.

Fryer, Mary Beacock. *King's Men, the Soldier Founders of Ontario.* Toronto, ON: Dundurn Press, 1980.

_____ and William A. Smy, compilers. *Rolls of the Provincial (Loyalist) Corps, Canadian Command, American Revolutionary Period.* Toronto, ON: Dundurn Press, 1981.

Herrington, W.S. *Pioneer Life Among the Loyalists in Upper Canada.* Toronto, ON: Macmillan Co. of Canada, 1915.

Loyalist Families of the Grand River Branch, United Empire Loyalist Association. Toronto, ON: Grand River Branch UELAC/Pro Familia Publishing, 1991.

Merriman, Brenda Dougall. *United Empire Loyalists: A Guide to Tracing Loyalist Ancestors in Upper Canada.* Campbellville, ON: Global Heritage Press, 2006.

Penrose, Maryly B. *Indian Affairs Papers, American Revolution.* Franklin Park, NJ: Liberty Bell Associates, 1981.

_____. *Mohawk Valley in the Revolution: Committee of Safety Papers and Genealogical Compendium*. Franklin Park, NJ: Liberty Bell Associates, 1978.

Potter-McKinnon, Janice. *While the Women Only Wept: Loyalist Refugee Women in Eastern Ontario*. Montreal QC/Kingston ON: McGill-Queen's University Press, 1993.

Reaman, G. Elmore. *The Trail of the Iroquois Indians: How the Iroquois Nation Saved Canada for the British Empire*. Toronto, ON: Peter Martin Associates, 1967.

Reid, William D. *The Loyalists in Ontario, Sons and Daughters of the American Loyalists of Upper Canada*. Lambertville, NJ: Hunterdon House, 1973 (reprints from Genealogical Publishing Company).

Russell, Bill. *Records of the Department of Indian Affairs at Library and Archives Canada: A Source for Genealogical Research*. Second edition. Toronto, ON: Ontario Genealogical Society, 2004.

Smy, William A., compiler. *An Annotated Roll of Butler's Rangers, 1777-1784*. St. Catharines, ON: Friends of the Loyalist Collection at Brock University, 2004.

Stuart, Donna Valley. *The Genealogy of the French Families of the Detroit River Region, 1701-1936*. Revised edition. Detroit, MI: Detroit Society for Genealogical Research, 1976.

Wallace, W. Stewart. *The United Empire Loyalists: A Chronicle of the Great Migration*. Toronto: Glasgow, Brook, 1920. See also the complete book at www.fullbooks.com/The-United-Empire-Loyalists.html.

Watt, Gavin K. and Jim Morrison. *The British Campaign of 1777, Volume 1, The St. Leger Expedition: The Forces of the Crown and Congress*. King City, ON: Gavin K.Watt, 2001.

_____. *The Burning of the Valleys: Daring Raids from Canada Against the New York Frontier in the Fall of 1780*. Toronto, ON: Dundurn Press, 1997.

Brock University Library. "Friends of the Loyalist Collection at Brock University." www.brockloyalisthistorycollection.ca

Paul Bunnell. *Loyalist Quarterly*. www.bunnellgenealogybooks.citymaker.com

Nan Cole and Todd Braisted. The Online Institute for Advanced Loyalist Studies. www.royalprovincial.com

Loyalist Cultural Centre & Heritage Park. www.uel.ca

The National Archives (England). www.nationalarchives.gov.uk/default.htm.

Marlene Simmons. Quebec and Eastern Townships Genealogy Page. simmons.b2b2c.ca

Quebec Family History Society. www.qfhs.ca

United Empire Loyalists' Association of Canada. www.uelac.org.

Appendix I

The Ontario Genealogical Society

The Ontario Genealogical Society (OGS) was formed in 1961 to serve the interests of genealogy in this province. The mission statement is "to encourage, bring together, and assist all those interested in the pursuit of family history." The attraction of this province as a destination for immigrants, starting with Loyalist times, is no doubt responsible for OGS being among the largest heritage organizations in Canada. The 25th Anniversary celebrations in 1986 included the granting of a coat of arms to the society by the Lord Lyon of Scotland. The accompanying motto *Multi Priores Multae Patriae* translates as Many Ancestors, Many Homelands, reflecting the diverse cultural background of our province over two centuries. OGS is a non-profit corporation that receives financial support from the provincial Ministry of Culture.

> Ontario Genealogical Society
> Suite 102, 40 Orchard View Boulevard
> Toronto, ON M4R 1B9
> Telephone 416-489-0734 Fax 416-489-9803
> Email provoffice@ogs.on.ca
> Website www.ogs.on.ca

OGS is governed by a board of directors and its executive officers. The major divisions are administration, finance, library, member services, publications, and special projects. OGS also has liaison with various federations and other heritage groups, as well as advocacy to represent our interests regarding government policy and legislation. At the head office in Toronto the executive and the board of directors meet regularly. All administration is coordinated here under an executive director, and committees meet to work on special projects. Publications and other OGS products can be purchased during routine business hours.

Membership

Membership is aligned with the calendar year. After 31 October, dues will apply to the following calendar year. New members receive useful information about OGS in a Members Handbook and of course are entitled to vote at the annual meeting. Benefits include the quarterly journal *Families,* the quarterly newsletter *Newsleaf,* and advance news of conferences and workshops. A members-only section is under development on the website. Branch publications lists are often inserted in *Newsleaf.* All members can submit two free research queries per year to The Name Game in *Families.* Group rates for home, automobile and medical insurance are available to members. Networking opportunities exist at several levels from meetings to volunteering. OGS members in Canada receive a tax receipt for the amount of their dues. Like many other societies, OGS is moving to provide even more electronic resources.

Research and Queries

While OGS has always encouraged the "do-it-yourself" approach, the society does provide some assistance for members or for enquirers. Advice on how to research your family history and an introduction to Ontario sources are available on the website. Please consult the site before sending general enquiries. For an hourly fee, a research services committee will undertake searches in a limited number of sources. For complex or extended research projects, OGS recommends approaching members of the Ontario Chapter of the Association of Professional Genealogists. The OGS website also has many links to resources and other societies.

Library

The society's library is in the Canadiana collection of the North York Central Library, located in the North York Centre at 5120 Yonge Street. For out of town visitors, North York is part of Metropolitan Toronto, and the name of the subway stop on the Yonge Street line is North York Centre. You are advised to call in advance to confirm their open hours. The OGS library is a large collection, basically for reference only. That means little material circulates through interlibrary loan. Planning a whole day for a preliminary visit is not unreasonable.

OGS Library
Gladys Allison Canadiana Room
North York Central Library
5120 Yonge Street
North York, ON M2B 5N9
Telephone 416-395-5623
www.torontopubliclibrary.ca/uni_can_index.jsp

The OGS library includes its own publications, branch publications, indexes, transcriptions, compilations, newsletter subscriptions from many other societies, and other genealogically related subjects. At the OGS website, you can search the catalogue online by author, title, or subject key words. A special goal of the OGS library is to encourage and collect family histories for people who lived in Ontario. Over 3,000 family histories are available and more donations are always welcome. OGS library complements North York's excellent Canadiana collection of books, microfilm and finding aids. The entire Canadiana collection is additionally enhanced by the libraries of the Société franco-ontarienne d'histoire et de généalogie, the Jewish Genealogical Society of Canada (Toronto division), and the Canadian Society of Mayflower Descendants.

Conference

The highlight of the year is the annual conference in May or June, with several days of lectures, workshops, meetings, and socializing. The annual meeting is also held at that time. A different site is chosen each year, usually organized by one or more of the branches. While a certain focus devolves on the host area and its genealogical resources, there is a range of topics to appeal to all registrants. Conference weekend is an unparalleled opportunity for personal contact with fellow members, expert speakers, and dozens of exhibitors. A syllabus of proceedings is part of the registration package, with synopses of the presentations. Following the conference, a number of the lecture manuscripts may be published in *Families*.

Publications

Families is the Society's quarterly journal of feature articles, book reviews, and queries. Contributors write about research trips, descriptions of sources, solving ancestral problems, and many genealogy-related subjects. Back issues are available through the OGS head office. *Families* has been indexed from its inception for names, subjects, and authors in two separate volumes. *Newsleaf* is the quarterly newsletter. The list of all publications for sale can be viewed on the website, with branch publications appearing on their individual pages. Past issues of *Families* are being added to the members-only section of the OGS website. This will facilitate finding articles cited in the text of this book.

Projects

OGS projects are powered by volunteers. New volunteers are always appreciated; even distant members can contribute by typing or indexing. A variety of skills are always being sought to fill volunteer positions in the head office or on committees. See the OGS website or notices in *Newsleaf* for updated information about projects and positions wanted. Helping can be a social as well as a learning experience with like-minded members. A few of the significant projects OGS has undertaken or continues to work on:

- *Index to the 1871 census of Ontario*
The Index to heads of household and strays for 1871 was completed in 30 print volumes, with each volume containing one or more counties and districts. It was the first electronic database created in partnership with Library and Archives Canada and is searchable on the Canadian Genealogy Centre website.

- *Index to the Upper Canada Land Books*
This undertaking was completed in 2005. More than 84,000 names with accompanying information have been extracted from an early series of land records. Published in nine print volumes, the entire series 1787-1841 is available on a searchable CD-ROM.

- *Ontario Cemeteries*
OGS is the acknowledged leader in the province in identifying cemetery locations and advocacy for the preservation of burial grounds. A long-range project involving every branch of the society is the transcription and indexing of over 6,000 cemeteries and burial grounds in Ontario. Many branches have completed all cemeteries within their areas. A few locations, especially big city cemeteries, still need volunteers to organize and assist. Copies of the transcriptions are deposited at the OGS Library, the Archives of Ontario, and Library and Archives Canada. More importantly, each transcription can be purchased for a nominal sum to support the branch which produced it. AO has microfilmed the OGS transcriptions and some made by other groups on 147 reels, current with material received by the end of

2001. The microfilms can be borrowed on interlibrary loan from AO.

In addition, OGS is providing two research aids on the website. Ontario Cemetery Ancestor Search is based on names being extracted from the branch transcriptions. It enables finding the relevant branch and the cemetery with the full gravestone inscriptions. Ontario Cemetery Locator is a searchable directory for a cemetery name, township or municipality, with drop down menus showing the choices.

- *Ontario Genealogical Society Provincial Index*

This ambitious and massive ongoing OGSPI project seeks to document information about ancestral families from a multitude of sources—census, vital records, newspaper notices, local histories, queries published in *Families*, an assortment of military sources, and more. It is also self-described as a hypertext library. Many of the submissions come from branch projects and participation. The main page has an alphabetical surname search menu and each entry gives the source of the information for follow up.

- *Places of Worship Inventory*

The mandate of this project is to catalogue all churches and places of worship in the province up to the early twentieth century. Each branch works in its own area for this project so some are more advanced than others. The Inventory is intended to show names and places of the congregations and the present locations of their existing vital records.

- *Independent Order of Oddfellows.*

The IOOF had an insurance program for its members with the former Empire Insurance Company. OGS is indexing the relief association record books 1875-1929 to create a database of information about approximately 59,000 names.

Retrospects of the society have appeared in *Families* to mark anniversary occasions, for instance, "The Ontario Genealogical Society: Twentieth Anniversary" by Kathleen M. Richards in Vol. 20, No. 4 (1981) and "Landmarks in Ontario Genealogy: A Twenty-five Year Retrospective" by Bruce Elliott in Vol. 26, No. 4 (1987). A brief historical summary can be seen on the website.

The OGS Endowment Fund is a special and important objective of the society to *preserve the past for families of the future* by creating a permanent source of revenue. Donations to the Endowment Fund can be made to the provincial office.

Branches

The 30 OGS branches represent nearly every area of Ontario, with their own newsletters, publications, meetings and projects. Branch membership entails an additional fee as outlined on the OGS membership form. Most branches have a library or resource collection, which may be housed within a nearby public library or other institution. Some have published guides to genealogical sources for their particular areas, among the numerous other work they initiate. Several branches form an OGS region for operational purposes. Day-long regional meetings or workshops are held at least once per year.

BrantCounty
114 Powerline Road
Brantford, ON N3T 5L8

Bruce & Grey
Box 66
Owen Sound, ON N0H 2C0

Durham (formerly Whitby-Oshawa)
Box 174
Whitby, ON L1N 5S1

Elgin County
Box 20060
St Thomas, ON N5P 4H4

Essex County
Box 2
Station A, Windsor, ON N9A 6J5

Haldimand County
Box 38
Cayuga, ON N0A 1E0

Halton-Peel
2441 Lakeshore Road W, Box 70030
Oakville, ON L6L 6M9

Hamilton
Box 904
Hamilton, ON L8N 3P6

Huron County
Box 469
Goderich, ON N7A 4C7

Kawartha
Box 162
Peterborough, ON K9J 6Y8

Kent County
Box 964
Chatham, ON N7M 5L3

Kingston
Box 1394
Kingston, ON K7L 5C6

Lambton County
Box 2587
Sarnia, ON N7T 7W1

Leeds & Grenville
Box 536
Brockville, ON K6V 5V7

London-Middlesex
1017 Western Road
London, ON N6G 1G5

Niagara Peninsula
Box 2224, Station B
St Catharines, ON L2M 6P6

Nipissing & District
Box 93
North Bay, ON P1B 8G8

Norfolk County
Box 145
Delhi, ON N4B 2W9

Ottawa
Box 8346
Ottawa, ON K1G 3H8

Oxford County
Box 1092
Woodstock, ON N4S 8A5

Perth County
Box 9
Stratford, ON N5A 6S8

Quinte
Box 153
Ameliasburg, ON K0K 1A0

Sault Ste. Marie & District
Box 1203
Sault Ste. Marie, ON P6A 6N1

Simcoe County
Box 892
Barrie, ON L4M 4Y6

Sudbury District
c/o Sudbury Public Library
Bag 5000, Station A
Sudbury, ON P3A 5P3

Thunder Bay District
Box 373
Station F, Thunder Bay, ON P7C 4V9

Toronto
Box 518
Station K, Toronto, ON M4P 2G9

Waterloo Region
Eastwood Square, Box 40030
Kitchener, ON N2H 6S9

Wellington County
Box 1211
Guelph, ON N1H 6N6

York Region
Box 32215, Harding Post Office,
Richmond Hill, ON L4C 9S3

OGS Coat of Arms granted 21 September 1985

Appendix II

Government Repositories and Resource Centres

Federal

Library and Archives Canada
395 Wellington Street
Ottawa, ON K1A 0N4
(613) 992-3884 or toll-free 1-866-578-7777
www.collectionscanada.ca/

Canadian Genealogy Centre
see Library and Archives Canada, above

Senate of Canada, Office of the Law Clerk
40 Elgin Street, Room 1310
Ottawa, ON K1A 0A4
(613) 992-2416

Head, Records Control
Citizenship Registration Branch
Box 7000
Sydney, NS B1P 6G5
[mail inquiries only]

Citizenship and Immigration Canada
Public Rights Administration
360 Laurier Avenue West, 10th Floor
Ottawa, ON K1A 1L1
[mail inquiries only]

Directorate of History and Heritage
National Defence Headquarters
101 Colonel By Drive
Ottawa, ON K1A 0K2
www.forces.gc.ca/dhh/
[mail or fax inquiries only; fax (613) 990-8579]

Veterans Affairs Canada
66 Slater Street
Ottawa, ON K1A 0P4
(1-877) 604-8489
www.vac-acc.gc.ca/remembers

Census Pension Searches Unit
Census Operations Division
Statistics Canada
B1E-34 Jean Talon Building
Tunney's Pasture
Ottawa, ON K1A 0T6
(613) 951-9483
www.statcan.org/ (Search term "1940" on website)

Pier 21 National Historic Site
1055 Marginal Road
Halifax, NS B3H 4P5
(902) 425-7770
www.pier21.ns.ca

Chief Herald of Canada
Canadian Heraldic Authority
Rideau Hall, 1 Sussex Drive, Ottawa, ON K1A 0A1
1-(800) 465-6890
www.gg.ca/heraldry/hldcan_e.asp

Provincial

Archives of Ontario
77 Grenville Street
Toronto, ON M5S 1B3
(416) 327-1582 and (416) 327-1600
Ontario residents: (1-800) 668-9933
www.archives.gov.on.ca

Office of the Registrar General
Box 4600, 189 Red River Road
Thunder Bay, ON P7B 6L8
Ontario residents: (1-800) 461-2156
Non-Ontario residents: (1-807) 343-7459
www.cbs.gov.on.ca/mcbs/english/forms.htm
(Service Ontario) www.gov.on.ca/GOPSP/en/graphics/About-English.html

Adoption Disclosure Register
Ministry of Community, Family and Children's Services
2 Bloor Street West, 24th Floor, Toronto, ON M7A 1E9
(416) 327-4730
mcss/gov.on.ca/mcss/english/pillars/community

Ministry of Natural Resources
Crown Land Registry
300 Water Street, Box 7000
Peterborough, ON K9J 8M5
(705) 755-2106
www.mnr.gov.on.ca/MNR

Ontario Court General Division – Estates
393 University Avenue, 10th Floor
Toronto, ON M5G 1E6
(416) 326-2940

Ontario Superior Court of Justice
Individual county and district courthouses
www.archives.gov.on.ca/english/interloan/c-courts.htm

Appendix III

Religious, Professional and Other Repositories

Religious Archives

The Anglican Church of Canada
www.anglican.ca/index.htm

Anglican Diocese of Algoma
619 Wellington Street East
P.O. Box 1168
Sault Ste. Marie, ON P6A5N7
(705) 256-5061
www.dioceseofalgoma.com/

Anglican Diocese of Huron
Verschoyle Philip Memorial Archives
Huron College, University of Western Ontario
1349 Western Road
London, ON N6G 1H3
(519) 645-7956
www.diohuron.org/

Anglican Diocese of Keewatin Archives
915 Ottawa Street
Box 567
Keewatin, ON P0X 1C0
(807) 547-03353
www.dioceseofkeewatin.ca/

Anglican Diocese of Moosonee
Box 841
Schumacher, ON P0N 1G0
(705) 360-1129
moosenee.anglican.org/

Anglican Diocese of Niagara Archives
William Ready Division of Archives & Research Collections
McMaster University
1280 Main Street West
Hamilton, ON L8S 4L6
(905) 525-9140 x22079
www.library.mcmaster.ca/archives/anglican/

Anglican Diocese of Ontario Archives
90 Johnson Street
Kingston, ON K7L 1X7
(613) 544-4774 x 28
www.ontarro.anglican.ca/archives/

Anglican Diocese of Ottawa Synod Archives
420 Sparks Street
Ottawa, ON K1R 6G6
(613) 232-7124 x 234
www.ottawa.anglican.ca/archives.shtml

Anglican Diocese of Toronto Archives
135 Adelaide Street East
Toronto, ON M5C 1L8
(416) 363-6021
www.toronto.anglican.ca/

Canadian Baptist Archives
McMaster Divinity College, McMaster University
1280 Main Street West
Hamilton, ON L8S 4K1
(905) 525-9140 x 23511
www.macdiv.ca/students/baptistarchives.php

Evangelical Lutheran Church in Canada, Eastern Synod Archives
Wilfrid Laurier University
75 University Avenue West
Waterloo, ON N2J 3C5
(519) 884-1970 x3414
library.wlu.ca/archives/

Mennonite Archives of Ontario
Conrad Grebel University College
200 Westmount Road North
Waterloo, ON N2L 3G6
(519) 885-0220 x238
grebel.uwaterloo.ca/mao/

Moravian Church Archives
41 W. Locust Street
Bethlehem, PA, USA 18018
(610) 866-3255
www.moravianchurcharchives.org/

Ontario Jewish Archives
4600 Bathurst Street
Toronto, ON M2R 3V2
(416) 635-2883 x170
www.jewishtoronto.org/

Presbyterian Church in Canada Archives
50 Wynford Drive
Toronto, ON M3C 1J7
(416) 441-1111
www.presbyterian.ca/archives/

Quaker Archives and Library of Canada
Dorland Friends Historical Collection, Pickering College
16945 Bayview Avenue
Newmarket, ON L3Y 4X2
(905) 895-1700 x 247
www.archives-library.quaker.ca/en/introduction.html

Canadian Conference of Catholic Bishops
www.cccb.ca/
(not all dioceses have archival facilities)

Roman Catholic Diocese of Alexandria-Cornwall
Box 1388, 220 Chemin Montréal
Cornwall, ON K6H 5V4
(613) 933-1138
www.alexandria-cornwall.ca

Roman Catholic Diocese of Hamilton
700 King Street West
Hamilton, ON L8P 1C7
(905) 528-7988
www.hamiltondiocese.com

Roman Catholic Diocese of Hearst
P.O. Box 1330, 76 rue 7e
Hearst, ON P0L 1N0
(705) 362-4903
www.hearstdiocese.com

Roman Catholic Archdiocese of Kingston
390 Palace Road
Kingston, ON K7L 4T3
(613) 548-4461
www.romancatholic.kingston.ca

Roman Catholic Diocese of London
1070 Waterloo Street North
London, ON N6A 3Y2
(519) 433-0658
www.rcec.london.on.ca

Roman Catholic Diocese of Moosonee
Box 40
Moosonee ON P0L 1Y0
(705) 336-2908

Roman Catholic Archdiocese of Ottawa
1247 Kilborn Place
Ottawa, ON K1H 6K9
(613) 738-5025 x 246
www.ecclesia-ottawa.org/

Roman Catholic Diocese of Pembroke
Box 7, 188 Renfrew Street
Pembroke, ON K8A 6X1
(613) 732-7933
wwwdiocesepembroke.ca/

Roman Catholic Diocese of Peterborough Archives
Trent Valley Archives, Fairview Heritage Centre
567 Carnegie Avenue
Peterborough, ON K9L 1N1
(705) 745-4404
www.trentvalleyarchives.com/diocese.htm

Roman Catholic Diocese of St Catharines Archives
Box 875, 3400 Merrittville Highway
Thorold, ON L2R 6Z4
St Catharines, ON
(905) 684-0154
www.romancatholic.niagara.on.ca

Roman Catholic Diocese of Sault Ste Marie
30 Ste. Anne Road
Sudbury, ON P3C 5E1
(705) 674-2727 x 237
www.diocesessm.org/en

Roman Catholic Diocese of Thunder Bay
Catholic Pastoral Centre
Box 10400, 1222 Reaume Street
Thunder Bay, ON P7B 6T8
(807) 343-9313
www.dotb.ca

Roman Catholic Diocese of Timmins
Catholic Information Centre
65 Jubilee Avenue East
Timmins, ON P4N 5W4
(705) 267-6224
www.nt.net/dioctims/

Roman Catholic Archdiocese of Toronto Archives
Catholic Pastoral Centre
1155 Yonge Street, Suite 505
Toronto, ON M4T 1W2
(416) 934-3400 x 501
www.archtoronto.org

United Church of Canada Archives
3250 Bloor Street West, Ste. 300
Toronto, ON M8X 2Y4
(416) 416-231-7680 x 3123   1-800-268-3781 x 3123
Fax 416-231-3103
www.unitedchurcharchives.ca

United Church of Canada
Montreal/Ottawa Conference Archives
Ottawa and Seaway Valley Presbyteries
c/o City of Ottawa Archives
110 Laurier Avenue West, Mail Code 19-49
Ottawa, ON K1P 1J1
(613) 580-2424 x 13333
www.united-church.ca/local/archives/mo/ottawa

United Church of Canada
Manitoba/Northwestern Ontario Conference Archives
University of Winnipeg Library
515 Portage Avenue, Winnipeg, MB R3B 2E9
(204) 783-0708
www.united-church.ca/local/archives/mno

Professional/Educational Resources

Ministry of Education
Ministry of Training, Colleges and Universities
Mowat Block, 14th floor
900 Bay Street
Toronto, ON M7A 1L2
(416) 325-2929
www.edu.gov.on.ca

Ontario Federation of Independent Schools
2199 Regency Terrace
Ottawa, ON K2C 1H2
(613) 596-4013
www.ofis.ca

Ontario Public School Boards Association
439 University Avenue, Suite 1850
Toronto, ON M5G 1Y8
(416) 340-2540
www.opsba.org

Ontario Catholic School Trustees Association
20 Eglinton Avenue West, Suite 1804
Toronto, ON M4R 1K8
(416) 932-9460
www.ocsta.on.ca

Law Society of Upper Canada Archives
Library Services, 130 Queen Street West
Toronto, ON M5H 2N6
(416) 947-3315 or 1-800-668-7380 x 3315
www.lsuc.on.ca/

College of Nurses of Ontario
101 Davenport Road
Toronto, ON M5R 3P1
(416) 928-0900
www.cno.org

Ontario Medical Association
525 University Avenue, Suite 200
Toronto, ON M5G 2K7
(416) 340-2914 x 2914
www.oma.org

Osler Library of the History of Medicine
McIntyre Medical Sciences Building
McGill University
3655 Promenade Sir-William-Osler
Montreal, QC H3G 1Y6
(514) 398-4475 x 09873
www.mcgill.ca/osler-library/

College of Physicians and Surgeons of Ontario
80 College Street, Toronto, ON M5G 2E2
(416) 967-2600 x363 fax: (416) 961-3330
www.cpso.on.ca

Canadian Institute for Health Information
495 Richmond Road, Suite 600
Ottawa, ON K2A 4H6
(613) 241-7860
secure.cihi.ca/cihiweb/splash.html

Brock University Library, Special Collections & Archives
500 Glendridge Avenue
St. Catharines, ON L2S 3A1
(905) 688-5550 x3264
www.brocku.ca/library/

Queen's University, W.D. Jordan Library Collection
Douglas Library
Union Street & University Avenue
Kingston, ON K7L 5C4
(613) 533-2839
library.queensu.ca/webmus/sc/

Trent University Archives, Bata Library
1600 West Bank Drive
Peterborough, ON K9J 7B8
(705) 748-1011 x 7413
www.trentu.ca/admin/library/archives

University of Toronto, Robarts Research Library
130 St. George Street
Toronto, ON M5S 1A5
(416) 978-8450
www.library.utoronto.ca/robarts/

J. J. Talman Regional Collection
D.B. Weldon Library
University of Western Ontario
London, ON N6A 3K7
(519) 679-2111 x 84821
www.lib.uwo.ca/weldon/

Other Repositories & Libraries

Allen County Public Library
900 Library Plaza
Fort Wayne, IN 46802
(260) 421-1200
www.acpl.lib.in.us/

Barnardo's After Care Section
Tanners Lane
Barkingside
Ilford, Essex IG6 1QG England

Dufferin County Museum & Archives
Genealogical Reference
Box 120
Rosemount, ON L0N 1R0
(705) 435-1881 fax: (705) 435-9876

Family History Library
35 North West Temple Street
Salt Lake City, UT 84150-3440
(801) 240-2584
www.familysearch.org/

Hudson's Bay Company Archives
Provincial Archives of Manitoba
200 Vaughan Street
Winnipeg, MB R3C 1T5
(204) 945-4949
www.gov.mb.ca/chc/archives/hbca

Knights of Columbus, Ontario State Council
393 Rymal Road West
Hamilton, ON L9B 1V2
(905) 388-2731 or 1-800-759-0959
www.osc-koc.com/

Loyalist Cultural Centre & Heritage Park
54 Park Road
Box 112, R.R. #1
Bath, ON K0H 1G0
(613) 373-2196
www.uel.ca/

Marine Museum of the Great Lakes
55 Ontario Street
Kingston, ON K7L 2Y2
(613) 542-2261
www. marmuseum.ca

Metropolitan Toronto Police, Force Historian
40 College Street
Toronto, ON M5G 2J3
(416) 808-7020
www.torontopolice.on.ca/museum/

Montgomery County Department of History and Archives
Old Courthouse
P.O. Box 1500
Fonda, NY 12068-1500
(518) 853-8186
www.amsterdam-ny.com/mcha/

Norfolk Heritage Centre
Eva Brook Donly Museum
109 Norfolk Street South
Simcoe, ON N3Y 2W3
(519) 426-1583
www.norfolklore.com/

North American Black Historical Museum & Cultural Centre
Box 12, 277 King Street
Amherstburg, ON N9V 2C7
(519) 736-5433
www.blackhistoricalmuseum.com

Ontario Association of Cemetery and Funeral Professionals
270 The Kingsway, Box 74568
Etobicoke, ON M9A 2T0
(416) 231-0855 toll-free (1-888) 558-3335
www.oacfp.com

Ontario Association of Children's Aid Societies
75 Front Street East
Toronto, Ontario M5E 1V9
(416) 366-8115
www.oacas.org/

Ontario Heritage Trust
10 Adelaide Street East
Toronto, Ontario M5C 1J3
416-325-5000
www.heritagefdn.on.ca/

Ontario Museums Association
50 Baldwin Street
Toronto, ON M5T 1L4
(416) 348-8672 or 1-866-OMA-8672
www.museumsontario.com/

Grand Orange Lodge of Canada
94 Sheppard Avenue West
Toronto, ON M2N 1M5
(416) 223-1690 or 1-800-565-6248
www.grandorangelodge.ca/

Penetanguishene Centennial Museum & Archives
13 Burke Street
Penetanguishene, ON L9M 1C1
(705) 549-2150
www.pencenmuseum.com/

Royal Canadian Military Institute
426 University Avenue
Toronto, ON M5G 1S9
(416) 597-0286
www.rcmi.org

Toronto Reference Library, Special Collections
789 Yonge Street
Toronto, ON M4W 2G8
(416) 393-7131
www.tpl.toronto.on.ca

Walpole Island Heritage Centre
Walpole Island First Nation
R.R. #3
Wallaceburg, ON N8A 4K9
(519) 627-1475
www.bkejwanong.com

Woodland Cultural Centre
P.O. Box 1506
184 Mohawk Street
Brantford, ON N3T 5V6
(519) 759-2650
www.woodland-centre.on.ca/index.php

Appendix IV

Other Genealogical and Historical Societies

Genealogical Societies

Bruce County Genealogical Society
Box 1083
Port Elgin, ON N0H 2C0
www.rootsweb.com/~onbcgs/

Detroit Society for Genealogical Research
c/o Burton Historical Collection
5201 Woodward Avenue
Detroit, MI 48202-4093
www.dsgr.org/

Dryden Family History Group
www.drytel.net/wvermeer/dfhg.html

Haliburton Highlands Genealogy Group
Box 834, 174 Bobcaygeon Road
Minden, ON K0M 2K0
www.rootsweb.com/~onhhgg

Jewish Genealogical Society of Canada (Toronto)
Box 91006, 2901 Bayview Avenue
Toronto, ON M2K 2Y6
www.jgstoronto.ca

Jewish Genealogical Society of Ottawa
www.jgso.org

Jewish Genealogical Society of Hamilton & Area
www.jgsh.org

Lakeshore Genealogical Society
Box 1222
Cobourg, ON K9A 5A4

Lanark County Genealogical Society
Box 512
Perth, ON K7H 3K4
www.globalgenealogy.com/LCGS

Manitoulin Genealogical Club
c/o Box 355
Little Current, ON P0P 1K0
www.rootsweb.com/~onmanito/club.htm

Muskoka Parry Sound Genealogy Group
www.mpsgg.com/

North Hastings Genealogy Club
members.shaw.ca/nhlist/home.htm

Sioux Lookout Genealogy Group
Box 1592
Sioux Lookout, ON P8T 1C3
www.rootsweb.com/~onslgc

Société franco-ontarienne d'histoire et de généalogie
Provincial Secretariat
2445, boulevard Saint-Laurent, B151
Ottawa, ON K1G 6C3
(613) 729-5769 or 1-866-307-9995
www.sfohg.com/en/
(13 regional centres)

Stormont, Dundas & Glengarry Genealogical Society
Box 1522
Cornwall, ON K6H 5V5
See www.rootsweb.com/~onglenga/

Temiskaming Genealogical Group
Box 1051
New Liskeard, ON P0J 1P0
www.nt.net/~timetrav/

Upper Ottawa Valley Genealogical Group
Box 972
Pembroke, ON K8A 7M5
www.uovgg.ca

Historical Societies

Chatham-Kent Black Historical Society
177 King Street East
Chatham, ON N7M 3N1
(519) 352-3565
www.ckblackhistoricalsociety.org/

Clans & Scottish Societies of Canada (CASSOC)
78-24 Fundy Bay Boulevard
Toronto, ON M1W 3A4
www.cassoc.ca

Great Lakes Historical Society
Box 435, 480 Main Street
Vermilion, OH 44089-0435
(440) 967-3467 or 1-800 893-1485
www.inlandseas.org

Historical Society of Mecklenburg Upper Canada
Box 1251, Station K
Toronto, ON M4P 3E5
www.german-canadian.ca/mecklenburg/historic.htm

The Markham Berczy Settlers Association
10292 McCowan Road
Markham, ON L3P 3J3
(905) 640-3906
markhamberczysettlers.ca

Multicultural History Society of Ontario
487 Spadina Avenue (temporary for how long??)
43 Queen's Park Crescent
Toronto, ON M5S 2C3
(416) 979-2973
www.mhso.ca/

Ontario Black History Society
10 Adelaide Street East, Suite 202
Toronto, ON M5C 1J3
(416) 867-9420
www.blackhistorysociety.ca

Ontario Historical Society
34 Parkview Avenue
North York, ON M2N 3Y2
(416) 226-9011
www.ontariohistoricalsociety.ca

Pennsylvania German Folklore Society of Ontario
c/o 10292 McCowan Road
Markham, ON L3P 3J3
www.pennsylvania-german-foloklore-society.com
(3 chapters)

Quebec Family History Society
Box 1026, 173 Cartier Avenue
Point Claire, QC H9S 4H9
(514) 695-1502
www.qfhs.ca/

Wisconsin Historical Society
816 State Street
Madison, WI 53706
www.wisconsinhistory.org/

Lineage Societies

Canadian Society of Mayflower Descendants
c/o Susan E. Roser, Society Historian
4137 Tremaine Road, R.R. 6
Milton, ON L9T 2Y1
www.rootsweb.com/~canms/canada.html

Royal Heraldry Society of Canada
Box 8128, Terminal T
Ottawa, ON K1G 3H9
www.heraldry.ca/
(7 branches)

United Empire Loyalists' Association of Canada
Dominion Headquarters
50 Baldwin Street, Suite 202
Toronto, ON M5T 1L4
(416) 591-1783
www.uelac.org/
(13 branches in Ontario)

Appendix V

Genealogical Publishers and Suppliers

Ancestry, Inc.
360 West 4800 North,
Provo, UT USA 84604
(801) 705-7000 or 1-800-262-3787
www.ancestry.com

Archives Association of Ontario
Box 46009, College Park P.O.
444 Yonge Street, Toronto, ON M5B 2L8
www.aao.fis.utoronto.ca

The Champlain Society
Box 507, Stn. Q,
Toronto, ON M4T 2M5
(416) 482-9635
www.champlainsociety.ca

Linda Corupe, UE
210 Allan Drive,
Bolton, ON L7E 1Y7
(905) 857-1759
www.lindacorupe.com

Dundurn Press
3 Church Street, Suite 500
Toronto, ON M5E 1M2
(416) 214-5544
www.dundurn.com/

Federal Publications, Inc.
165 University Avenue, Suite 102
Toronto, ON M5H 3B8
(416) 860-1611
www.fedpubs.com

Genealogical Publishing Company, Inc.
1001 North Calvert Street
Baltimore, MD USA 21202-3897
(410) 837-8271 or 1-800-296-6687
www. genealogical.com

Global Genealogy/Global Heritage Press
43 Main Street South, P.O. Box 569
Campbellville, ON
(905) 854-2176 or 1-800-361-5168
globalgenealogy.com

Heritage Productions
416-861-0165 or 1-800-580-0165
www.genealogystore.com

Hunterdon House: This company no longer exists. See Global Heritage Press and Genealogical Publishing Company.

Interlink Bookshop and Genealogical Services
4687 Falaise Drive
Victoria, BC V8Y 1B4
1-800-747-4877
www.interlinkbookshop.com/

Iroqrafts
1880 Tuscarora Road, R.R. #2
Ohsweken, ON N0A 1M0
(519) 445-0414
www.iroqrafts.com/

Log Cabin Publishing, Robert Mutrie
9 Sauer Avenue
Welland, ON L3B 5G8
www.nornet.on.ca/~jcardiff/lps/

The MacDonald Research Centre: See Global Heritage Press.

McGill-Queen's University Press
3430 McTavish Street
Montreal, QC H3A 1X9
(514) 398-3750
mqup.mcgill.ca/index.php

Natural Heritage Books: This company has merged with the Dundurn Group.
www.naturalheritagebooks.com/

Ontario Government Publications (ServiceOntario Centres)
777 Bay Street, Market Level
Toronto, ON M5G 2C8
Ottawa City Hall
110 Laurier Avenue West
Ottawa, ON K1P 1J1
(416) 326-5300 or toll free in Canada 1-688-9938
www.publications.serviceontario.ca/ecom/

Ontario Historical Society
34 Parkview Avenue
North York, ON M2N 3Y2
(416) 226-9011
www.ontariohistoricalsociety.ca

Ontario Indexing Services
351 Pommel Gate Crescent
Waterloo, ON N2L 5X7
(519) 885-0031

Ontario Ministry of Natural Resources
Information Centre, North Tower
300 Water Street
Peterborough, ON K9J 8M5
1-800-667-1940
www.mnr.gov.on.ca/MNR/mapmenu.html

Perly's Maps: See Rand McNally

Pro Familia Publishing
128 Gilmour Avenue
Toronto, ON M6P 3B3
(416) 767-2804
(designer & typesetter; limited edition family histories)

Rand McNally Canada Inc.
90A Royal Crest Court
Markham, ON L3R 9X6
(905) 477-8480 or 1-800-205-6277
www.randmcnally.ca/

University of Toronto Press
10 St. Mary Street, Suite 700
Toronto, ON M4Y 2W8
(416) 978-2239
www.utpress.utoronto.ca

Russ Waller's Genealogy Books
(mail or email orders only)
www.angelfire.com/journal/loyalgen/

Index